Code Red

David Dranove

Code Red

AN ECONOMIST EXPLAINS

HOW TO REVIVE

THE HEALTHCARE SYSTEM

WITHOUT DESTROYING IT

PRINCETON UNIVERSITY PRESS

PRINCETON AND OXFORD

Published by Princeton University Press, 41 William Street, Princeton, New Jersey 08540

In the United Kingdom: Princeton University Press, 3 Market Place, Woodstock, Oxfordshire OX20 1SY

Library of Congress Cataloging-in-Publication Data

Dranove, David.
Code red : an economist explains how to revive the healthcare system without destroying it / David Dranove.
p. ; cm.
Includes bibliographical references and index.
ISBN 978-0-691-12941-9 (alk. paper)
1. Health care reform—United States.   2. Insurance, Health—United States.
3. Medical economics—United States.   4. Medical care—United States.   I. Title.
[DNLM: 1. Managed Care Programs—economics—United States.   2. Managed Care Programs—trends—United States.   3. Ethics, Medical—United States.
4. Health Care Reform—economics—United States.   5. Health Care Reform—methods—United States. W 130 AA1 C669 2008]
RA395.A3D743   2008
362.1'0425—dc22   2007037180

British Library Cataloging-in-Publication Data is available

This book has been composed in Utopia and Avant Garde Typefaces

Printed on acid-free paper. ∞

press.princeton.edu

Printed in the United States of America

10   9   8   7   6   5   4   3   2   1

✚ CONTENTS ✚

✚ ACKNOWLEDGMENTS ✚

I DREW INSPIRATION for this book from my mother, Dorothy Dranove, and my father-in-law, Sandor Salgo, both of whom passed away in 2007. They received outstanding medical care during their final days and weeks without enduring financial hardship. I hope that I am able, through this book, to help all Americans be so fortunate.

I would also like to acknowledge the research support provided by Michael Hu, Eliot Weinstein, and, especially, Christa Van der Eb. They ventured deep into areas that I had never previously explored.

Diagnosing the Condition

*Our health-care system is the envy
of the world because we believe in
making sure that the decisions are
made by doctors and patients, not
by officials in the nation's capital.*

—PRESIDENT GEORGE W. BUSH, 2004.[1]

*Let's face it—if we were to start
from scratch, none of us, from
dyed-in-the-wool liberals to rock-
solid conservatives, would fashion
the kind of health care system
America has inherited. So why
should we carry the problems of
this system into the future?*

—SENATOR HILLARY CLINTON, 2004[2]

ENVY OF THE WORLD or not, no one seriously believes that the U.S. healthcare system has fully achieved the three main goals that any nation aspires to: access, efficiency and quality. For the better part of the past one hundred years, the story of healthcare reform has been one of trying to achieve these goals. For all of our efforts, they remain as elusive as ever.

For much of the twentieth century, quality and efficiency took a back seat to access. Private sector health insurance in the United States began in fits and starts prior to the 1930s, expanded to cover 10 million Americans by the start of World War II, and then took off in the 1950s. Despite several failed efforts to enact national health insurance, the federal government played largely a secondary role in promoting access during this time. While the federal government dragged its feet, states and local governments created a modest safety net for those who could least afford to pay for their own care.

In 1965, Congress finally enacted two major health insurance programs: Medicare, which insures nearly all elderly and disabled Americans, and Medicaid, which covers the medically indigent. These programs expanded access to tens of millions of Americans while contributing to rising costs. Since the 1970s, public and private payers have focused less on access and more on cost containment. By the end of the 1990s, it looked like the cost problem had been licked (or at least mitigated) by managed care, but patients and providers rebelled. In 1999 and 2000, the Institutes of Medicine released two studies warning about problems with healthcare quality.

In the early days of the twenty-first century, we are still troubled by the same problems of access, quality, and efficiency. Despite the best of intentions, about forty-seven million Americans lacked health insurance at some time in the past year. After a brief respite in the 1990s, costs have resumed their relentless climb. And while we are healthier than ever, we have become more aware of unacceptable discrepancies in the quality of care. The $2 billion American healthcare system is in critical condition.

Like any patient in critical condition, the first step to finding a cure is proper diagnosis. This is what the first half of the book is all about. Beginning with the landmark 1932 report of the Committee on the Costs of Medical Care, I describe how researchers have identified myriad systemic problems with the healthcare system and their root causes. I will also describe the many attempts at cures; there is much we can learn from our past mistakes (and occasional successes.) In the second half of the book, I will talk about ongoing efforts to revive the system. In the final chapter, I offer some suggestions of my own.

Directions for Change

Unlike many other books about healthcare reform, I will not offer any sweeping proposals for universal coverage. This is not for lack of ideas. For the better part of the past century, policy analysts from across the political spectrum have presented comprehensive proposals, ranging from a market-based initiative offered by the conservative Heritage Foundation to a single-payer initiative offered by the liberal Physicians for Responsible National Health Insurance. There are many complex reasons why these proposals have failed to achieve the consensus required to become law. Perhaps the most compelling is offered by the late Columbia University policy guru Eli Ginzberg, who observes that the healthcare industry had too many power centers, including physicians, hospitals, insurers, pharmaceutical companies, and other suppliers.[3] I would add employers, who are the de facto purchasers of health insurance for most Americans, and patient advocacy groups, especially advocates for the elderly. It seems that no one has offered a health reform proposal that does not adversely affect at least two power centers. Insurers and suppliers oppose proposals that rely on significant expansion of government powers, while providers and patient advocates have shown little interest in market-based solutions, especially if they promote managed care. The result is perpetual legislative gridlock.

When President Clinton unveiled his Health Security Act in 1993, some of my colleagues who should have known better assured me that this proposal would succeed where others in the past had failed. Politicians insisted that the plan would get through Congress because there were new voting blocs. "Things are different," they said. But as I thought back over the history of failed health reform and the need to appeal to multiple power centers, I realized that I had heard those sentiments before. It seemed that the more things changed, the more they stayed the same. Sure enough, optimism about the plan's chances faded and ultimately disappeared in 1994. By November 1994, Republicans were firmly in control of Congress and national health reform was a dead issue. It has come back to life, and analysts are once again suggesting that "things are different."

I do not expect Congress to break its century-long political logjam and enact a sweeping program for national health reform. This is not a revelation. In their remarkable 1974 study of the origins of the Medicaid program, Robert and Rosemary Stevens argue that we will at best achieve piecemeal legislation, or what I call "creeping incrementalism."[4] Stevens and Stevens have proven to be correct so far, and there is nothing to suggest any immediate sea change. That is why I am not offering a single comprehensive solution. Besides I do not believe that there is a magic bullet cure for the U.S. healthcare system. But I do believe that we can revive the system and get things moving in the right direction again. For example, I believe that it is possible to cut the number of uninsured in half or better with minimal federal intervention. A number of states have taken the initiative and a polite shove from the federal government is all it will take to make this a national reality. Having reduced the problem of the uninsured to a manageable size, smaller scale initiatives can fill in most of the remaining holes in the safety net.

Many proposals to solve the access problem get bogged down in efforts to simultaneously reduce costs. There is a false premise at work here, namely that cost reduction is a necessary condition for improving other aspects of the healthcare system. The success of Medicare and Medicaid in improving access for tens of millions of Americans is prima facie evidence that we can focus on one problem at a time. Besides it is not obvious that we should lower costs per se, but rather that we should be sure to spend our money wisely. I will suggest several simple ways to make us wiser shoppers.

If we focus excessively on costs, then quality is sure to suffer. It is reassuring that employers, payers, and the government are working hard to find ways to measure and reward the highest quality providers and payers. But this movement may be stopped dead in its tracks unless we get better data and improve the methods used to analyze them. Even this will not be enough. Providers and patients must radically rethink the meaning of quality; otherwise third-party oversight will have little impact and quality will forever take a back seat to costs. I do not pretend to know how to perfectly measure quality, reward the best providers, and encourage the worst to do better. But I will offer a few suggestions for how we can do these things better.

Is This a Sequel?

I published *The Economic Evolution of American Health Care* in 2000. Targeted to both industry experts and a lay audience concerned about America's most important industry, that book chronicled the rise and uncertain future of managed care. I think *Economic Evolution* did a good job of laying out where the U.S. health economy was heading and explaining how managed care could hold the line on costs. At the same time, I identified serious obstacles to the continued success of HMOs (Health Maintenance Organizations) in the market. While the conventional wisdom is that managed care has failed, the reality is that many managed care strategies are thriving, including the nearly universal adoption of provider networks and drug formularies, innovations in provider payments, and disease management. Even so, a public backlash against the heavy handed oversight and narrow provider networks of some managed care plans has caused a shift away from tightly managed HMOs into looser forms of managed care. The result has been a predictable sharp increase in healthcare costs. At the same time, concerns about quality have intensified and there is heightened interest in solving the access problem.

This book both updates *Economic Evolution* as well as broadens its focus to include public sector efforts to cope with quality and cost and, especially, access. There is some overlap in the two books, especially in the first half of this book where I discuss basic health economics topics such as demand inducement and moral hazard. The first half of this book also presents a lot of new material on access to care and insurance markets. The second half is strictly a sequel to *Economic Evolution*, describing new efforts to deal with cost, quality, and access via consumer directed health plans, provider report cards, and state health reform initiatives. The final chapter in which I offer recommendations is a culmination of my efforts in both books. I hope it contains something useful.

The Accidental
Healthcare System

[Every member of the population]
has a right to adequate medical
care (and) adequate protection
from the economic fears of sickness.

—PRESIDENT HARRY S. TRUMAN,

Message to Congress, 1945[1]

Early Symptoms

In the late nineteenth century, the average American spent less than $4 per year on healthcare (less than $100 in today's dollars.) Americans spent so little mainly because providers could do little to heal them. Ether had been available as an anesthetic since 1847, but the risk of infection ruled out surgery in all but the direst of cases. Medicinal drug use was widespread, but it was difficult to distinguish efficacious drugs from snake oil. (One of the most popular medications of the late nineteenth century was mercury!) Most patients received their drugs at home; hospitals were for the poor and the homeless.[2]

As the twentieth century dawned, medical technology was advancing and healthcare spending was increasing as a result. Pasteur advanced the germ theory of disease in 1870 and by 1900, providers could detect and treat diphtheria and other communicable diseases.

Wilhelm Röntgen discovered practical uses for high voltage radiation in 1895. One of the first applications of Röntgen's discovery was to take a picture of a person's bones on a photographic plate. These "X-ray" pictures reduced the time required to set broken bones, greatly improving the odds of surviving surgery. Hospitals also began using carbolic acid (discovered by Lister) as an antiseptic, reducing the risk of postoperative infection, further improving survival rates. As hospitals added to their technological arsenal, more and more patients viewed them as a viable option for life-saving treatment.

These new technologies came at a cost. The average American in 1900 spent $5 on medical care, but many spent much more and a few were forced to use up their life savings to pay for care. Those unable to pay for "state-of-the-art" care had to rely on charity or go without. Some ended up at on poor farms, which comforted but did not treat the sick and dying.

Health insurance would have prevented such catastrophes, but few Americans had health insurance as we know it today. Employers in high risk industries such as mining and the railroads often covered the costs of their workers' industrial injuries. But employers saw this as a way to maintain productivity.[3] Health insurance as a means to protect wealth and assure access for nonwork related illnesses was nonexistent.

Even as affordability was becoming an issue, healthcare costs continued to rise. The famous Flexner Commission Report of 1910 added urgently needed scientific rigor to medical education, but the stiffer educational requirements increased the cost of a medical education and served as an entry barrier into the profession. The number of physicians per capita declined by 27 percent in just twenty years, from 173 per 100,000 in 1900 to 125 per 100,000 in 1920.[4] This was accompanied by a sharp rise in physician fees and incomes. At the same time, the pace of medical innovation began to quicken, with technological advances such as urinalysis and blood testing simultaneously driving up the demand and costs of care.

As more and more families faced the prospect of financial ruin in the event of a major illness, governments felt pressure to provide some kind of protection. By 1915, half of the states had enacted worker compensation laws and progressive organizations like the American Association for Labor Legislation (AALL) began a strong push for national health coverage for all working Americans and their families. The president of the AALL, Alexander Lambert, was a physician and was also chairman of the Judiciary Council of the American Medical Association (AMA). Lambert encouraged the two organizations to work together to promote access.

In early 1916, the AALL, with help from AMA leadership, drafted model legislation that would provide comprehensive insurance to all workers. The insurance would be funded jointly by government, employers, and the workers themselves. The AALL proposal attracted considerable support from a wide range of constituents, including the *New England Journal of Medicine*, the United States Public Health Service, numerous state medical societies, and a conference of state health officers. The *Journal of the American Medical Association* even remarked that "the time for the medical profession to interest itself in social insurance legislation is now."[5]

Employers (who did not want the additional expense) and insurance companies (which were not yet selling health insurance and did not want to be told whether and how to do so) opposed the proposal. The president of the Insurance Economic Society of America asked, "Can you imagine the horde of constables necessary to enforce such a law?" and attorney Philemon Tecumsah Sherman (son of the Civil War general) warned that the success of the new German national health insurance system, which was a model for the AALL proposal, was due to "the iron discipline of the German government."[6] This was not meant as a ringing endorsement. Sherman also noted that insuring workers would leave those most in need of coverage still wanting.

Although the AMA helped draft the AALL proposal, it never officially endorsed it. Many physicians were disenchanted with worker compensation programs, objecting to the low fee schedules and disruptions to the physician/patient relationship. They now had second thoughts about the wisdom of socialized medicine. Hearing the objections of its members, AMA leadership backed down and, in 1920, adopted a resolution opposing socialized medicine. The AMA has held this position ever since.

Opposition from the AMA was just one factor that stood in the way of the AALL national health insurance proposal. Most Americans blamed Germany for starting World War I, and opponents of the AALL plan were only too happy to point out where the idea originated.

The Committee on the Costs of Medical Care

In 1927, a consortium of private foundations organized the Committee on the Costs of Medical Care (CCMC). The fifty member CCMC was comprised mainly of healthcare providers but also included six Ph.D. social scientists. The chair, Dr. Ray Wilbur, had an illustrious past. He received his M.D. degree in 1899 from Cooper's Union and shortly thereafter moved to Germany to study under Paul Erlich, who would later discover chemotherapy. Wilbur moved back and forth between Europe and the states until 1909 when he was selected to be the inaugural chair of the Department of Medicine at the new Stanford University Medical School. He was promoted to dean of the medical school in 1911, became Stanford University president in 1916, and remained there until 1943. By 1927 Wilbur was no stranger to politics. He had been President Warren Harding's personal physician and was at his bedside in San Francisco when Harding died in 1923. Shortly after taking charge of CCMC, Wilber graced the cover of *Time* magazine. Two years later, he was tapped by President Herbert Hoover (a personal friend) to be secretary of the interior. Between 1927 and 1932, Wilbur wore three hats: university president, CCMC chair, and cabinet secretary.

Although Wilbur was not an accomplished researcher—his publication record is virtually nonexistent—he firmly believed in the value of rigorous empirical research. While at Stanford, he raised significant funds to support a full-time research faculty and training of doctoral students. He followed the same academic instincts during his tenure as head of the CCMC. Under Wilbur's direction, the CCMC produced the first major studies of the U.S. healthcare industry. The committee gathered detailed information about spending, resource availability, and the organization of provider practices. Its final report, released in 1932, summarizes over two dozen research studies and addresses many issues that remain salient today.

The CCMC report describes how the burden of healthcare costs had been growing over time. Total health spending in 1929 was $3.6 billion, or about $30 per capita ($340 in today's dollars) and just 3.5 percent of gross domestic product (GDP). (See table 1.1.) Though small in both absolute and relative terms, these figures masked considerable variation across the population. The committee's analysis of spending data confirms that some Americans faced considerable financial risk: "If an illness requires hospital care in addition to professional services, it alone may entail costs which are catastrophic to the family."[7] In fact, average hospital receipts per patient in 1929 (just prior to the stock market crash) exceeded $200, or nearly one-third of annual per capita income.[8] In terms of affordability, this would equate to about $15,000 today.[9] Few patients had insurance of any kind, so they either paid the bills themselves or appealed to the charity of the hospital.

The CCMC called for a public sector plan to eliminate "all or nearly all of the variation (of medical costs) for every family."[10] From that moment, eliminating the financial risk associated with catastrophic illness has been a principal goal of healthcare reformers. It is a goal that makes a lot of sense.

The Value of Insurance

When it comes to money, most of us are "risk averse." This means that we prefer to pay an actuarially fair insurance premium rather

Table 1.1. Annual Health Spending: 1929–60

Year	Total health spending ($billion)	Per capita spending	Real per capita spending (today's dollars)	Annual inflation in real per capita spending	Health spending as percent of GDP
1929	$3.6	$29	$340	N/A	3.5%
1935	2.9	23	330	−0.5%	4.1
1940	4.0	30	420	4.9	4.0
1950	12.7	82	670	4.8	4.4
1960	26.9	146	960	3.7	5.3

Source: Cathy Tallon at OA/CMS and CMS current reports.

than face the possibility of huge financial loss.[11] The financial peace of mind that insurance affords may be intangible, but it is highly valuable. Most Americans willingly pay premiums for health, home, auto, and life insurance that exceed the actuarially fair value of the benefit by 10 percent or more. Health insurance not only provides financial peace of mind, it also grants us access to care, because many providers are rightfully reluctant to treat the uninsured. Why should providers bear the financial consequences of broad failures of social policy?

While we usually think of insurance as something that we obtain on an annual basis, the logic of risk aversion holds over our entire lifetimes. When we are young, we know that we may one day experience some costly illness such as diabetes or stroke. Without insurance, this could lead to financial ruin. Many young individuals might welcome the opportunity to obtain financial protection by paying a steady health insurance premium over their lifetime. In effect, they would cross-subsidize their own care, paying a premium that exceeds actuarially fair rates when they are young to be certain they can cover all their medical expenses when they are old.

Our employer-based health insurance system provides something resembling lifetime coverage. Young insured workers usually cross-subsidize their older coworkers. Payroll deductions for Medicare work the same way. (So do nationalized healthcare systems; young taxpayers cross-subsidize care for the elderly.) As I will describe in chapter 5, a new type of insurance product may allow workers to cross-subsidize themselves over time, by allowing them to keep some of the difference between what they pay in insurance and what they spend on medical care, and use that difference to cover future medical needs. In all of these ways, health insurance provides financial protection both at a given point in time and over a lifetime.

The CCMC Proposals

At the time of the CCMC report, there was hardly any health insurance to speak of. The private health insurance market that we know today was not quite on the horizon. The kind of protection recommended by CCMC would therefore require some form of comprehensive government-sponsored insurance.

The CCMC critique of the U.S. healthcare system did not stop with access. The CCMC devoted most of its report to a second problem—inefficiencies in the healthcare system. It criticized "widespread waste" and "unnecessary medication." In one telling passage, it expressed concerns about fee-for-service compensation, whereby physicians were paid additional fees for each service they rendered: "One of the worst results of the present method of remunerating physicians is that practitioners may have, or may be thought to have, an economic incentive to create unnecessary medical service or to prolong illness."[12]

The CCMC studied options for streamlining the delivery of healthcare and listed its first policy priority as follows: "The Committee recommends that medical service, both preventive and therapeutic, should be furnished largely by organized groups of physicians, . . . and other associated personnel."[13]

The CCMC suggests that these organized groups receive prepayment from local populations as a way to provide financial security to patients, improve quality, and limit unnecessary treatments. These ideas presaged the development of HMOs as well as national health insurance (NHI) proposals centered on HMOs or other organized delivery systems.

The prescience of the CCMC did not stop with the promotion of organized group practice. The CCMC recommended an emphasis on prevention. It also called for additional formal training for specialists while limiting the number of specialists. These ideas have remained on the policy radar screen ever since.

The CCMC report received considerable attention when released, but not all of it was positive. The *New York Times* and other key newspapers criticized the report, as did the AMA. It would be decades before discussions of access and cost were once again intertwined and even longer before health policy leaders would seriously question fee-for-service medical care.

Decades of Debate about National Health Insurance

When Franklin Roosevelt replaced Herbert Hoover in 1933, the Great Depression was more than three years old, 25 percent of America's workers were unemployed, and the average household income was below today's poverty level (adjusted for inflation). Health spending had fallen from pre-1929 levels, but had actually increased as a percentage of GDP. President Roosevelt wanted to "explore the possibilities of a unified social insurance system affording protection against all major personal hazards which lead to poverty and dependency."[14] In June 1934, Roosevelt appointed his Secretary of Labor Frances Perkins to head a Committee on Economic Security (COES), which was charged with developing ideas for a national social safety net.

Perkins, America's first female cabinet secretary, began her career as a social worker and was involved in Jane Addams's famous Hull House, which provided social services to the residents of its surrounding Chicago immigrant community. Prior to joining Roosevelt's cabinet, Perkins was the head of New York State's Department of Labor where she championed minimum wage laws and unemployment insurance. Perkins had spent her entire career dealing with the problems of poverty; the related problem of access to healthcare had not been a priority, and Roosevelt's decision to ask Perkins to head the COES reflected his own priorities.

By December 1934, the COES outlined a national social insurance program including unemployment insurance, public relief, and old age security. Their report also listed eleven principles for NHI, including:[15]

- Patients should have free choice of provider
- Medical professions should choose the method of remuneration
- The professions should have responsibility for improving quality
- Health insurance should exclude commercial agents
- Each state should administer its own health insurance plan "under a Federal law of permissive character"

Taken together, these principles would have two major implications for healthcare markets: (1) The provision of healthcare would remain free from meddling by third parties, and (2) the government would play an expanded role in the financing of care. We eventually learned that these are incompatible principles; whoever foots the bill for medical care inevitably wants to oversee how the money is spent. Meddling would be unavoidable.

Although a national consensus supported using tax dollars to expand access, organized medicine opposed any effort that appeared to socialize medicine. Unwilling to burn political capital at this critical juncture, President Roosevelt put NHI on the back burner. Despite identifying principles for NHI, even the COES stated that it was "not prepared at this time to make recommendations for a system of health insurance."

Roosevelt and Perkins instead focused on the centerpiece of his New Deal agenda: the Social Security Act of 1935. The act created two major programs: Social Security and Welfare. The federal Social Security program was to be administered uniformly across the nation and provide a measure of income security for all seniors. Federal rules about welfare had a much more "permissive character." Despite federal cost sharing and minimum federal requirements, states were permitted to vary in the generosity of welfare programs. This would weigh heavily on subsequent efforts to create a nationwide healthcare safety net.

The Social Security Act of 1935 also created Old Age Assistance (OAA) programs that augmented payments to low income seniors. Like it did for welfare, the federal government gave states considerable flexibility in administering OAA, resulting in big differences across the states. In 1940, for example, the percentage of elderly receiving assistance varied from 10 percent in New Jersey to over 50 percent in Oklahoma, while annual benefits per recipient ranged from under $100 in Arkansas to $455 in California.[16]

Roosevelt did not entirely give up on healthcare. After passage of the Social Security Act, he appointed an Interdepartmental Committee to Coordinate Health and Welfare Activities. That committee presented a report in 1938 calling for states to establish health insurance programs with financial assistance from the federal government. Roosevelt endorsed the idea but it met with stormy protests and went nowhere in Congress.

NHI Remains an Elusive Goal

As the nation emerged from the Great Depression and transitioned to a war time economy, healthcare spending began to rise once again and national health insurance remained a prominent domestic policy issue. Politicians from both parties introduced legislative proposals to expand coverage. Setting a precedent for today's health insurance debate, Democrats proposed a government-sponsored insurance program whereas Republicans offered to subsidize purchases of private sector health insurance.[17]

Neither regulatory nor market-based proposals could win enough support to get very far in Congress. Opposition by the AMA was certainly a factor. President Roosevelt's preoccupation with the developing war in Europe was another. After World War II, public opinion turned against labor unions (whose postwar strikes disrupted the recovering economy) and their political agenda, which included nationalizing healthcare.

Despite these political setbacks, access continued to be a major concern among elected officials; a survey conducted in the late 1940s identified the absence of medical coverage as the most significant problem in government assistance programs.[18] After winning the election of 1948, President Truman threw his weight behind a proposal by Oscar Ewing, the head of the Federal Security Administration (the forebear of today's Center for Medicare and Medicaid Services.) The Truman-Ewing plan called for expanding the Old Age Assistance (Social Security) program to cover up to sixty days of hospital care annually. Republicans were unanimous in opposing the plan and the AMA once again trotted out the label of "socialized medicine." The plan withered on the vine.

When World War II ended, Congress envisioned a surge in the demand for hospital care. To meet this need, Congress in 1946 created the Hill-Burton program, which over the next three decades would pump over $6 billion into the construction and expansion of non-profit hospitals. In exchange for Hill-Burton funds, hospitals agreed to treat patients who lacked insurance and could not afford to pay for care themselves. Over the years, this became a critical (if somewhat obscure) feature of the U.S. healthcare safety net, as hospitals used the profits earned on privately insured patients to cover the costs of care for the uninsured.

Long after Hill-Burton mandates for charity care have expired, the nonprofit hospitals that the program created dominate the market. Hill-Burton funds are surely part of the reason for the success of non-profits, but there are others, including the trust that many Americans place in their community and faith-based nonprofit providers, and the fact that nonprofits are exempt from paying state and local taxes.[19] There is an ongoing debate, and some legal battles, about how much charity care nonprofits should provide in exchange for their tax exemptions. This is a cumbersome way to maintain the safety net, but it is the American way.

Truman remained keen on enacting some kind of national health insurance program. In 1951, he appointed a Commission on the Health Needs of the Nation and named a Republican physician and medical administrator, Paul Budd Magnuson, to chair it and appoint its members. A year later, the commission recommended scrapping the Truman-Ewing plan once and for all. It instead called on all employers to provide coverage to their employees while subsidizing the purchase of private health insurance for those of limited means. The expected federal price tag for guaranteeing health insurance for all Americans: about $1 billion. That may sound like a lot of money, but it might cost 100 times that or more to cover all the uninsured today. The proposal also promoted group practices (shades of CCMC) and grants to encourage construction and expansion of medical and nursing schools. This time, Truman met opposition from his own party and yet another proposal to cover all Americans faded into the background.

In the meantime, the forecast increase in the demand for medical care came to fruition. This partly reflected the return to civilian life of millions of veterans (and the subsequent baby boom.) But medical technology continued to be a major cost driver, as doctors brought into everyday practice the advances in surgical techniques that emerged on the World War II battlefields. Thanks to new anesthetics and antibiotics, patients could fully expect to survive invasive surgery. Other innovations included dialysis and pacemakers. Hospital admissions grew from eighteen million in 1950 to twenty-five million by 1960, and healthcare spending doubled, approaching $150 per capita by 1960 (about $1,000 in today's dollars). Many seniors spent far more than this amount.[20] Social Security retirement benefits averaged under $1,000; hardly enough to cover the basic necessities of life *and* medical costs.

The safety net at this time consisted of nonprofit/Hill-Burton hospitals providing charity care, county hospitals serving as providers of last resort, and a hodge-podge of state "vendor payment" programs that helped defray medical bills for individuals receiving Old Age Assistance (OAA). These left gaping holes. Some states in the 1950s expanded their vendor payment programs and a few covered low income individuals of all ages. But many states had meager programs and ten states offered no assistance whatsoever. Even as the private health insurance market was beginning to flourish, the problems of the uninsured were intensifying.

Kerr-Mills

In 1960, Senator Robert Kerr and Congressman Wilbur Mills sponsored legislation to unify vendor payment programs. This was an unusual but effective partnership. Born in Chickasaw Indian Territory, Kerr made a fortune in oil (he is the Kerr of Kerr McGee Oil Industries) before entering politics in the 1930s. He was a traditional conservative southern Democrat who opposed most social welfare legislation. Mills was also a southern Democrat (from rural Arkansas) who entered politics in the 1930s, but his political views rarely aligned with Kerr's. As a county official during the Depression, he started a program to pay medical bills for the poor and he continued to champion liberal causes during his forty-year tenure in Congress. Mills rose to the powerful position of chairman of the House Ways and Means Committee but his career effectively ended in 1974 when he was involved in a scandal that featured the reflecting pool of the Washington Monument, large quantities of bourbon, and a nightclub stripper named Fanny Foxe.

Kerr and Mills frequently disagreed about social welfare programs, but they did agree on one subject. The elderly were becoming a powerful voting bloc and the disappointing performance of the OAA vendor payment programs created a political opportunity for Democrats seeking to keep control of Congress and win the White House in the November 1960 election. The Kerr-Mills Act of 1960 created the Medical Assistance to the Aged program. Following the model of the welfare programs created under Roosevelt, MAA used federal matching grants to encourage states to expand vendor payment programs but otherwise took a hands-off approach to regulating the healthcare system.

The carrot of matching grants proved to be insufficient to propel most states into action. Only a few states developed large Kerr-Mills programs and some states did nothing at all. In the meantime, the financial struggles of the uninsured were intensifying. Millions of elderly and poor Americans had no insurance and healthcare cost inflation showed no signs of abating with real annual increases exceeding 5 percent.[21] These problems represented a political opportunity for President Johnson and his "Great Society."

At Long Last: Medicare and Medicaid

Lyndon Johnson was a newly styled southern Democrat who, like Wilbur Mills, believed that the federal government should provide an expanded social safety net. He called his vision the Great Society and the centerpiece of his legislative agenda was the 1965 Social Security Amendments that created Medicare and Medicaid. Medicare is the healthcare counterpart to Social Security. Open to virtually all elderly and disabled Americans regardless of their ability to pay, it initially covered hospital and physician services but notably excluded long-term care and prescription drugs. There were several reasons for these exclusions. These two categories accounted for only 15 percent of healthcare spending and were not deemed essential. Some feared that covering drugs and long-term care would drive up spending in these categories. (The conventional wisdom at the time was that the demand for hospitals and physicians would not be substantially affected by insurance.) Finally the AMA and American Hospital Association wielded considerable political muscle; as long as government paid the bills and otherwise stayed out of the way, doctors and hospitals wanted to be included in the program and were happy to see other potential claims on federal funds excluded.

Table 1.2. Growth of Government Healthcare Spending after 1965

Year	Total Health Spending (in $billions)	Government (all sources)	Government as percentage of total
1965	$35.9	7.9	22.1%
1970	65.4	22.4	34.3
1975	117.1	46.3	39.5

Source: Health Insurance Association of America, *Source Book of Health Insurance Data 1989,* Washington, DC: HIAA.

Medicaid is the healthcare counterpart to welfare. Medicaid covers the "medically indigent"—those individuals of limited financial means who fall into one of several categories including the aged, disabled, and families with dependent children. It is up to the states to finalize eligibility and coverage, and to this day there remains some variation among states (but not nearly as much as in Kerr-Mills.) All states are required to cover long-term care and drugs. Medicaid continues to be the largest source of insurance for long-term care, paying for nearly half of all nursing home bills.

With the creation of Medicare and Medicaid, federal and state governments became the nation's largest purchasers of healthcare, accounting for one-third of all spending by 1970 (see table 1.2). For the first time, government had a vested interest in cost containment. It would not take long before federal and state legislators would question whether they could continue to maintain a hands-off approach to healthcare delivery. As I describe in chapter 3, the era of healthcare regulation was fast approaching.

Expanding Access through the Private Sector

The CCMC identified the financial perils faced by the uninsured in 1932. A third of a century later, Congress finally made a meaningful response. Fortunately the private sector had not been waiting.

Recognizing that consumers would value the risk reduction afforded by insurance, private companies were finding a way to thrive in the marketplace while delivering that value. By the time Medicare and Medicaid came along, most Americans were already covered by private health insurance.

The origins of private health insurance trace back to industrial medicine coverage of the late nineteenth century. Employers covered work-related healthcare costs but rarely covered other medical costs incurred by workers or their family members. In the early 1900s, fraternal orders began prepaying physicians about $2 annually (or less than $20 in today's dollars) to provide primary care and minor surgery for lodge members. The two largest lodge practices, the Foresters and Fraternal Order of Eagles, contracted with over 2,000 doctors to care for over 600,000 members.[22]

These lodge practices were the forerunners of capitated medical care that is a hallmark of Health Maintenance Organizations. Both lodges and HMOs paid physicians an upfront capitated (per patient) fee that limits the payer's financial exposure while giving the physicians incentives to hold the line on costs. Another similarity was that the lodges forced doctors to compete for contracts, in the process obtaining their services at below market rates. HMOs and lodge practices also shared a common enemy, organized medicine. Physician associations complained publicly about the quality of doctors who contracted with lodges while muttering privately about the depressing effect of lodge practice on physician fees. State and local medical societies expelled lodge doctors and worked to deny them admitting privileges to hospitals. By the 1920s, lodge practice had died out and private sector health insurance all but disappeared.

The Birth of the Blues

As the Great Depression descended, healthcare had become a big business, accounting for about 4 percent of the gross domestic product by the early 1930s. Hospitals alone accounted for one-third of the total healthcare bill. It hardly served the interest of hospitals if patients could not afford to pay for care yet this is exactly what was happening.

Average hospital receipts per patient fell by 75 percent and hospitals searched for a new financial model to replace traditional fee-for-service payment.[23] They found it in the ideas of University of Chicago economist Rufus Rorem.

Rorem was an expert on healthcare costs and the chairman of the American Hospital Association's Committee on Uniform Accounting. In 1933, Rorem published a study on the financial burden of illness on behalf of the CCMC.[24] He reported that the overall burden of healthcare costs was not excessive and even suggested that healthcare was a bargain when one considers the value of the lives saved. But the centerpiece of the report was analysis of the uneven distribution of spending. This analysis confirmed earlier CCMC arguments about the value of insurance.

Rorem offered a novel win-win solution for hospitals and patients. He suggested that hospitals charge individuals a modest monthly prepayment—about $2 a month in most cases—in exchange for guaranteed free access. A handful of hospitals gave it a try, most notably Baylor University Hospital, which offered prepayment to local schoolteachers. This is widely credited to be the first Blue Cross insurance plan, although the first plan to use the Blue Cross name and symbol was offered by hospitals in St. Paul, Minnesota.[25]

Rorem continued to publish articles on the theory and practice of prepayment. Some of his most important work explained how to predict healthcare spending in a community. Hospitals needed to develop this expertise if they were to avoid losing money on prepayment; such "medical underwriting" remains one of the core tasks of any insurance company today.[26] With the access problem worsening with each passing year of the Depression, more and more hospitals banded together to offer Blue Cross plans. By 1935 there were fifteen plans in eleven states and by 1940 there were fifty-six plans with six million enrollees covering nearly every state. The plans quickly evolved to cover both workers and their dependents. They even covered maternity care, which had previously been thought of as a "predictable" expense and therefore uninsurable.

In addition to prepayment of pooled premiums, the Blue Cross plans had three other features that came to define "indemnity" health insurance. Enrollees could choose any hospital. The plans paid hospitals on a fee-for-service basis and did they not require patients to make copayments. This assured that financial considerations would not intercede in medical decision making. It would take decades before policy makers understood how these combination of features contributed to the never-ending cost spiral.

Soon after the first Blues were established, commercial for-profit insurers began offering their own versions of indemnity health insurance. Aetna, which started as a life insurance company in 1850, offered its first hospital insurance policies in 1936.[27] Cigna, whose eighteenth-century forerunner insured boat owners against transoceanic shipping disasters, began offering hospital coverage in 1937. These and other plans grew rapidly and by 1940, the commercial indemnity insurers had matched the Blues combined enrollments of six million.[28] Like the Blues, they offered free choice of provider and paid all reasonable charges. It is notable that approximately two-thirds of policies were sold to groups, mainly through employers. By selling to employer groups, insurers were assured a representative risk pool with predictable costs. Predictable costs meant predictable profits.

From the enrollee's perspective, there were a few differences between the Blues and commercial plans. State laws allowed the Blues to operate as nonprofits and they were exempt from a variety of taxes including premium taxes. In exchange, the Blues were required to community rate, that is, they had to charge the same premium to all enrollees. This created an opportunity for commercial insurers to "cherry pick" healthier enrollees by offering lower premiums. Some commercial insurers also required patients to make modest copayments, reasoning that healthier enrollees would accept copayments in exchange for reduced premiums. Such reasoning has not been lost on today's health insurers.

Physician Coverage

The early Blue Cross plans were careful not to antagonize organized medicine. The AMA had adopted a resolution opposing prepaid medical care and the AMA was not lacking for political clout. Fear of the AMA contributed to Roosevelt's decision to drop NHI from his New

Deal legislation and the AMA even convinced a few states to prohibit the Blue Cross plans from covering physician services. Blue Cross plans in other states voluntarily took the same course. But patients wanted to know why they could not prepay for physician services and many physicians wanted to follow the lead of hospitals and pool patient prepayments to guarantee their earnings.[29]

These concerns came into focus in the fall of 1938 when newly elected California Governor Culbert Olson promised to seek compulsory health insurance for all residents of the state. The California Medical Association (CMA) had always echoed the AMA's opposition to prepayment in the private sector but was even more fearful of interference by the public sector. The CMA's solution was to offer its own private insurance plan that allowed patients to prepay for physician services while continuing to pay physicians on a fee-for-service basis. Five thousand physicians agreed to participate and in February 1939, the California Physicians' Service, soon to be renamed Blue Shield of California, was born. The pressure for compulsory insurance diminished and Olson's proposal was defeated. Blue Shield plans soon emerged in Michigan, New York, and Pennsylvania and by the 1950s they had blanketed the nation.

The Blue Cross and Blue Shield plans required special state "enabling" legislation. The enabling laws allowed hospitals and doctors to act as nonprofit insurers, but they usually were written to keep each from the other's turf. Blue Cross sold hospital insurance; Blue Shield covered physician services. States would eventually permit Blue Cross and Blue Shield to offer comprehensive coverage. Over time, many commercial carriers added physician coverage to their hospital insurance policies.

Employer Coverage

The Blues and commercial health insurers that arose in the middle of the twentieth century sold most of their policies to employer groups. Given that many of today's health reform proposals seek to sever the link between employment and health insurance, it is helpful to understand why the link existed in the first place. Mark Pauly, a University of

Pennsylvania economist who is today's leading academic authority on health insurance, has observed that employers do not offer health insurance out of the goodness of their hearts.[30] Firms offer insurance because it is an effective way to attract and retain workers. If employers are offering insurance rather than workers buying it on their own, then it must be that employers can get a better deal than workers (tax considerations included). In fact, employers probably have to get a noticeably better deal, otherwise workers would prefer to purchase an individual policy that best met their needs instead of the one chosen for them by their employer.

Employer coverage is usually cheaper than individual coverage. By selling to employer groups, insurers can economize on marketing, sales, and administrative expenses. Insurers also know that employer-sponsorship creates natural risk pools both at a given point in time (workers who are healthy today subsidize those who are sick today) and over time (young workers subsidize the old). In contrast, insurers worry that enrollees who want to purchase individual health insurance are disproportionately likely to have substantial medical needs. This is known as adverse selection. (A good example of adverse selection is when a young couple plans to start a family; they may know it but their insurer would not.)

Insurers try to cope with adverse selection by "experience rating"—charging a premium based on the enrollee's past healthcare spending experience. But experience rating is imperfect—it is based on past needs while enrollees base their demand for insurance on their own expected future needs. Moreover experience rating in individual insurance markets causes the sick and the old to pay higher premiums than the healthy and the young, eliminating the "insurance" afforded by cross-subsidization. To further protect against adverse selection, insurers have imposed preexisting condition exclusions, refusing to cover the costs for medical conditions that were present at time coverage was purchased. Even these precautions do not allow insurers to charge the same amount for individual and group coverage.

For all of these reasons, two-thirds of Americans who had health insurance before World War II received it through their employer. Events that transpired during World War II would further promote employer-based coverage.

The Tax Subsidy

President Roosevelt created the National War Labor Board (NWLB) in 1942 to assure that potential labor market unrest would not affect wartime production. In September 1942, the NWLB imposed a wage freeze to prevent inflation. This made it difficult for firms to attract and keep workers, so employers increasingly offered nonwage benefits, including health benefits, which the NWLB exempted from the freeze. At the same time, the Internal Revenue Service ruled that certain payments by employers for healthcare benefits were not taxable as employee income.[31] The ruling was limited in scope but the Revenue Act of 1954 made the tax exemption permanent and comprehensive.

The cumulative effect of these events was profound. By 1944, hospital insurance coverage jumped to twenty-nine million. Ten years later, more than one hundred million Americans had hospital coverage and fifty million had coverage for physician expenses. At the same time, the percentage of insured with group coverage edged up to 70 percent.

Most economists today complain about the tax exemption, and for good reason. For a typical American making $75,000 annually, the income tax on an additional wage of $8,000 would be about $2,000. When the employer gives that individual $8,000 in health benefits, the worker pays nothing in taxes. Wealthier workers, who are in higher tax brackets, get an even bigger tax break. Overall the federal and state governments forego nearly $200 billion in tax revenue every year and almost the entire "tax subsidy" goes to middle-class and wealthy households.[32]

The tax exemption creates other problems. There is currently an uneven playing field in the health insurance market. The added cost of expensive plans and the extra healthcare that comes with them can be paid with before-tax dollars. Almost everything else we buy is paid for with after-tax dollars. This makes it cheaper to buy a dollar's worth of healthcare than to buy a dollar's worth of other stuff. The employer-centered health insurance system also insulates workers from the economic consequences of their healthcare choices, because their employers tend to pay most of the added cost of expensive plans. Moreover, employer-sponsored coverage creates obstacles to workers seeking to change jobs or retire early, as I describe in the next chapter.

Employer-sponsored insurance has wreaked some havoc, for sure. Some critics argue that employer coverage is purely an artifact of the tax exemption and propose that all individuals be responsible for purchasing their own insurance. But this ignores the fact that the marketplace favored employer-based coverage before there was a tax exemption, for the reasons of cost reduction and risk avoidance. Those reasons have not disappeared, and it would be overly simplistic to dismiss the employer-based system as the unwelcome vestige of a distortionary tax. Any private sector solution to our nation's health problems will be well-served if there is a role for employer-sponsored coverage.

Where Things Stood

This was the U.S. healthcare system, circa 1970: Nearly 90 percent of Americans, including virtually all of the elderly, had reasonably complete health insurance. While there were some gaps in many insurance policies, most Americans could sleep comfortably at night without worrying about whether they could afford to pay their medical bills. There was also a viable safety net for those who lacked insurance. Nonprofit hospitals, bound by Hill-Burton requirements and the desire to keep their tax exemption, but also motivated by their sense of mission, used the "profits" they earned from their privately insured and Medicare patients to cross-subsidize coverage of the uninsured. Local government hospitals served as providers of last resort. It was a complicated way to deal with the access problem, and few Americans were aware of the fact that their private insurance was subsidizing care for the uninsured, but it seemed to be working.

The pressure to do something about access was off, at least for the time being. For the first time, healthcare policy analysts began to pay attention to rising costs. New technology was, as always, a prime culprit. By the mid-1970s, patients were beginning to enjoy the benefits of combination chemotherapy, CT scans, ultrasound, open heart surgery, joint replacement surgery, and organ transplants. The quality of medical care had taken yet another quantum leap, but so did spending. This did not seem to bother most Americans who felt spending on medical care should be even higher.[33] But it bothered those who were writing the checks to providers.

This was just about the time when a new wave of health services research showed evidence of enormous waste in the U.S. healthcare system. Policy makers, insurers, and employers took notice and made profound changes. We are still feeling the effects.

Paging Doctor Welby

*The main cause of the unjustified
and unnecessary increase in costs
is the complex of perverse
incentives inherent in the system
of . . . fee-for-service for doctors,
cost reimbursement for hospitals,
and third-party intermediaries to
protect consumers.*

—ALAIN ENTHOVEN, *New England
Journal of Medicine* 1978[1]

Marcus Welby Medicine

Most Americans in 1970 thought that the healthcare system was
working well.[2] Americans had especially high regard for physicians,
as reflected in the top-rated television program of that year, *Marcus
Welby, MD*. The fictional Marcus Welby had a private office in Santa
Monica, California. He also saw patients at Lang Memorial Hospital, a
nonprofit hospital. Dr. Welby and the specialists at Lang had unques-
tioned decision making authority; no hospital administrators looked
over their shoulders as they made life and death decisions. If patients
could not make it into the office or the hospital emergency room,

Dr. Welby paid them a house call. Patients had financial peace of mind because insurance covered all the expenses. And no one cursed at HMOs for refusing coverage! The quality and personal attention that Dr. Welby delivered to his television patients, unfettered by insurance red tape or worries about costs, resembled the kind of medical care that all Americans perceived they were receiving from their own physicians and hospitals. To some extent, Americans still long for the days of "Marcus Welby medicine."

Before starring as Marcus Welby, actor Robert Young portrayed Jim Anderson in another top-rated show, *Father Knows Best*. I do not think it was a coincidence that America's physician was also America's dad. Americans trusted their healthcare system and Marcus Welby *cum* surrogate father personified the reasons for that trust: he was compassionate, he was in control, and he seemed to provide the best possible quality of care.

On the first two dimensions, I think America's trust was well-founded. It is often said that medicine is a calling and I do not think that this is the mere stuff of television drama. The young men and women who graduated from college with terrific grades and lofty career ambitions had their choice of career paths and could probably make more money (in net present value) in law or business. What often led them into medicine was the desire to do well by doing good. No one is immune from pursuing selfish goals, but doctors, more than most other professionals, probably do care deeply about the well being of their "customers." Americans were also right to trust in the control asserted by their doctors, who called the shots at real world hospitals just as Dr. Welby and his associates did at Lang Memorial. In the words of economist Victor Fuchs, the doctor was "the captain of the ship."[3]

I am less convinced about the unquestioning trust in the quality of Marcus Welby medicine. I sometimes imagine the following ending to an episode of *Marcus Welby, MD*. Unbeknownst to anyone, Dr. Welby has messed up a diagnosis causing a patient to die despite the heroic efforts of the specialists at Lang Memorial. The final scene takes place at the cemetery where the grieving family lays their loved one to rest. As they leave the graveside, they notice Dr. Welby standing nearby. Do they confront him with anger? No. Do they threaten him with a lawsuit? No. They thank Dr. Welby for being so compassionate, for always "being there" for the family. They do not blame him for their loved one's death, because they do not believe it possible that Dr. Welby could make such a horrible mistake.

Dr. Welby's patients were not alone in their blind trust. We all believed our physicians were as infallible as Dr. Welby. It would take years before Americans would begin to understand that doctors, like everyone else, can make mistakes, and that some doctors are better than others. But long before Marcus Welby entered into the American consciousness, a few academics studying the costs of medical care were beginning to question whether the "captain of the ship" was always charting the best course.

Incentives and Medical Decision Making

Roemer's Law

Milton Roemer was a renaissance man. Between 1939 and 1943, he received a bachelor's degree in public health from the University of Michigan, a master's degree in sociology from Cornell University, and an M.D. degree from New York University. He supervised venereal disease clinics in New Jersey and worked for the U.S. Public Health Service on rural health needs. In 1951, Roemer assumed a leadership position at the fledgling World Health Organization where he wrote a seminal comparative analysis of world health systems. He even launched Canada's first social health insurance program in Saskatchewan. But his most important contribution to the evolution of the U.S. healthcare system comes from a short research article that he published in 1961 while teaching healthcare administration at Cornell.[4]

Roemer's research at the time examined the effects of the Hill-Burton fueled growth in hospital capacity on access and costs of care. Focusing his attention on a region of upstate New York near where he taught, Roemer observed something peculiar in the data. Whenever hospitals added beds, the beds seemed to fill up. To a medical man like Roemer, this observation did not make sense—he had found no evidence to suggest that patients were unable to obtain hospital care before the bed expansions or that their medical needs had dramatically increased. To this day, health services researchers and policy analysts continue to cite Roemer's Law: "A bed built is a bed filled."[5]

Roemer's Law had a troubling implication: hospitals must have convinced patients to use services that they did not need. What makes this more disturbing was the implication for physicians, who have always been directly responsible for admitting patients. Physicians must have been admitting patients solely to fill the empty beds. What fed the mythology of Marcus Welby medicine was our belief that physician decision making was based solely on medical considerations; finances were not supposed to matter. Maybe we were wrong.

Roemer's study involved just one small part of the United States and used fairly rudimentary statistical tools that might have biased his conclusion. Even so, his findings challenged the conventional wisdom that the only problems with the U.S. health economy pertained to access. And they made a certain amount of intuitive sense. It was unreasonable to expect physicians to be immune to the same venal financial incentives that affect all of us. If they (and their hospitals) could make more money filling empty beds, then we ought to expect them to try to do so. Patients lacked the medical knowledge necessary to challenge their physicians' recommendations, and would naturally comply. "A bed built is a bed filled" became a mantra for policy makers seeking to hold the line on healthcare costs.

The impact of Roemer's Law is felt today in Canada, England, and other places where access to technology is limited out of fear that physicians will "fill up" any services that are available, regardless of the underlying needs of the population. But Roemer did more than inspire a generation of policy makers. Thirty years after the CCMC first raised doubts about the efficiency of traditional fee-for-service medicine, Roemer's study set the stage for a new wave of health services research. By the 1970s, researchers had produced substantial evidence that the U.S. healthcare system was plagued by perverse incentives that unnecessarily drove up costs. Policy makers used these findings to justify a host of rules and regulations that continue to govern how our health dollars are spent.

While it was Roemer's curious facts that inspired the debate about the efficiency of the U.S. healthcare system, it was a brilliant mathematical economist's lone detour into the world of healthcare economics that would provide an even more powerful framework for understanding the strengths and limitations of Marcus Welby medicine.

Kenneth Arrow and the Importance of Uncertainty

Every year, the International Health Economics Association awards the Kenneth Arrow Prize for outstanding research. The prize is named for economics Nobel Prize winner Kenneth Arrow who, in 1963, wrote his first and only health economics paper, "Agency and the Welfare Economics of Medical Care."[6] It is impossible to overstate the impact of this paper on the way researchers and policy analysts think about the physician-patient relationship. The paper continues to be widely cited and is required reading for nearly all students of health management.

Arrow received the Nobel Prize for his "theorems of welfare economics." These theorems describe the conditions under which free markets are efficient and best serve the interests of consumers.[7] Arrow explained why it is essential for consumers to have full information about their options and to be able to freely buy and sell all goods and services. In economics parlance, this means that there must be perfect information and complete markets. Otherwise resources can be misallocated and consumers may face needlessly high prices. Because information is often imperfect and markets are often incomplete, Arrow's work is often cited to justify government intervention.

In "Agency and the Welfare Economics of Medical Care," Arrow applied these ideas to healthcare. He explained that the healthcare "market" really consists of two distinct kinds of markets. One is the kind we normally think about—markets for the provision of goods and services including hospitalizations, physician care, and drugs. According to Arrow's theories, if consumers can choose from a large number of providers and are well-informed about their options, then provider markets should function just fine without government intervention. These are big "ifs" and Arrow acknowledged that the asymmetry of information between physicians and patients can lead to the kinds of distorted choices that Roemer described.

The other kind of market eliminates unwanted risk. This includes unwanted financial risk, and free market healthcare can not live up to the competitive ideal unless consumers can obtain health insurance at actuarially fair prices. But Arrow reminds us that patients face more than financial risk—they also face a profound risk to their health. Unlike financial risk, the risk to health may be uninsurable. After all, we cannot normally give up a little bit of health in order to insure against losing our lives.[8] In Arrow's words, the market to protect against health risks is incomplete.

Arrow's next argument was his most profound and controversial. He stated that institutions evolve in response to the inefficiencies of the free market. This is a kind of Darwinian view that presupposes that over time, innovative ideas and new ways of doing business will topple failed ideas and institutions. Politics do sometimes intervene to protect the status quo, but politicians who support an ineffective status quo are eventually replaced. Thus if we observe an institution survive for an extended period of time, it is reasonable to conclude that it has successfully addressed at least some of the inefficiencies of the institutions that preceded it. The dominant institutions of healthcare markets in the 1960s were the physician-patient relationship, epitomized by Marcus Welby medicine, and indemnity insurance that paid the medical bills but otherwise butted out. Following Arrow's logic, a healthcare system dominated by Marcus Welby medicine and indemnity insurance must have been doing a decent job of addressing the problems of asymmetric information and incomplete insurance markets.

A decent job, yes, but far from perfect. Patients were in no position to diagnose and treat their own illnesses, so it made sense for them to trust in compassionate, knowledgeable experts. Arrow even observed that "compassion and competence are their [physicians'] stock in trade."[9] But this trust came at a cost. Physicians still made mistakes. Some physicians might even exploit their informational advantage for financial gain. And insured patients might ignore the financial consequences of their decisions at the expense of insurers who paid all bills without asking questions. Of course, individuals with no insurance faced financial risk and it was impossible to fully insure against health risks. Patients were damned if they had insurance and damned if they didn't. Health services researchers would soon document how these problems were driving up costs and leaving millions of Americans in financial peril.

Demand Inducement

In 1974, Canadian health economist Robert Evans introduced a new theory that was inspired by Roemer's research about hospital utilization. Evans motivated the theory of "supplier induced demand" as follows: "The professional relationship arises from the significant information differential between physician and patient, and permits the physician to exert direct, non-price influence on the demand for his own services."[10]

This theory puts a very different spin on Arrow's ideas about physician agency. It begins with the same premise—physicians know a lot more about medicine than do their patients. It reaches the same initial conclusion—physicians must act as their patients' agents. But where Arrow believed that physicians acted as near perfect agents doing what is best for their patients, Evans and other inducement theorists were more cynical. They noted the physician/agent has an inherent conflict of interest. Not only does the physician diagnose the patient's ailment, the physician also recommends a course of treatment and gets paid to deliver that treatment. Inducement theory states that physicians facing such incentives will tend to over-prescribe costly services.[11]

Evans's demand inducement theory is consistent with Roemer's Law. According to inducement theory, physicians fill new hospital beds not because more patients are sick, or because access is more convenient, but because filling the beds boosts their incomes. Evans offered additional evidence on inducement by examining different regions in Canada. He discovered that physicians seemed to be able to generate the same amount of work regardless of the physician/population ratio in their region. Evans's explanation is simple but alarming: when physicians are abundant, they induce more demand so as to maintain their incomes. This became known as the "target income" hypothesis and often goes hand-in-hand with inducement theory.

There is an alternative explanation for Evans's findings, one offered by my colleague Mark Satterthwaite, who suggested that physician migration would tend to even out incomes.[12] That is, physicians would tend to relocate from low paying areas to high paying areas. As long as there are any demand or cost differences across regions, you would see different physician/population ratios but comparable incomes. Satterthwaite's sound but boring economic argument was generally ignored in favor of Evans's more controversial theory.

If Evans's inducement theory was true, this would be a serious blow to all the patients and policy makers who had placed their trust in Marcus Welby medicine, as it would mean that doctors were performing unnecessary treatments for the sole purpose of boosting their incomes.[13] And as the supply of physicians continued to increase, so would the amount of unnecessary treatment. Taking the most pessimistic view of Evans's results, a 10 percent increase in the supply of physicians would result in a 10 percent increase in the number of unnecessary procedures.

Inducement theory provided a provocative explanation for the rapid increase in healthcare costs, especially in the United States where increases in physician supply were accompanied by increases in bed availability. Perhaps increases in spending had nothing to do with patient needs and everything to do with this expanding supply. This problem was even self-reinforcing. Physicians and hospitals would always be busy and prosperous, encouraging the training of more physicians and the opening of more hospitals. Yet no matter how many more doctors or hospitals were added, there would always seem to be a need for more! Demand inducement would cause spending to spiral out of control.

More Evidence on Inducement

The publication of Evans's research spawned a cottage industry of inducement studies by research economists. Perhaps the most important follow-up study was published by Stanford University economist Victor Fuchs. Fuchs is a renowned scholar in the field of public finance, which studies the economic role of the public sector and has served as the president of the American Economic Association. His seminal book, *Who Shall Live?*, offers a sobering look at the crucial tradeoff between health and wealth that all nations must confront.

Fuchs noted that both Evans's and Roemer's work required more sophisticated statistical techniques if the theory of inducement was to be accepted by those who took a more positive view of physician agency. He was particularly concerned about the direction of causality in the relationship between physician supply and patient demand; perhaps physicians located in areas of high demand, and not vice versa. Fuchs applied updated research methods to data on surgeons in the United States and found an inducement "elasticity" of 0.28. That is, a 10 percent increase in the number of surgeons was associated with a 2.8 percent increase in the number of surgeries. Subsequent studies using even richer data and more refined methods also find statistically significant evidence of inducement, though the reported elasticity is closer to 10 percent. This seems too low for inducement to be more than a partial explanation for the cost spiral. Some scholars, including myself, question the statistical validity of even these smaller findings, doubting whether the methods of Fuchs and others truly resolve causality.[14]

Despite the sketchy empirical support for the Roemer/Evans/Fuchs view that supply creates its own demand, there is an incontrovertible idea at the heart of inducement theory: physician financial incentives affect medical decision making. I call this the "First Axiom of Incentives in Medical Care":

If you pay providers to do more X, they will do more X

This logic behind this axiom is self-explanatory and is why most economists (including myself) believe that physicians induce demand to some extent.

Few people today would be surprised to learn that a physician's judgment can be clouded by the promise of thousands of dollars in fees. But thirty or forty years ago, we held our physicians to a higher standard and the healthcare community was jarred by the inducement evidence. Perhaps we should have paid more attention to the Committee on the Costs of Medical Care, which observed in 1932 that fee-for-service medicine gave doctors "an economic incentive to create unnecessary medical service." The CCMC even offered a solution—prepayment. A considerable body of recent research confirms that physicians paid a fixed salary provide fewer services than those paid fee-for-service.[15]

One of the most important strands of the inducement literature pertains to physician ownership of diagnostic testing equipment.[16]

Physician-owners tend to order many more tests than nonowners—some studies suggest they order twice as many. Facts like these have led some states to ban physician ownership of testing equipment. But these facts present another chicken and egg problem—does ownership lead to more testing, or do physicians who tend to order a lot of tests find it worthwhile to own the equipment? A 1990 study by David Hemenway and colleagues avoided this problem by doing a before-and-after analysis of physicians who purchased diagnostic equipment.[17] They found that after becoming owners, physicians increased test ordering by about 10 to 20 percent. The effect of ownership may not have been as strong as previously claimed, but it was still there and still fairly substantial.

A combination of factors—the need to come to terms with rising spending, the intuitive appeal of the theory, and the prominence of Evans and Fuchs—convinced health policy makers that demand inducement was a major source of inefficiency. It is difficult to overstate the resulting impact of the theory in public policy. Governments have used it to justify limiting the supply of physicians and to ration patient access to costly technologies. Private insurers have used it to justify controls on utilization and to tout the efficiency of Health Maintenance Organizations.

Economies of Scale

Inducement theorists discouraged the proliferation of hospitals on the grounds that it would encourage unnecessary utilization. This argument complemented the findings from another line of research emerging at this time. During the 1960s, economists began estimating "cost functions" that related a business's efficiency to its size and product mix. Because hospitals were a major part of the economy and because data on hospital costs were widely available, dozens of researchers estimated hospital cost functions. Most of the early studies indicated that there were substantial economies of scale in hospitals overall as well as for specific services such as open heart surgery.[18] There was also evidence of a link between provider outcome and volume that suggested an important learning curve in the delivery of complex treatments.[19] The upshot from these studies was that it might good for our wealth and our health to concentrate the delivery of care in a few large hospitals. As I will soon discuss, policy makers were keen to oblige.

Insurance and Patient Incentives

Moral Hazard

Inducement theory seems to dismiss the role of patients in medical decision making. But even if patients are unwittingly complicit in allowing inducement, they are still complicit. Most patients have a good reason not to object to their physicians' costly recommendations—insurance pays the bill. Physicians might not even need to induce demand for costly tests and procedures. Insured patients would demand them.

Regardless of whether we believe physicians face the right incentives, it is certain that insured patients face the wrong incentives. Free care invites overutilization. Patients may visit providers when their conditions do not warrant medical attention, buy unneeded drugs, demand batteries of tests when simpler diagnostics would do, and ignore prices when selecting providers. When patients behave as if price does not matter, everyone's costs increase. Insurers have a name for this behavior—moral hazard. Economists have been studying the problem of moral hazard for decades.

Economist Mark Pauly was studying for his Ph.D. when Kenneth Arrow published his paper on physician agency. Inspired by Arrow, Pauly's research provided an economic foundation for thinking about how insurance affects the demand for medical care.[20] He observed that when it came to price, the demand for medical care is not unlike the demand for any other good or service. In particular, if the price of medical care falls, consumers will want to buy more of it. It is also likely that they will purchase some medical services that cost more than they are worth. In economic parlance, this creates a "deadweight loss" to society.

Pauly observed that the deadweight loss could be curtailed if insurers imposed copayments in the form of deductibles (payments that must be made upfront before insurance coverage kicks in) and coinsurance (a flat fee or flat percentage of charges for each additional service rendered.) The only way to completely eliminate the deadweight loss would be to do away with insurance altogether, but this would eliminate the benefit of risk spreading. In other words, we can have well-functioning provider markets and poorly functioning insurance markets, or vice versa. They cannot both function perfectly at the same time.

The idea that price affected medical utilization did not sit well with the medical community, which had long held to the medical model in which utilization was based on the medical judgments of doctors and not the financial considerations of patients. Physicians did not fully dismiss the role of economics; most understood that insured patients were more likely to seek care and consent to treatment.[21] But most physicians did not believe that this effect was strong enough to justify the copayments described by Pauly.

The RAND Study

To economists, the question was not whether moral hazard existed, but whether the effect was large. If price did play a big role in medical decision making, then the potential benefits of imposing copayments could be huge. By the late 1960s, events on the national stage made it imperative for lawmakers to find out whether price mattered. Despite the passage of Medicare and Medicaid, supporters of universal access in the United States were unhappy with the state of affairs. There were still some gaps in coverage for those under age sixty-five. Even the safety net provided by nonprofit hospitals was wearing a bit thin, as rapidly rising costs and lagging Medicaid payments made it increasingly difficult for them to provide uncompensated care.

To plug these gaps, Senator Ted Kennedy and Congressman Wilbur Mills proposed a comprehensive federally operated national health insurance system. This would complement the Marcus Welby system of providing care, with its autonomous providers practicing fee-for-service medicine. The Kennedy-Mills proposal would cost billions of dollars to implement so they suggested a coinsurance rate of 20 percent and a deductible of $1,000.

Seeking a way to expand coverage without a federal takeover of the health insurance systems, President Nixon offered to instead increase the Medicaid income limit. Nixon wanted to limit the cost of this expansion, so he asked the Office of Economic Opportunity (OEO) to find out how much money could be saved through copayments. Because published research did not provide a reliable answer, the OEO solicited proposals to conduct a nationwide Health Insurance Experiment (HIE).[22]

In 1970, the OEO selected the RAND Corporation to conduct the experiment. The RAND study was led by Joseph Newhouse, considered by his colleagues today to be the "dean" of health economists. Newhouse assembled a remarkable team of social scientists and academic physicians, many of whom used the HIE as a springboard to successful academic careers at leading universities.[23] The broad array of their interests and skills is reflected in the wide range of issues addressed by the HIE.

The HIE had a simple research design. Beginning in the mid-1970s, thousands of enrollees in six areas of the country were randomly assigned to different insurance plans in which they remained enrolled for three to five years.[24] Random assignment helped assure that each plan had a cross-section of patients, some healthy and some with severe medical problems. All the plans covered virtually all healthcare services, including mental health, drugs, and long-term care.

The main difference among the plans was the degree of patient cost sharing. Some patients were assigned to "free care" plans that covered all costs. Other patients had to make copayments of up to 50 percent. Some paid substantial deductibles.[25] Cost sharing was capped at 15 percent of family income, or $1,000 in total family expenses, whichever was lower. This was a fairly high cap, considering that per capita spending on healthcare at the time of the study was about $700. (Today, per capita spending exceeds $7,000.) RAND offered substantial "participation incentives" to potential enrollees. These financial incentives worked—over 80 percent of the roughly 7,000 individuals contacted by RAND agreed to participate in the HIE.

The HIE resulted in over one hundred publications.[26] The most highly publicized result, first disseminated in the early 1980s, can be summarized very easily: *price matters*. The typical enrollee receiving free care incurred about 40 percent higher healthcare costs than did the typical enrollee who made copayments. More care was not necessarily better care. After the HIE ended, those patients who received free care were generally no healthier than those who made copayments. Low income participants with initially poor health status were an important exception. Price mattered for them as well, but the savings from copayments were accompanied by poorer health outcomes.

The HIE results had many important nuances. The biggest savings occur when individuals move from completely free care to making 25 percent copayments. Further increases in copayments impose greater financial risk but only modest additional savings. Over half the savings in any given year accrued from individuals who did not use any medical services that year. In other words, the biggest effect of cost sharing is to keep patients from seeing providers altogether. It is fair to ask whether this is the best place to focus cost containment efforts. In a similar vein, RAND found that cost sharing had virtually no impact on inpatient expenses for those patients who found their way into a hospital. If we are looking to make hospitals more efficient, then the HIE results indicate that cost sharing is not the solution. We should not make too much of this finding, however. HIE enrollments were a tiny fraction of the total in each area studied. Providers probably did not even notice that the study was ongoing and would have had no reason to reduce prices or try to enhance efficiency. If all individuals faced HIE-style cost sharing, providers might have to sit up and take notice.

By the time the HIE results emerged, the motivation for the study was moot. Neither the Kennedy-Mills nor Nixon proposals went anywhere in Congress. Even so, the HIE has important lessons for today's health policy debate. The craftsmanship displayed by Newhouse's team at RAND leaves little doubt that price does matter and that free care is *wasteful* care. RAND even provided valuable estimates of how much money can be saved when patients have to pay part of the medical bill.

Insurance and Provider Competition

If fully insured patients ignored prices when deciding what medical services to purchase, then they probably ignored prices when choosing a provider. As a result, market forces, such as they were, would not prevent providers from raising their prices. Upon hearing about this situation, a colleague of mine asked why providers did not charge infinite prices. I explained that given the rate of medical price inflation, we were getting awfully close.[27] Fed up with the situation, insurers introduced a payment model that was in widespread use in the utility industry. Electric companies and local phone companies were usually granted monopoly status so as to reduce capital costs. In order to prevent these monopolists from price gouging, state regulators set prices based on their costs of doing business, plus an allowance for a return on capital.

Led by the large Blue Cross and Blue Shield plans, insurers applied the same logic to hospitals. Hospitals were not monopolists in the sense of being the sole providers in their markets, but they may well have been, given the lack of patient price sensitivity. Rather than pay hospitals what were perceived to be exorbitant charges, health plans began to pay on the basis of accounting costs (plus an allowance for modest profits). Plans were also concerned about price gouging by physicians. Instead of paying the physicians' charges, they paid them the least of the "usual, customary, and reasonable" (UCR) charge, thereby basing prices on local market norms.[28] Early on, Medicare and Medicaid also relied on cost-based reimbursement to hospitals and UCR payments to doctors.

Cost-based reimbursement seemed like a reasonable way to keep hospital payments in line with costs. Unfortunately it created a new set of perverse incentives. Accountants quickly learned how to allocate costs so as to maximize reimbursements without actually saving any money. (As an MBA student in 1980, I took a course in hospital accounting that seemed to be entirely about exploiting loopholes in cost-based reimbursement.) Hospitals also learned that whenever their costs went up, their payments would go up as well. The results were all too predictable. Eager to attract physicians and their patients, hospitals receiving cost-based reimbursement added new technology and additional support staff. Costs were not an issue.

I am not certain where the term "medical arms race" originated, but it was first called to my attention in 1979 by my dissertation advisor, Alain Enthoven. He pointed out that there were nearly as many open heart surgery providers in Santa Barbara, California as there were in all of Canada, and he blamed this on competition fueled by cost-based reimbursement. A few years later, University of California economists Harold Luft and James Robinson published systematic evidence that hospitals were competing for the favors of physicians by adding CAT scanners, dialysis units, and open heart surgery suites, and by expanding nursing staffs.[29] It was a hard pill for economists to swallow, but it seemed that competition was yet another culprit in the cost spiral.

The Healthcare Quadrilemma

Indemnity insurance was supposed to protect consumers against the cost of illness. By contributing to moral hazard and the medical arms race, indemnity insurance helped to drive up medical costs. Economist Burton Weisbrod saw an even broader pattern of connections in the health economy, describing the links between insurance, costs, medical technology, and quality, as the "health care quadrilemma."[30] Weisbrod is a leading scholar in two fields closely related to health economics—the economics of the nonprofit sector and the economics of technology. As the director of the Center for Health Economics and Law at the University of Wisconsin in the 1980s, he conducted extensive research on the economics of medical research and was honored with membership in the National Academy of Sciences and the American Academy of Arts and Sciences, a rare combination for an economist.

Weisbrod argued that the types of research projects selected by drug companies and other medical R&D firms depended on the expected market rewards and not just the scientific potential. This is the received wisdom today, of course, but it was a revelation at the time. Because insured patients received blanket protection against medical costs, medical research firms knew that cost would be no object when it came time to sell their discoveries. If anything, high cost treatments meant high profits, so R&D was conducted without regard to cost. The resulting technological improvements were impressive and the quality of care improved. But they came with steep price tags and the higher costs further fueled the demand for insurance. This cycle would repeat itself unless insurers changed the incentives for R&D. Weisbrod did not pass judgment on this process—after all, the health benefits of new technology might be worth the cost—but he identified yet another reason for the ongoing cycle of medical cost inflation.

A Legacy of Confusing Prices

Cost-based reimbursement has left one more legacy that any patient can observe by looking at a hospital bill, where they will find a long list of daily charges for each of the hospital's many "cost centers"—the med/surg acute-care bed day, the intensive care day, surgery, drugs, supplies, physical therapy, occupational therapy, laboratory, radiology, and so forth. This system of setting charges dates back fifty years or more, but became institutionalized with the onset of cost-based reimbursement, which required hospitals to keep track of the services provided by each cost center.

Unfortunately hospital charges often bore no relationship to costs. Charges for diagnostic tests might have exceeded costs by a factor of three or more and charges for intensive care might have been less than costs. These oddities hardly mattered to hospitals because payers rarely paid what the hospitals charged. (Payments were based on a complex formula that involved "cost to charge ratios" computed by accountants.) But most patients had no idea that their medical bill was merely window dressing, and more than a few were quite distressed to see a $50 "charge" for aspirin. Although the era of cost-based reimbursement is long behind us, Medicare still requires similar calculations so that it can set payment rates. Today's hospital bills report charges for each of the Medicare cost centers and continue to confuse and frustrate patients who do not understand how the system works. There have been many calls for simplifying pricing, and for good reason. As I will explain in chapter 5, this may be easier said than done.

Practice Variations

Like Milton Roemer, Jack Wennberg began his career as a public health officer. Wennberg completed both his MD degree and a Master's in

Public Health in the early 1960s. After completing his residency at Johns Hopkins University, he joined the faculty of the University of Vermont, where he directed the state's Regional Medical Program. In order to promote more effective allocation of Vermont's health resources, he set up an epidemiological data system that measured how patients across the state utilized hospital and other medical services. To his surprise, he discovered that the rate at which patients used services varied widely. Even more surprising, the variation apparently had very little to do with their underlying medical needs. The rates of intervention for even simple surgical procedures such as tonsillectomies varied substantially from one town to the next. Wennberg used the term "medical practice variations" to describe this phenomenon. After moving to Dartmouth Medical School, Wennberg has devoted his life to researching variations. For his efforts, Jack Wennberg has been dubbed both the "Christopher Columbus" and "Johnny Appleseed" of medical practice variations.[31]

Wennberg and numerous other scholars have published dozens of articles documenting the extent of practice variations in regions all around the world. They show that rates of interventions for a wide range of procedures such as appendectomies, caesarian sections, hip replacements, prostatectomies, and tonsillectomies can vary across cities and towns by a factor of two or more. End-of-life spending also shows enormous variation; so, too, does spending on prevention. Practice variations cannot be explained by differences in insurance coverage, other economic factors, or supply availability. They are just as prevalent in nations with socialized healthcare systems as they are in the United States.

The most likely explanation for practice variations is that individual physicians have their own practice styles, for example a preference for performing caesarian deliveries. These styles may be based on differences in education, ongoing training, and personal preferences. A dominant provider in a community, such as a department head in a major teaching hospital, can influence the style of local doctors and attract into the community those doctors who are already predisposed to that style. The end result is that within a hospital, or even within an entire community, most of the doctors may have a similar style.

As Wennberg describes it, the initial response to the research on practice variations was "muted."[32] People were more concerned with physicians' and patients' financial incentives than with the possibility that doctors might disagree about what constitutes proper medical process. In 1982, Wennberg published an article about variations in *Scientific American*. Two years later, the influential policy journal *Health Affairs* published a theme issue on practice variations that was accompanied by a press conference at the U.S. Capitol at which Wennberg and several Congressmen spoke. Policy makers were finally taking notice of Wennberg's variations.

In Wennberg's opinion, practice variations were prima facie evidence that something was wrong with medical decision making. Assuming there is a right and wrong way to deliver medical are, he questioned how different communities could experience such widely different standards of care. Policy makers began to understand that medical practice variations might be just as big a source of inefficiency as demand inducement, moral hazard, and the medical arms race.

Thus far I have catalogued a host of inefficiencies associated with the market for healthcare services. In the chapters ahead, I will describe how policy makers have sought to address these problems. Before doing so, I will consider another important market—the market for health insurance to protect against financial risk. This market is plagued with its own set of problems, leading to even more policy prescriptions.

Breakdowns in Insurance Markets

Adverse Selection and Cream Skimming

Through the 1970s and 1980s, most health services researchers focused their research on inefficiencies in provider markets. But a theoretical study of insurance published in 1976 by two mainstream economists, Michael Rothschild and Joseph Stiglitz, served notice that insurance markets were also plagued with inefficiency.[33] It is now widely recognized that it may be impossible to prevent the breakdowns in free market health insurance that Rothschild and Stiglitz identified.

Rothschild and Stiglitz model the behavior of insurance companies and insurance purchasers (either individuals or firms) when the latter have "private information" about their healthcare needs. (This means that individual insurance purchasers know about their own medical needs but insurance companies know only about the aggregate needs of a population.) Insurance companies would naturally like to sign up customers who expect to be healthy and avoid those who expect to incur large medical bills. This is known as "cream skimming," a pejorative term but also an inevitable tactic for any profit-seeking insurer. Conversely those expecting the biggest medical bills will be most eager to buy insurance. This is the problem of adverse selection that I described in chapter 1, and is another inevitable consequence of free market health insurance.

Rothschild and Stiglitz show that cream skimming and adverse selection can be avoided if insurers can perfectly experience rate, that is, set premiums in accordance with each enrollee's expected medical needs. But this makes a shambles of the financial protection that insurance is supposed to provide. Once someone gets a chronic illness, their premiums would skyrocket. Insurance provides true financial protection only if it pools risk among the healthy and the sick.

Markets that pool risk are inherently unstable. Within any risk pool, healthy enrollees necessarily subsidize the purchases of sicker enrollees. This creates a business opportunity—a new insurer can come along and cream skim the healthy enrollees by offering a policy with lower benefits and lower premiums. Sicker enrollees, who prize their benefits, will remain with the incumbent insurer, who will experience adverse selection as a result. The incumbent will have to raise premiums, driving even more low risks from the pool.

The Rothschild and Stiglitz model suggests that insurers could use marketing tactics to further skim off the healthiest enrollees. My favorite example, albeit an apocryphal one, is of the insurer who allegedly placed their offices on the sixth floor of an old building with no elevator. Anyone not fit enough to climb the stairs could not sign up for the policy! Better examples may be found in the advertisements for health insurance found in fitness and travel magazines, just the sort of reading material favored by the young and healthy.

Many researchers have added theoretical twists to the Rothschild and Stiglitz model, but they all confirm that risk pools are prone to bouts of cream skimming and adverse selection. Only large employers, whose employees represent a stable risk pool with relatively average medical needs, are likely to be immune from these tactics. The constant churning of insurance products, combined with sharp increases in the premiums charged by insurers who suffer from adverse selection, contributes to an even more vexing problem with private health insurance—the persistence of a large population that has no insurance coverage at all.

The Uninsured

According to two authoritative national surveys, about forty-seven million Americans—16 percent of the population—have been without health insurance at some point in the past year.[34] Virtually all of the uninsured are ineligible for Medicare or Medicaid. If they are to obtain coverage, it will most likely be through the private sector. This is hardly a new problem. Private health insurance markets have never come close to covering everyone.

Piecing together data from different sources, it is possible to examine trends in insurance coverage from the middle of the last century, before Medicaid and Medicare were created. The number of individuals with private insurance coverage for hospital expenses grew from twelve million in 1940 to 153 million in 1965. (See table 2.1.) The total U.S. population in 1965 was about 190 million, so about thirty-seven million (20 percent of the population) lacked private hospital insurance. Kerr-Mills and other government programs covered hospital costs for a few million people, leaving at least thirty million Americans without any hospital coverage. Coverage for physician and other medical expenses outside the hospital was considerably sparser, and very few Americans were insured for prescription drugs or long-term care.

Medicare and Medicaid were introduced in 1966. Medicare had an immediate enrollment of twenty million. It took time for some states to ramp up their Medicaid programs, but the number of Medicaid recipients also reached twenty million by the early 1970s.[35] Many of the

Table 2.1. Private Health Insurance Coverage: 1950–65

Year	Number with Hospital Coverage	Percent with Hospital Coverage	Number with Physician Coverage	Percent with Physician Coverage
1940	12.3 million	9.3%	3.0 million	2.3%
1950	76.6	50.6	21.6	14.3
1960	130.0	72.5	86.9	48.5
1965	153.1	80.6	111.7	58.8

Source: Health Insurance Association of America, *Sourcebook of Health Insurance Data*, various years. These data are drawn from insurance company reports of enrollment and may not accurately adjust for individuals who are covered under more than one plan.

Medicaid recipients were also on Medicare and many Medicare and Medicaid enrollees previously had Kerr-Mills coverage or private health insurance. Thus the number of net newly insured was far less than forty million.

Many holes remained in the safety net. Medicare did not cover drugs or long-term care and required deductibles and copayments for everything else. Medicare allowed private insurers to sell "wraparound" plans to fill in the gaps. Elderly poor and disabled individuals could also use Medicaid to pay for what Medicare did not. There was a catch to getting Medicaid coverage, however. To become eligible, individuals would have to spend down their wealth. This meant that qualifying for Medicaid effectively required a deductible equal to one's lifetime savings. This remains a key concern for anyone today who has accumulated some retirement savings but is seeking eligibility for Medicaid.

In addition to supplementing Medicare for indigent elderly and disabled individuals, the most important Medicaid category is "Aid to Families with Dependent Children."[36] In practice, this was restricted to children in single parent households where the parent did not work full time. As I will discuss, there have been a number of patches to expand Medicaid coverage beyond these initial categories.

By 1970, about twenty-five million Americans—roughly 12 percent of the population—still lacked health insurance at some time during the year. An estimated one in six children lacked health insurance.

Counter to the stereotype, the majority of uninsured children lived in situations where the head of the household was employed. The same was true for the majority of uninsured adults. The ranks of the uninsured have increased fairly steadily as the U.S. population has grown, with slight declines during business upturns and increases during recessions. It is disturbing that the number of uninsured has continued to climb in the last few years during an economic recovery.

The Inequities of Employer-Based Coverage

Despite the success of Medicare and Medicaid, most Americans continue to rely on their employers to buy health insurance for them. This works pretty well if you work for a large firm; 98 percent of firms employing two hundred workers or more offer health insurance.[37] Things do not look so good if you work for a smaller firm, where offer rates are below 60 percent. We cannot assess solutions to the problems of employer-sponsored insurance without getting to the root cause of this differential.

Bear in mind that insurers set premiums to at least cover the expected health costs, administrative and selling costs. There are two factors that might drive a wedge between the premium and the amount that an employer (and its employees) is willing to spend. The first is any difference between the insurer's and enrollee's expectations about health spending. If a potential enrollee is healthy but the insurer thinks otherwise, the premium may be more than the individual is willing to bear. (This is just a restatement of the problem of adverse selection.) The second is the cost of selling insurance, including sales, administration and the medical underwriting performed by the insurer to limit adverse selection.[38]

For an average worker at a large firm, the wedge is small. One reason is that insurers view large companies as having stable, representative risk pools that pose less of a threat of adverse selection. Another reason is that insurers can spread their costs over more workers. For workers at small firms and the self-employed, the wedge can be much larger. Obviously insurers cannot spread their fixed costs quite so far. This can add hundreds of dollars to the costs of each policy, enough to give pause to many potential enrollees. Insurers also have more reason to be concerned about adverse selection. Sometimes they will be able to experience rate premiums. Large companies benefit from the law of large numbers and are unlikely to have wild swings in the average needs of employees. Small companies are not so fortunate, especially when we bear in mind that a single catastrophic illness can require medical bills in the hundreds of thousands of dollars.

Even if insurers do not experience rate, large companies have a decided advantage. Large companies are in the market for insurance every year and their risk profiles do not change very much. But small companies and individuals go in and out of the market with changeable risk profiles. Insurers are always asking why a firm that did not purchase insurance in the past is seeking coverage now. Could it have one or two employees who have serious medical needs? Anticipating adverse selection, insurers raise their premiums to all small employers and individuals. Those in good health may find the price of insurance is too much to bear and prefer to remain uninsured.

Following the same logic, it is easy to see how premiums can be even larger for part-time and temporary workers. Moreover these workers tend to have low earnings, so they may have more important spending needs. Only 30 percent of U.S. firms offer insurance to part-time workers; only 3 percent offer insurance to temporary workers.

Despite these obstacles, many uninsured individuals appear to have enough discretionary income to purchase individual coverage, but simply choose not to. A recent study by Kate Bundorf and Mark Pauly suggests that anywhere from 60 to 80 percent of the uninsured can afford to purchase coverage.[39] Many of them are offered insurance that is heavily subsidized by their employers and further subsidized through the federal tax exemption, yet do not take up the offer. Why would they choose to remain uninsured? Some of the uninsured might underestimate their medical needs. Others might prefer to risk a big medical bill than pay a steep insurance premium. If they continued to run up huge medical bills, they might become eligible for Medicaid or arrange with their providers to accept periodic partial payments. Individuals with few assets to protect might be willing to face the risk of bankruptcy, which would effectively limit the downside of a big medical bill. Many individuals are willing to seek out charity care or visit providers of last resort. I recall a colleague some years ago commenting that he had yet to encounter a taxi driver who had health insurance because they always knew where to go for free care. The exaggerated claim made a valid point.

No matter how hard one tries to dismiss the problems of the uninsured, it is certain that millions, if not tens of millions of Americans lack health insurance through no fault of their own. Many, perhaps most, are one illness away from financial catastrophe, forced to sell their homes, spend down their retirement savings, or go bankrupt.[40] That is just the financial side of the equation. The uninsured are far less likely to have a personal physician. They get less preventive care. Those who become seriously ill may delay the start of treatment. Once treatment commences, they have less access to the best providers and the latest technologies. As a result, the uninsured have lower "health capital"—they are less productive when alive and die sooner. The Institutes of Medicine estimates that the human capital lost by the uninsured exceeds $65 billion annually.[41]

Insurance Market Spillovers

The employer-based health insurance system creates problems that spillover into the entire economy. One obvious problem is that smaller firms are at a competitive disadvantage when trying to hire workers. Smaller firms can pay higher insurance premiums and reduce either wages or profits to make up the difference. Or they can choose not to offer insurance at all. Either way, they suffer in comparison with bigger rivals. This is not necessarily unfair, at least it is no less fair than when small firms have to pay more than large firms for other inputs into production. But it is small firms that stand to gain the most from government efforts to improve the way that insurance markets function.

Unfortunately some of the rules and regulations governing employer-sponsored health insurance put small firms at an even bigger disadvantage. A key provision of the 1974 Employee Retirement Income Security Act (ERISA)—the legislation that created Individual Retirement Accounts—exempts "self-insured" firms (i.e., firms that assume the financial risk from their employees' medical bills) from state health insurance regulations, including taxes and mandates to cover services such as acupuncture, podiatry, drug abuse treatment, and hair prostheses.[42] The average state health insurance tax is 2 to 3 percent of premiums, hardly enough to make or break a small firm. But the costs of mandates are another story. A few mandates, such as well-child care, could save money but most add to costs and a few, such as in vitro fertilization, can add several percentage points to premiums. Taken together, mandates can drive up premiums by 30 percent or more.[43] As it turns out, most insurance policies already cover many mandated services, such as chemotherapy and mastectomies, so the actual impact may be smaller. Economists Gail Jensen and Michael Morrisey have conducted extensive research on mandates and estimate that they increase premiums by about 10 percent.[44] It is no wonder that most large firms choose to self-insure, thereby becoming "ERISA exempt" from state insurance mandates.

Despite the attraction of avoiding mandates, smaller firms are often unable to bear the risk of self-insurance. Small businesses may face bankruptcy if just one employee runs up big medical bills. Larger firms benefit from the law of large numbers and can more easily bear the risk of self-insurance. Unable to self-insure, small businesses must purchase traditional health insurance, complete with taxes and all the mandated benefits. Whenever a state legislature considers another mandate, for autism, fertilization, hearing aids, or colorectal cancer screening, the debate is not really about whether that service is important or not—the employer and employees could decide that for themselves. The real debate is whether the interest group representing the mandated service has more clout than the interest group representing small businesses. All too often, small businesses lose.

Job Lock

Employer-based insurance not only distorts competition between big and small firms, it distorts worker job choices. For the economy to be at maximum efficiency, workers ought to go where they can be most productive. But when choosing a job, many workers consider whether they can obtain health benefits.[45] They may turn down a job that is perfectly suited to their abilities in favor of another that offers better insurance. That would never happen if insurance coverage was divorced from employment.

Things can be even dicier for workers who have insurance and are contemplating changing jobs. Until recent legislative changes that I describe in the next chapter, workers had to face waiting periods and preexisting condition exclusions that might cause them to think twice before switching employers. Some studies suggest that the resulting "job lock" reduced labor market turnover by as much as 20 percent, though a few studies suggest the problem is far smaller. This is a serious problem; we all benefit when workers are able to change jobs in order to maximize their potential. Job lock stifles this mobility. Again this would never happen if insurance was divorced from employment and it represents a real drag on the economy.

The impact of the employer-based insurance system extends throughout a worker's career. Most Americans contemplate taking early retirement and nearly 20 percent retire before they turn sixty-five and are eligible for Medicare. Those who do retire early are disproportionately likely to have retiree health benefits. The early retirement rate for those with benefits is 6 to 8 percentage points higher than for those without.

Anything but Free

Since the enactment of Medicare and Medicaid, the United States health economy has been a patchwork quilt of federal, state, and private sector insurance programs, while provision of care has remained almost exclusively in the private sector. The healthcare market studied by health services researchers in 1960s and 1970s—the market of Marcus Welby medicine—hardly lived up to the ideals of a free market described by Arrow. Plagued by demand inducement, moral hazard, practice variations and a medical arms race, the medical care market may have been "free" of third-party interference, but it lacked the discipline required for efficiency and effectiveness. Ironically the "free" healthcare market was proving to be remarkably expensive. In response, payers sought ways to tie the hands of Doctor Welby and his patients. I will describe these rules and regulations in the next chapter.

For all that Americans have spent on healthcare, it remains a national disgrace that so many lack health insurance and the protections it affords. The adverse spillovers to labor markets only amplify the need to fix the problems of employer-based health insurance markets.

Arrow predicted that if a market's key institutions did not serve the interests of consumers, then those institutions would be replaced. By the 1970s, there was a growing consensus that Marcus Welby medicine was failing. The regulatory and market institutions that replaced it were developed by impatient payers and reluctantly embraced by exasperated enrollees. All the while, the policy goals of high quality, efficient healthcare for all Americans seemed as elusive as ever.

Therapy for an Ailing Health Economy

There are now ominous signs appearing which seem to suggest that all which was gained for the poor and elderly may soon be lost under the guise of "economy."

—Senator John Tunney
(Democrat, California), 1971[1]

A Stealth System

Marcus Welby, MD depicted a vibrant American healthcare system. Most Americans bought into the mythology, and why not? The system seemed to work, at least for those with insurance. Mainstream America was largely unconcerned about cost or quality, even if a growing number of academics were raising red flags.

The signs of trouble were easy to spot, if anyone bothered to look. Spurred on by the Medicare and Medicaid expansions of insurance coverage, per capita spending in the United States increased from $126 in 1960 to more than $300 by 1970. (See table 3.1.) At the same time, about 12 percent of Americans under age sixty-five still lacked insurance. It was no badge of honor that the United States had higher costs and a higher rate of uninsurance than any other developed nation.

Table 3.1. Annual Health Spending: 1960–80

Year	Total health spending ($billion)	Per capita spending	Real per capita spending (today's dollars)	Annual inflation in real per capita spending	Health spending as percent of GDP
1960	$27.6	$146	$960	3.7%	5.2%
1970	75.1	357	1800	6.5	7.2
1980	254.9	1110	2640	3.9	9.1

Source: CMS current reports. Note that there is a change in the way the data is computed starting in 1970. This causes a slight discrepancy between older and newer data.

There were other signs of problems. When compared with other developed nations, Americans had average life expectancy and infant mortality. While a nation's healthcare system does not fully determine the health status of its people, it was difficult for supporters of the status quo to argue that Americans were getting a reasonable bang for their healthcare bucks.

Facts like these drew the attention of commercial insurers and government regulators. But what really captured their attention was that healthcare was consuming an ever increasing percentage of employer labor costs and government budgets. Payers believed the situation was unsustainable and it was time for them to impose themselves on the healthcare system. The era of Marcus Welby medicine was coming to an end.

Origins of Managed Care

The physician-patient relationship in the United States has never been completely free from outside influence. Recall that the AMA's historic opposition to national health insurance was due, in part, to the heavy-handed manner in which states operated their worker compensation programs a century ago. Government intervention in healthcare has even deeper roots. Physician licensure began in the mid-eighteenth century when would-be physicians had to petition their colonial governor for permission to practice. Physician licensure disappeared for a time during the early nineteenth century but returned a few decades later. States eventually imposed licensing restrictions on virtually all the medical professions as well as institutional providers such as hospitals and nursing homes. Patients have never had totally free choice of provider; only government-approved providers would do.

These restrictions are ostensibly designed to assure quality but have had the additional effect of limiting entry, reminding us that regulation sometimes serves the interests of the regulated. State and local governments did little else to regulate medical practice. There was some self-regulation through practices such as physician peer review and facilities accreditation.[2] Beyond these, however, third-party restrictions on medical practice were few and far between.

To most Americans this meant that they could freely choose among any licensed provider to deliver their care. Providers sold their services directly to patients, receiving fee-for-service payments that were not subject to third party review. Beginning in the 1890s, a very different model of healthcare delivery began to emerge in isolated pockets around the nation. A handful of physicians offered "lodge practices"—prepaid medical care given to fraternal orders, unions, and other associations of workers. By 1920, two dozen clinics in Oregon and Washington offered prepayment arrangements to employee groups.

From an economic perspective, the most important difference between lodge practice and traditional practice was prepayment. Patients may have been ignorant of this important change in financial incentives, but they were surely aware that lodge practice meant an end to free choice. If an employer offered a lodge practice, then the employees could only obtain free care from that practice's medical staff. If they obtained care outside the practice, they had to pay the entire bill themselves. It had to be this way. Physicians who accepted prepayment could not open their practices to every provider, lest they lose control of spending. Prepayment and limited choice went hand in hand.

The 1932 report of the Committee on the Cost of Medicare Care had nothing but praise for these practices. CCMC observed that prepayment was a form of insurance that relieved employees of the financial risks associated with illness. CCMC also applauded the fact that prepayment limited incentives to provide unnecessary care, anticipating

Roemer and Evans by thirty years. CCMC strongly encouraged physicians to practice in groups, citing four main benefits:

1. Physicians in groups could bear the financial risk of prepayment.

2. Physicians in groups could specialize their practices.

3. Physicians in groups could afford to make capital investments in technology.

4. Physicians in groups could afford professional management.

The benefits paralleled similar changes in business practice that were fueling the post–World War I growth of corporate America—risk spreading, specialization, technology investment, and professional management. The CCMC recommended nothing less than a thorough transformation of the entire U.S. healthcare system, from a fledgling profession into an efficient business enterprise. It would take another forty years or more before these ideas would enter the mainstream.

Kaiser and the Group Health Cooperative

In the intervening decades, prepaid practices popped up here and there, mainly on the West Coast. The first large prepaid group was the Ross-Loos Clinic in Los Angeles, which had nearly 40,000 enrollees by the mid-1930s. In 1980, Ross-Loos was acquired by Insurance Company of North America, which would, in turn, merge with Connecticut General to become CIGNA, now one of the nation's largest managed care insurers.

Kaiser plans grew out of the need to provide medical care to tens of thousands of West Coast shipyard workers during World War II. When the workers dispersed at the end of the War, Kaiser was stuck with modern hospitals and highly trained physicians, so it opened its facilities to the public. The Kaiser Foundation Health Plans and their affiliated Permanente Medical groups were an immediate success, with over 150,000 members by 1950. By the 1970s, Kaiser was in five states with total enrollments exceeding three million.

The Group Health Cooperative (GHC) of Puget Sound began shortly after World War II as an experiment in taking lodge practice into a local community. A consumer cooperative in Seattle approached Dr. John Garfield, who had established a successful lodge practice in Oklahoma. Together they created the GHC and convinced four hundred families to contribute $100 each toward the purchase of the Seattle Medical Securities Clinic and a sixty bed hospital. Growing slowly at first, the GHC gained popularity in the 1950s and had 250,000 enrollees in the Seattle area by 1960. There was a smattering of other successful prepaid practices, most notably HIP of New York, which began in the 1940s and had 500,000 members by 1960. Despite these big successes, there were only about forty prepaid group practices by 1970 and most Americans were blissfully unaware that there was an alternative to Marcus Welby medicine.

HMOs

The Father of Managed Care

In May 1970, Paul Ellwood coined the term Health Maintenance Organization (HMO) and slowly but surely, the entire nation began to take notice. Ellwood, a Stanford Medical School graduate and pediatric neurologist by training, had by this time transformed himself into a health policy expert. An admirer of the prepaid group practice model, he had the opportunity to promote his ideas after a chance meeting on an airplane with a top advisor to President Nixon. The meeting came at a propitious time because the Nixon administration was seeking an alternative to the Kennedy-Mills NHI proposal. Ellwood was invited to Washington for further talks with administration staffers where he coined the term Health Maintenance Organization "as a way of describing an organization that would compete on the bases of price and quality and combine insurance and healthcare in a single organization."[3] Ellwood convinced the administration to put its weight behind a proposal to increase enrollments in prepaid groups. This led to the HMO Act of 1974, which helped catalyze their growth.

Ellwood went on to form the consulting firm Interstudy, which gathers and interprets data on HMO performance. Interstudy clients include most of the nation's top health insurers, as well as many employers and academic researchers. On the policy front, he created the "Jackson Hole Group," a healthcare reform policy think tank whose semipermanent membership consisted of prominent supporters of managed care and independent business leaders. The group met off and on during the 1980s and 1990s at Ellwood's vacation home in Jackson Hole. The group's ideas formed the genesis of President Clinton's ill-fated Health Security Act proposal. As of 1970, however, not even Paul Ellwood could anticipate the prominent role that HMOs would play in future debates about health policy.

HMO Strategies

The few policy analysts who were paying attention could identify several strategies that HMOs used to set them apart from traditional fee-for-service medicine. The most obvious and important was prepayment. A 1971 report about Kaiser HMOs touted "the absence of a fee-for-service incentive to do what, by judicious surgical standards, constitutes unjustified surgery."[4] Kaiser and GHC also built their own hospitals, thereby eliminating the conflict inherent in Roemer's Law. As a result, the supply of beds per enrollee and the length of stay per admitted patient have been much lower at Kaiser and GHC than in the fee-for-service sector, and more closely approximate the numbers seen in Canada and other nations that tightly control bed supply.

The integration of insurer and provider under one organizational umbrella encouraged other cost saving innovations. Kaiser built dedicated rehabilitation hospitals and started its own home nursing care programs. Patients got out of the hospital faster and the total costs of care fell. Kaiser hospitals were among the first in the nation to offer full time emergency care teams (rather than rotate physicians and nurses off their wards.) GHC introduced a telephone nurse consulting program and created "rapid care units" where physicians and nurses monitored patients as an alternative to conventional hospitalization. Through the 1970s and 1980s, Kaiser and GHC continued to emphasize outpatient care by offering freestanding surgery and emergency care facilities. These innovations were described as a way to "wring maximum health out of every dollar instead of maximum dollars out of every illness."[5] Nearly all of these innovations have become standard practice throughout medicine.

HMO supporters also touted their emphasis on prevention.[6] One of the founders of the GHC, Dr. Sandy MacColl, wrote that he and his colleagues sought "a system of family care . . . directed towards a goal of good care, health maintenance, and preventive services."[7] The term Health Maintenance Organization reflected Paul Ellwood's belief that prepayment rewarded providers who kept their patients healthy. Dr. Cecil Cutting, the executive director of the Kaiser Permanente Medical Group in Northern California called this "the Reversal of Economics," stating that with prepayment, "both the hospitals and doctors are better off if the patient remains well."[8] Although this is the conventional wisdom even among many critics of HMOs, it requires a somewhat cynical view of traditional medical practice, implying that fee-for-service doctors are "better off " if their patients get sick. They may be better off financially (assuming their patients don't leave them), but it is hard to believe they are better off in the broader sense of professional fulfillment. Even so, the evidence that I will describe in the next chapter strongly supports the argument that HMOs have done a better job at prevention.

What many saw as a major limitation of HMOs—restrictions on provider choice—also worked to their advantage. Whereas state laws effectively forbade indemnity insurers from excluding any licensed providers from their panels, HMOs were closed panel plans. This meant that if you wanted Kaiser or GHC insurance, you had to receive care from Kaiser-Permanente or GHC physicians. It was widely perceived that HMOs took advantage of this by recruiting physicians with conservative practice styles. Physicians who preferred vaginal deliveries to caesarian sections, physical therapy to joint replacement, and drugs and watchful waiting to heart surgery could save the HMOs a lot of money. These physicians could also make more money for themselves by accepting prepayment, lending new meaning to the expression "less is more." If HMOs recruited conservative physicians, this left the "liberal" ones to treat everyone else. It seems like this would be a wash for the overall healthcare system until we consider that the success of HMOs put pressure on other insurers to find ways to be cost competitive.

HMOs were very sensitive on the subject of quality and did their best to allay consumer fears. For example, Kaiser described physician recruitment as a "continuous talent hunt" and boasted of both the technical competency and communication skills of its physicians.[9] One Kaiser report stated: "To the trained observer, Permanente physicians-in-chief are indistinguishable from the divisional and departmental chiefs to be found in the clinical faculties of medical schools, except that they appear further advanced in their understanding and appreciation of community medical care organization."[10]

An Incomplete Legacy

Sixty years after they began, Kaiser, GHC, and HIP remain important players in the U.S. healthcare system. Kaiser is far and away the nation's largest fully integrated insurer/provider, currently serving nearly eight million members in nine states. Kaiser remains strongest in its home base on the West Coast but during the 1990s, it attempted an eastward expansion. Kaiser lacked the scale to own its own hospitals and specialty groups so instead it contracted with local providers. Kaiser could not control provider costs and potential enrollees had lingering doubts about quality.[11] Amid staggering losses of several hundred millions of dollars, Kaiser folded most of these plans. GHC and HIP remain close to their home markets—GHC currently has 600,000 members in Washington and parts of Idaho while HIP enrolls about 800,000 in the New York metropolitan area.

There are a variety of reasons why large prepaid group practice did not grow much beyond their original markets. Remember that Kaiser, GHC, and HIP got started before commercial insurance became firmly established. They were able to quickly sign up enrollees and achieve scale economies in their local markets while establishing good reputations for quality. Once the Blues and commercial plans proliferated, the demand for coverage by prepaid groups declined.

HMOs also struggled to recruit physicians who feared ostracism and worse from organized medicine. The medical establishment routinely criticized the quality of HMO physicians and scorned the "unethical" practice of limiting patient choice of provider. Local medical societies urged members and hospitals to boycott group practice physicians and their patients. In 1943, the U.S. Supreme Court concluded that the boycotts were illegal restraints of trade. The AMA responded by adopting "Twenty Points" for approving prepaid practices that seemed to satisfy the courts, but many local medical societies refused to cooperate. One of these was the King County Medical Society, which denied membership to GHC physicians. Because it was deemed unethical for society members to assist nonmembers, this amounted to a thinly veiled boycott. In a unanimous 1951 decision, the Washington State Supreme Court ordered the society to admit GHC members. By then, the indemnity insurance sector had taken off and it would take another three decades before HMOs would pose a serious threat to traditional fee-for-service medicine.

Medicaid "Reform"

Budget Busting

Through the 1960s, indemnity insurance and its hands off approach to paying for healthcare dominated the market, which meant that physicians retained complete autonomy over the practice of medicine. But even as Marcus Welby was dominating the television ratings, the era of Marcus Welby medicine was coming to an end. A new era of regulation and healthcare planning was dawning.

Not surprisingly, it all had to do with money. Prior to 1965, federal and state involvement in healthcare financing was fairly limited. The creation of Medicaid and Medicare changed everything. In the decade between 1960 and 1970, total state and federal health spending increased more than fourfold. There has been no similar increase either before or since.

Medicaid represented a two-edged sword to the states. All states welcomed federal subsidies for local spending. But federal matching only goes so far, and the Medicaid entitlement has placed an enormous strain on state budgets. As early as 1971, Medicaid enrollments exceeded sixteen million and total spending exceeded $6 billion (in nominal dollars). Both figures doubled initial estimates. Not surprisingly, the states with the largest Kerr-Mills programs, including Massachusetts, New Jersey, New York, Washington, and Wisconsin, tended to have the most costly Medicaid programs. This created a dilemma for legislators in these states—how could they maintain the healthcare safety net without raising taxes? Insurers and employers also voiced concerns about rising private sector health spending, intensifying the pressure for some kind of cost containment regulation.

Any state looking to rein in health spending did not have to be particularly inventive. It is well-known that cost-containment strategies come in two flavors—you can limit quantities or you can limit prices. Government-funded healthcare systems in Canada and Europe were already experimenting with both flavors with some apparent success. Americans would soon get a taste for themselves.

Limiting Quantities through Health Planning

Canadian and European nations have purposefully avoided free market healthcare. Rightly or wrongly, most health policy makers outside of the United States are skeptical of markets and optimistic about the ability of government to manage healthcare systems. One of their most important tools is health facilities planning. Through facilities planning, the government decides how many hospitals, beds, and services there will be and where they will go.

Health facilities planning in the United States began in earnest with the 1948 Hill-Burton program, whose purpose was to prevent an expected shortage of hospital beds. Industry experts at the time believed that every region in the United States needed 4.5 hospital beds per 1,000 population (well above then current levels). Hill-Burton money for new hospitals was targeted toward those regions that were furthest from this 4.5 per thousand "ideal." By 1970, the nation had reached the Hill-Burton objectives and occupancy rates began to decline, even as the number of beds continued to climb.

Planners next turned their attention to a projected shortage of physicians. A 1965 report to the American Association of Medical Colleges claimed that it was "not likely that America will ever be able to produce all the physicians that the nation would like to have."[12] Federal and state governments poured several billion dollars into programs to in-crease medical school enrollments and build new schools. Surging physician incomes, fueled in part by Medicare and Medicare, encour-aged record numbers of college students to apply. The federal govern-ment also eased restrictions on immigration and licensure by graduates of overseas medical schools. The combination of government interven-tion and market forces worked too well; by 1980, planners were claim-ing that the United States had a physician surplus, a claim that many still make.

Federal health planning through the 1960s and 1970s was often at odds with the efforts of state health planners. With Medicaid budgets growing out of control, states sought to reduce supply. They targeted hospitals, because, to paraphrase bank robber Willie Sutton, that was where the money was. Roemer's Law and Evans's inducement theory gave planners some academic legitimacy; limiting the supply of hos-pital beds and services would limit the ability of physicians to induce demand.

New York became the first state to place limits on hospital growth when, in 1964, it required government approval for expansion or new construction. The planning council charged with reviewing applications considered medical need and the availability of alternative providers. Any provider who built without being granted a "certificate of need" (CON) risked losing medical payments or even its license. The federal Comprehensive Health Planning (CHP) Act of 1966 encouraged state and local agencies to engage more fully in facilities planning and by 1972, over twenty states had CON requirements.

Those hoping that CON would contain costs pointed to Roemer's Law. For all of the attention that Roemer had received in academic circles, this was a rather thin reed to grasp. Roemer's Law was more of an interesting observation than a systematic fact. Besides most of the ongoing increase in health spending was likely due to demo-graphic changes and technology, not supply. Even if Roemer was partly correct, CON could hardly be expected to make more than a dent in rising costs.

There was also the matter of implementation. There was nothing to guarantee that planning councils would deny requests for more hospi-tal funding. These decisions would be made by political appointees who received advice from planners but had to answer to stakeholders. Political appointees might be expected to favor concentrated interests like local hospitals over diffuse taxpayer interests. The hospitals quickly learned how the game was played. They refused to object to each other's proposals for expansion (although they usually opposed entry by new hospitals.) Just in case political pressure did not work, hospitals submitted multiple applications with the hope of winning approval for just one or two, or located new facilities outside of hospitals, and thus beyond the jurisdiction of CON. The resulting diseconomies of scope might actually have driven total system costs higher, even as hospital costs were contained.

None of these possibilities deterred the planners. The Social Security Amendments of 1972 required states to review hospital construction and expansion as a condition for receiving Medicare and Medicaid funds. The 1974 National Health Planning and Resources Development Act (PL 93-641) centralized the rules for national health planning. PL 93-641 divided the nation into two hundred Health Services Areas, each with its own Health Systems Agency (HSA). HSAs had responsibility for reviewing all facilities expansion, modernization, and capital acquisition in excess of $150,000. The Health Care Financing Administration (HCFA), which oversaw Medicare and Medicaid, could deny payments to facilities that expanded without CON approval.

Historians Anne Somers and Herman Somers stated that the provisions of PL 93-641 provided "the first serious possibility for a comprehensive approach to the entire 'national health care system.' "[13] It did not take long, however, for most observers to conclude that PL 93-641 was not working. Researchers found that CON requirements might have slightly limited bed growth, but otherwise had little or no impact on the health economy.[14] In a recent review of the literature on CON, Michael Morrisey concluded that "rather than controlling costs, if anything, CON programs tended to increase costs."[15]

The Death and Life of Health Planning

By the mid-1980s, President Ronald Reagan was trying to reduce government intervention into markets. CON was an obvious target and at his urging, the federal government repealed PL 93-641 in 1986. Since then, about half of the states have repealed or significantly watered down their own CON laws. A 1998 study by Christopher Conover and Frank Sloan found no evidence of any increase in facilities acquisition or in total healthcare spending following these repeals.[16] CON as a national healthcare policy was dead.

Survivor: Illinois

A few states still have tough CON laws and my home state of Illinois has one of the toughest, having recently approved the first greenfield hospital construction in over twenty years. CON notwithstanding, the hospital sector in Illinois has continued to expand. But rather than build anew, Illinois hospitals have metastasized from their original facilities. Many hospitals in Illinois look like Rube Goldberg creations, with new wings here and new surgery suites there. The benefits of rational hospital design exist elsewhere but not in Illinois. Moreover Illinois hospitals today are located where Illinoisans lived in the 1950s, and the hospitals that received Hill Burton licenses fifty years ago dictate which of today's growing suburbs get to have local hospital services.

It makes no sense to invest so much in incumbent hospitals. Imagine if U.S. car makers could block entry by Japanese and Korean competitors, claiming that they had more than enough capacity to meet our automotive needs! It is just as ludicrous to allow incumbent hospitals to block entry. Defenders of the CON process will say that "healthcare is unique" without explaining how the public benefits when hospitals are protected from the discipline imposed by potential entry.

Some planning rules are even more infuriating. I have heard members of the Illinois Health Facilities Planning Board argue that it is acceptable for patients to travel forty-five minutes to a hospital because residents in rural states sometimes must travel further. Should we apply the same logic to education, forcing students in Illinois to travel thirty miles to school because some children in Montana do the same?

It is no surprise to locals, but corruption has also played a part in Illinois CON. A few years ago, Edward Hospital in suburban Naperville applied for a CON to build a new hospital in rapidly growing Plainfield. Just before the planning board was to vote on the application, board member Michael Levine seemed to enter into private consultation with other board members. The board denied the CON application, after which Edward CEO Pam Davis stormed out of the meeting, promising that "things were going to change." It turned out that a few weeks before the hearing, representatives from a developer and an investment firm had allegedly told Davis that if she wanted to obtain board approval, she would be well advised to use their services. Little did they know that Davis had already suspected such shenanigans and was wearing an FBI wire! After it was alleged that the developer and banker had close ties to Levine, the entire planning board was dismissed.

CON lives on in Illinois, at least for now. The state is conducing hearings on whether to sunset the policy and the current board appears open to allowing new hospital construction. But the board seems to favor hospitals that are struggling financially and especially those serving the medically indigent. This is a clever political move in a state that cannot find the funds to prop up its Medicaid program. Safety net hospitals that win CON approval can generate new revenue from privately insured patients. This revenue will offset shortfalls in Medicaid funding, letting the state legislature off the hook for finding more direct ways to shore up the program.

This may be good politics, but it is dangerous economics. CON perpetuates hospital market power and drives up insurance premiums, which taxpayers then blame on their insurers. In the process, the state gets to pick hospital winners and losers. This is no way to encourage hospitals to meet the needs of their populations.

Dictating What Doctors Must Do

Physicians have never been fully autonomous. Their decisions have always been subject to peer review. (It is the medical profession, not individual physicians, that has sought to preserve autonomy.) All hospitals had internal peer review processes to make sure that medical staff followed established norms of care. In addition, many physicians sought second opinions before admitting a patient to a hospital or performing surgery. Medical specialty societies also participated in professional self-policing by establishing guidelines for treatment of various diseases. For example, the AMA criteria for hospitalizing diabetes patients included institution of insulin therapy, uncontrolled vomiting, and several other criteria. Patients who did not meet one of these criteria were not supposed to be admitted to a hospital.[17]

Policy makers did not think that the medical community had gone far enough in establishing guidelines, and the mounting evidence of medical practice variations pointed to the potential benefits of standardizing physician practice. The 1972 Social Security Amendments established a process for achieving them. The law created Professional Standards Review Organizations (PSROs), which were local organizations of physicians charged with monitoring the necessity, appropriateness, and quality of care provided to hospitalized Medicare and Medicaid patients.[18] PSROs established standards of care for a wide range of diseases based on their review of the research literature and could direct HCFA to withhold payment from physicians whose treatment decisions did not measure up to these standards.

PSROs proved to be ineffective. It took more than five years for most PSROs to form, and even longer for them to establish standards. PSROs were reluctant to penalize physicians who were statistical "outliers" and rarely took action beyond withholding payments on a case-by-case basis. The Health Care Financing Administration concluded that PSROs reduced hospital inpatient stay by no more than 2 percent.[19] Medical practice variations persisted.

It is not clear if PSROs had a real chance of success. They represented the first large scale third-party effort to limit the autonomy enjoyed by the medical profession, and had to do so with limited data and funding. But PSROs did not fully die out. In 1983, they morphed into Professional Review Organizations (PROs) charged with monitoring Medicare's newest cost-containment program. These PROs, in turn, spun off private sector companies that would provide utilization review services, perhaps the most hated of all managed care practices.

The legacy of PSROs and practice standards lives on in today's pay-for-performance movement.

By the early 1980s, planning had fallen out of fashion in Washington. Economic incentives were all the rage, and the federal government was soon to embrace the use of incentives for healthcare cost containment. As with CON, it would let the states take the lead.

Price Controls

State Rate Setting Programs

I mentioned earlier how insurance made patients insensitive to prices. Hospitals might have charged "infinite prices" had insurers not stepped in with cost-based reimbursement. But cost-based reimbursement was not working; healthcare spending was still on the rise. Facing pressure to hold the line on Medicaid, some states sought another way to contain hospital payments.

Once again, New York with its outsized Medicaid program was the first to act. The state proposed replacing cost-based hospital reimbursement for Medicaid with a flat per diem rate. Private insurers, concerned that hospitals receiving low Medicaid payments might try to make up the shortfall by raising their prices for everyone else (a tactic known as cost-shifting) asked to be included in a comprehensive payment system. In 1970, with HCFA's blessing, New York introduced the first all-payer, prospective rate setting system. Within five years, seven more states with big Medicaid programs and large budget deficits obtained HCFA approval to begin all-payer rate setting programs of their own.

While there were many differences among the programs, they all included incentives for hospitals to reduce costs. But they also had limitations. New York's per diem rates encouraged hospitals to increase lengths of stay. Complex payment rules in other states invited various forms of accounting legerdemain. Research showed that the state rate-setting programs were modestly successful, reducing the rate of growth of hospital expenses by about 1 percent annually relative to states without them.[20]

The Medicare Prospective Payment System

Between 1970 and 1980, federal spending for Medicare Part A, which mainly covers hospital expenses, increased from $5 billion to $25 billion. HCFA needed a way to slow down further growth and found inspiration in the state rate setting programs. Despite its modest success, HCFA believed that a modified rate setting program could turn the tide on hospital inflation. HCFA's key innovation was to pay a fixed fee per admission. This would have two positive effects. First, it would limit HCFA's financial exposure. Second, and more importantly, it would give providers an incentive to reduce the costs for each inpatient stay. If hospitals did this, then HCFA could reduce its payments in the future without jeopardizing hospital finances.

It would be unfair if HCFA paid the same fee to every hospital for every admission. The cost of doing business varied by region, so HCFA added local cost adjustments. Teaching hospitals received a bonus to offset the cost of training residents. HCFA also recognized that the cost of hospital care varied dramatically according to the type of treatment delivered. For example, the cost of treating a patient with a broken hip is about ten times higher than the cost of monitoring someone with chest pain. HCFA needed to calibrate the payments according to each patient's clinical needs and the expected cost of treatment. Fortunately the tools for grouping patients into diagnostic categories with comparable medical needs—soon to be dubbed "diagnosis related groups" (DRGs)—were being developed by researchers at Yale University. In 1975, HCFA authorized New Jersey to test a prospective payment system using DRG-like adjustments. After ironing out many of the glitches, including learning about the possible ways that hospitals might game the system, HCFA unveiled its Medicare Prospective Payment System (PPS) in 1983.

The basic economics of the PPS have not changed in twenty-five years: hospitals stand to prosper if they can reduce the costs of inpatient stays. Hospitals have responded to these incentives by shortening lengths of stay, reducing staff, and limiting tests and procedures. Hospitals have also found a number of ways to game the system. They have manipulated diagnostic codes to move patients into more remunerative DRGs (this is known as "upcoding"), provided services on an outpatient basis (so as to generate additional payments), discharged patients to their own long-term care facilities (again to generate additional payments), and unnecessarily extended lengths of stay to trigger special "outlier" payments.

Anticipating such abuses, HCFA transformed PSROs into Peer Review Organizations (PROs) to monitor hospital responses to the PPS. (If the Medicare alphabet soup is getting too confusing, there is a glossary of these and other acronyms at the end of the book.) Even with PRO review, by the early 1990s red flags were being raised, especially about upcoding. A *New England Journal of Medicine* article reported on systematic upcoding by New England hospitals.[21] A *Boston Globe* exposé suggested that "of all the areas under investigation (by the Department of Health and Human Services), it is coding fraud that might be the most prevalent and costly" and Senator William Cohen stated that Medicare fraud cost Americans as much as $100 billion annually.[22]

In response, the Federal Bureau of Investigation ramped up its healthcare antifraud efforts, tripling the number of agents working on health probes.[23] The crackdown on Medicare fraud netted some big fish. The Department of Justice brought fraud charges against both HCA (Hospital Corporationn of America) and Tenet, two of the nation's largest provider systems. The systems ended up paying nearly $1 billion to settle the claims.

Despite the best efforts of some hospitals to game the system, the PPS seemed to be controlling costs. From 1985 to 1987, Medicare spending for hospital services rose at an annual rate of 8 percent. This was a welcome respite from two decades of double digit growth. There was some apparent substitution from inpatient to outpatient care, however, so that overall Medicare spending between 1985 and 1987 rose at an annual rate of 9.5 percent. When thinking about their many efforts to contain costs, policy makers began to use the analogy of squeezing a balloon—you can squeeze at one end but it will just expand at the other.

The Drawback of Cutbacks

Many observers had hoped that PPS would force hospitals to engage in total quality management (TQM) and similar practices that could simultaneously reduce costs and boost quality. Most hospitals tried TQM with varying degrees of success. But PPS rewarded hospitals for cost cutting whether they were cutting fat or lean. Critics of the PPS complained that hospitals were discharging patients "quicker but sicker." Systematic research failed to support this criticism; lengths of stay may have fallen but patients seemed to be no worse off at discharge.[24] Other research paints a more somber picture. Reductions in Medicare hospital payments have been associated with increases in mortality rates.[25] The same has been found for Medicaid.[26] It seems that not every dollar squeezed from the system had been going to waste.

Because hospitals tend to offer the same level of quality to all of their patients, cutbacks in Medicare or Medicaid can affect the quality of care delivered to all patients.[27] Private insurers were obsessed with the idea that government cutbacks would affect pricing; they should have been equally concerned about the impact on quality.

None of this discussion about quality is meant to justify the cost spiral, but rather as a reminder that there is no free lunch, not even in hospital care. If we elect to pay less for healthcare without paying careful attention to quality, then we should not be surprised when quality suffers. This may be a tradeoff we are willing to accept, but it is one we should not ignore. We need to bear this in mind as we consider the new Consumer Driven Health Plans that I describe in chapter 5.

Another way that providers might react to Medicare and Medicaid cutbacks is to refuse to treat Medicare and Medicaid patients. Thus far, Medicare payments have largely held there own against managed care, but Medicaid payments in many states are very low, with often devastating effects on access. I have worked closely with Children's Memorial Hospital in Chicago. Their policy has always been to admit all patients regardless of ability to pay. When Illinois cut its Medicaid payments, Children's saw an increase in referrals from distant neighborhoods whose local hospitals "dumped" their unprofitable cases onto Children's. The good news is that these patients have received world-class medical care. Other patients are not so fortunate, often getting dumped into overcrowded and understaffed county hospitals that must make do with their own limited budgets. In the extreme, Medicaid cutbacks can cause hospitals to close, forcing patients to find an alternate provider.[28]

Low payments also affect access to physicians. In a 1991 study, Anne Schwartz, David Colby, and Anne Reisinger documented substantial interstate variation in Medicaid physician payments and reported that "Medicaid beneficiaries in different states may face different degrees of access to medical care simply because of where they reside."[29] As Medicare contemplates dramatic reductions in payment rates as a way to close a projected gaping deficit, many doctors are reporting that they may stop taking on new Medicare patients. I will say it again: there is no free lunch, only tradeoffs. If we want better quality and access, we will have to pay for it. Our goal should be to find the most effective way to do so.

Rationing

We do not have unlimited resources to devote to healthcare. Once we set limits on what we are willing to spend, we must, by definition, ration. Normally we ration goods and services by price—in a free market, goods and services are purchased by those with a combination of the greatest means and greatest desire. But it does not usually work this way in healthcare, because insured patients are not deterred by prices. So we must ration in other ways, by regulating the availability of supply (CON) or changing provider incentives (HMOs). The only way to ration by price would be to eliminate insurance, but this solution is even worse than the problem.

Politicians may view any explicit mention of rationing as the third rail of healthcare politics, but rationing is inevitable. As I will describe in chapters 7 and 8, one U.S. state (Oregon) and many other nations are rather explicit in the use of cost-effectiveness criteria to ration services. This may prove far better than the other heavy handed approaches that I have described in this chapter. We are already rationing access to care; it can do no harm to try to get more bang for our healthcare bucks.

Mending the Insurance Safety Net

Creeping Incrementalism

Even after the passage of Medicare and Medicaid, tens of millions of Americans remained uninsured. At the same time, millions of Americans with private insurance had to think twice before changing jobs or retiring early. Comprehensive national health insurance would correct these problems but the past four decades have instead been marked by a kind of creeping incrementalism, with modest legislation to fill in some of the holes in the safety net.

Some of the biggest holes were associated with Medicaid. Many uninsured individuals and families did not belong to a qualifying Medicaid category. Those who did fall into a Medicaid category still had to "pass" a means test; in the 1980s, the average income threshold was 60 percent of the federal poverty level (FPL). The result was that many low-income families and their children were left without coverage.

In the past two decades, the federal government has taken a number of steps to broaden coverage. In the late 1980s, the income cutoff for families with children increased to roughly 133 percent of the FPL; some states chose even higher cutoffs. In addition, pregnant women and younger children were covered regardless of family structure. Prior to these changes, 18 percent of children and 21 percent of women age 15 to 44 were eligible for Medicaid; by 1992, these figures increased to 27 percent and 45 percent respectively. Even with this expansion, approximately 14 percent of the nation's children remained uninsured by the late 1990s.[30]

In 1997, the federal government moved to further reduce the number of uninsured children by creating the State Children's Health Insurance Program (SCHIP). Like Medicaid, SCHIP is a program administered by the states under federal rules with joint funding. States had the option of further expanding Medicaid, creating a new program, or doing both; about equal numbers of states chose each option. Under SCHIP, income limits increased to an average of 200 percent of the FPL for children of all ages. SCHIP also mandates that states advertise their programs and simplify applications. SCHIP was immediately successful;

the number of children covered by either Medicaid or SCHIP increased from 30 percent of the population in 1997 to 40 percent by 2000. SCHIP remains popular and, as of this writing, politicians from both parties espouse further expansion of the program.

Crowd Out

Even with Medicaid expansions and SCHIP, millions of Americans remain uninsured, including 11 percent of the nation's children. One reason is both simple and discouraging—increases in public sector coverage have been partially offset by declines in the private sector. Economists call this "crowd out."

Crowd out is an old and familiar problem in public finance. The promise of social security payments discourages investment in private pension plans. The possibility that the government might pay for hurricane damage discourages individuals from purchasing private sector flood insurance. By the same token, the availability of publicly funded health insurance reduces the demand for private sector insurance. In all of these examples, the question is not whether crowd out occurs; it does. The more crucial policy question is whether crowd out is severe. If public programs largely replace private programs, then the public gains absolutely nothing except for a larger government bureaucracy and higher taxes.

There are two ways that public health insurance could crowd out private insurance. Remember that employers offer health insurance benefits as part of a comprehensive wage/benefit package. If employees can obtain their insurance through a government program, then the employers' calculus tilts in favor of giving their workers higher wages, and letting the government provide the insurance. Even if employers do not change their offerings, their employees might prefer keeping the money they would normally contribute toward their employer plan and instead opt for Medicaid or SCHIP coverage. We might even see a combination of the two, whereby employers increase the required contribution, anticipating that some employees will opt out.

Research conducted after expansions of Medicaid and the creation of SCHIP shows that crowd out is substantial. For every ten individuals enrolled in these government programs, about five gave up private insurance.[31] Although there is some variation in the nature of crowd out based on age and income, there seems to be a good rule of thumb to follow if we are to evaluate future proposals to expand public insurance programs: we will have to spend about $2 in taxpayer money to provide $1 in additional benefits to the uninsured.

A shift private to public insurance programs would also create general economic distortions that might rival the labor market distortions caused by employer-based coverage. To put it simply, when health insurance is funded by employers, individuals have greater incentive to work. When funded by taxes, especially income taxes, individuals have less incentive to work. This is why many policy makers have sought ways to reduce labor market distortions while maintaining employer-based coverage.

Reducing Labor Market Distortions

COBRA and HIPAA

There have been two major efforts to reduce labor market distortions that might spill over from employer-sponsored health insurance. The first was included in the Comprehensive Omnibus Budget Reconciliation Act (COBRA) of 1985. Under COBRA, an individual who left a job that provided health insurance coverage would be eligible to continue purchasing insurance through the old employer's group for a period of up to eighteen months. The old employer could charge that individual no more than 102 percent of the average group premium. The eighteen months covered the typical waiting period for coverage with a new insurer. If the individual got a new job, the new employer could pay for the COBRA coverage until the waiting period ended.

Only about 20 percent of eligible workers took advantage of COBRA coverage. This seems very small, but many of those who did not use COBRA had an alternative source of insurance, such as through their spouse or their new employer. Economists Brigitte Madrian and Jonathan Gruber found that about 65 percent of workers without an alternative source of insurance chose to obtain COBRA coverage.[32]

Madrian and Gruber also found that the availability of continuous coverage increased the likelihood of early retirement by a third.[33] For younger workers, COBRA cut the magnitude of job lock almost in half.[34]

Despite these findings, it was clear that COBRA was not reaching everyone it could. About one-third of individuals who lacked alternative coverage chose not to invoke it. Many of these were unemployed and preferred to spend their money elsewhere. Assuring that these individuals had coverage would require more than applying a Band-Aid to COBRA. There were other problems with COBRA that would also have to be fixed. COBRA failed to protect individuals who had dropped out of the labor force for more than eighteen months. It also did nothing for employees whose companies stopped offering coverage (including workers whose companies went out of business.)

Perhaps the biggest complaint about COBRA was the administrative burden. Employers had to collect and process COBRA payments from ex-employees for a period of up to thirty-six months. The burden proved to be substantial—Gruber and Madrian placed it at over $10 billion annually. COBRA also exposed employers to adverse selection, as it was the sickest employees who were most likely to ask for COBRA coverage. Finally, COBRA was so complex that it triggered scores of lawsuits.

Although COBRA is still in place to provide access for displaced and transferring workers, many of the provisions have been superseded by an even more ambitious law, the Health Insurance Portability and Affordability Act (HIPAA) of 1996. While HIPAA is best known for establishing rules protecting the confidentiality of patient data, it also contains provisions addressing insurance coverage. The most important of these allows workers to count past uninterrupted insurance coverage toward any waiting periods required for new coverage. Most workers who change jobs can now obtain immediate coverage from their new employer. They do not have to worry if their old employer stops offering coverage and old employers do not need to keep close tabs on workers who take new jobs.

COBRA and HIPAA have filled in the gaps in employer-based coverage, making it easier for employees to keep coverage when they change jobs or retire. These are important accomplishments but Gruber and Madrian admit that it is difficult to put an exact dollar figure on the benefits of fluid labor markets.[35] HIPAA also creates some new problems. Employers used waiting periods to defend against adverse selection; without this weapon, employers are vulnerable if they hire individuals with substantial medical needs. HIPAA may now give pause to many smaller employers who currently offer insurance but cannot afford the exposure to a major claim by a new employee. This may explain why insurance offer rates by small employers have declined from 68 percent in 2000 to 59 percent in 2007.[36] And while HIPAA reduces the need for employers to track the insurance status of old employees, it now requires employers to learn about prior insurance status of new employees.

HIPAA's provisions go beyond providing protection for job changes. HIPAA requires insurers to offer policy renewals and sharply restricts medical underwriting, making it difficult for insurers to rapidly adjust premiums in response to the claims experiences of individual employers or set high prices for an employer group that is buying insurance for the first time. Though intended to limit adverse selection by artificially increasing the size and diversity of an insurer's risk pool, it may also deter insurers from pursuing the small group market altogether. Thus far, research on the consequences of these HIPAA reforms for overall coverage rates and coverage rates within risk categories—research that focuses mainly on similar reforms previously enacted in many states—is decidedly mixed.[37]

The Managed Care Prescription

Many Americans worry that lower costs mean lower quality.

—PRESIDENT BILL CLINTON in support of the Patient Bill of Rights[1]

If this is a back door to reassert the Clinton health-care plan again, forget it.

—LARRY NEAL, spokesperson for Republican Senator Phil Gramm

A Tragedy

In the 1990s, employers turned toward managed care to control costs. Managed care enrollments soared—from under 30 percent of the population in the late 1980s to over 90 percent a decade later. Americans enjoyed a respite from runaway medical cost inflation, but many worried that managed care was placing profits above lives. As more

Americans heard stories such as that of Massachusetts teenager Janet Thieriot, these worries intensified into an all-out backlash.

A diabetic, Thieriot began experiencing pain in her thigh in 1988 that sometimes left her unable to walk. Doctors and nurses attributed the pain to her diabetes. Her father asked their HMO to pay for a referral to an out-of-town specialist, but the HMO refused and her condition worsened. A visit to an emergency room revealed that she had Ewing's sarcoma, a rare but often curable form of cancer. Mr. Thieriot again asked the HMO to allow her daughter to be treated elsewhere, but it refused, saying that the family did not "go through proper channels." Janet Thieriot died of Ewing's sarcoma in 1989.

Tragedies like these were not new to the U.S. healthcare system. What was new was the reaction. In the days of Marcus Welby medicine, the death of a loved one was more often than not a matter for private mourning. The chances of recriminations against the provider, let alone a lawsuit, were remote. Few people blamed the entire healthcare system. During the 1980s, the frequency of malpractice suits increased, but this malpractice "crisis" soon died down. Managed care presented a new and easy target. As quickly as managed care won the battle for market share, it lost the battle for public trust and was forced to change its tactics or disappear from the market altogether.

The Rise of HMOs

Taking Health Benefits Costs Seriously

The business success of managed care reflected the ability of HMOs to meet the demands of the market. Up through the early 1980s, employers had been largely passive about their health benefits. Most offered their employees a single indemnity insurance plan chosen from among seemingly cloned competitors on the basis of slight differences in premiums and service. As premiums began to take a noticeable bite out of total labor expenses and researchers exposed the inefficiencies of the healthcare system, some employers wondered if they ought to treat health insurance as an expense to be controlled rather than an open-ended employee benefit.

Large companies competing in global markets were especially concerned about how healthcare benefits affected their competitiveness. The Detroit auto makers took it on the chin more than most, because their union contracts obligated them to provide generous health benefits to current *and* retired workers. As a result, they were spending more than $5,000 per employee on health benefits—adding roughly 5 to 10 percent to the cost of every vehicle sold.[2] Chrysler's chairman, Lee Iacocca, warned that unless healthcare spending moderated, "You'll see a lot of broke companies."[3]

Mark Pauly's observation about health insurance—that it is part of an employment package—suggests that that Iacocca's argument is a bit misleading. Rising healthcare costs threatened worker wages as much or more than they threatened corporate profits. Theoretical arguments aside, what matters is that U.S. employers believed their viability was at stake and that when it came to healthcare benefits, business as usual was no longer acceptable.

Seeking New Solutions

One of the first steps taken by large employers was to form "business groups on health." The Washington Business Group on Health began in 1974, and regional groups in the Midwest, New York, Texas, and California formed during the 1980s. Early on, the business groups kept members informed about the features of different health plans and lobbied for legislation that might reduce costs. Nowadays business groups focus at least as much on quality and the Pacific Business Group on Health has become a national leader in the quality report cards movement.

Apart from forming these groups, businesses in the 1970s still counted on government regulation and health planning to control costs. When government intervention failed, business looked elsewhere for solutions. They drew some inspiration from the RAND Health Insurance Experiment. By the early 1980s, indemnity insurers were already adding deductibles and copayments to their policies and the publication of the HIE results accelerated the trend. The percentage of employers requiring a deductible for hospital services increased from

30 percent in 1982 to 63 percent in 1984.[4] The percentage requiring a further copayment increased from 58 to 74 percent.

The dollars involved were usually small. Typical deductibles were about $150 (about $300 in today's dollars) and copayments were 10 to 20 percent. Out of pocket expenses were usually capped at around $1,000 ($2,000 in today's dollars). These were a bit below the levels that RAND researchers determined would optimally balance cost sharing and risk bearing. Joseph Newhouse suggests that the tax deductibility of insurance explains why real world insurance was more generous than "optimal."[5] He also wonders if across-the-board cost sharing might have done more harm than good by discouraging cost reducing preventive care and compliance with drug regimens. In any event, these modest cost sharing requirements did little to reduce overall healthcare spending.[6]

Turning to HMOs

Employers wanted an alternative to Marcus Welby medicine that could promise radical reductions in spending. HMOs offered the possibility of such radical change. Up to the 1980s, HMOs had been considered a "West Coast thing," and for good reason. Of an estimated nine million HMO enrollees nationwide in 1980, nearly five million lived in just three states, California, Oregon, and Washington.[7] Another 1.6 million lived in Colorado, Minnesota, and New York. To the rest of the nation, HMOs were not on the radar screen. This would soon change.

Some of the early impetus for change came from unlikely places. In 1967, the newly appointed president of the Blue Cross Association, Walter McNerney, urged member plans to support research and hold discussions about prepaid group practices. By 1973 there were six operational Blue Cross HMOs, and the "Blues" brand name was a key factor in helping them gain customer acceptance. During this time, Richard Nixon was seeking an alternative to centralized health planning. Thanks to the efforts of Paul Ellwood, Congress enacted Nixon's HMO Act of 1974, which required employers to offer their employees the option to enroll in "federally qualified" HMOs.

HMOs received a further boost in 1978 when economist Harold Luft published a study in the *New England Journal of Medicine*, entitled "How Do HMOs Achieve Their Savings?"[8] Luft presented "virtually all the evidence of the last 25 years concerning HMO 'savings' . . . and examine(d) various explanations of how such 'savings' are achieved."[9] The evidence, which mostly pertained to the Kaiser, GHC, and Ross-Loos prepaid group practices, indicated that total medical expenditures per enrollee were anywhere from 10 to 40 percent lower in HMOs than in traditional indemnity plans. Luft offered a number of possible answers to the question posed in the title of his paper: HMO enrollees had substantially fewer hospital admissions and shorter lengths of stay, though these were occasionally offset by higher levels of outpatient utilization. Luft also conjectured that HMO quality might be lower and HMO patients might be healthier than indemnity patients.

Research such as this caught the eye of secretary of Health, Education and Welfare, Joseph Califano, who began urging large corporations to consider offering HMOs to reduce health spending. As more employers became aware of the potential savings, HMO enrollments quickly began to increase, as reported in table 4.1. Despite this growth, most Americans remained enrolled in traditional indemnity plans and healthcare spending continued its relentless climb.

Table 4.1. HMO Enrollment Data

Year	HMO Enrollment	Healthcare $$ as Percent of GDP
1970	2.9	7.2
1975	5.7	8.3
1980	9.1	9.1
1985	18.9	10.5

Source: Interstudy Edge, various years. Note that HMO enrollment data is notoriously difficult to validate, due in part to the lack of a consistent definition of an HMO. The Interstudy data are largely derived from insurance company filings with state regulatory agencies.

A Different Kind of HMO

Kaiser, Group Health Cooperative, and other large prepaid group practices benefited from the surge in interest in HMOs. But most of the growth in enrollments came from new plans. The Blues offered plans with names like HMO Illinois and HMO Kansas. (To this day, a plan generically named "HMO Statename" is likely to be a Blue Cross plan.) For-profit indemnity insurers such as Aetna and Cigna also became big players. By the early 1980s, two new firms had entered the HMO market, United Healthcare and Humana (which was, at the time, the nation's largest hospital company.)

The new HMOs used a very different business model than the old prepaid group practices. Kaiser and the GHC were integrated organizations that controlled all aspects of the healthcare vertical chain. Enrollees typically had just one local hospital to choose from and had to visit physicians who were employed by or worked exclusively for the HMO. To contain costs, these older HMOs put most of their physicians on a fixed salary and limited the availability of costly new technologies. The new HMOs were vertically disintegrated. Rather than build their own hospitals and employ their own physicians (or contract with large groups on an exclusive basis), they assembled networks of providers in each local market and required their enrollees to stay within their networks. To contain costs, the new HMOs relied on contractual incentives coupled with judicious choices of network providers.

The new HMOs had to entice providers who previously worked exclusively in the traditional indemnity sector. They promised an increase in patient volume, albeit at a lower rate of reimbursement and with strings attached. (Viewed another way, physicians feared that if they did not contract with HMOs, they would lose volume.) One of the most important strings was the requirement that the provider had to obtain prior approval from a utilization review (UR) agency before hospitalizing a patient, performing surgery, or initiating long-term treatment of a chronic condition such as diabetes or AIDS. These UR agencies, typically offshoots of the Medicare PROs, developed standards based on cost-effectiveness research and used the standards to evaluate requests for treatment.

Physicians deplored utilization review. Although over 80 percent of physicians in one survey thought that cost-effectiveness was an appropriate criterion for medical decision making, nearly the same percentage did not believe that insurers should be involved in judging cost-effectiveness.[10] This opinion may have derived from prior experience with third-party oversight. Hospital peer review and PSROs had done little to alter medical decision making, so why would insurer UR make a difference?[11] As physicians gained experience with UR agencies, their opinions changed for the worse. Physicians found that they could always appeal a UR agency denial of a treatment request, and they usually won. This made it seem that the main purpose of UR agencies was to force physicians to jump through hoops to treat their patients regardless of whether the proposed treatment was cost-effective.

Following the lead of the prepaid groups, the new HMOs also relied on the "reversal of economics" to contain utilization. They paid primary care physicians a capitated fee—essentially a fixed monthly fee for every enrollee who selected that PCP as their source for primary care. Depending on the HMO, the capitated fee might be expected to cover the PCP's office expense, as well as any drugs, tests, or specialist referrals ordered by that physician. HMOs tried to risk adjust the capitated fee, but had to rely on limited risk adjusters such as age and sex. It also proved difficult for HMOs to find a reasonable way to capitate specialists, so specialists continued to receive fee for service payment.

Capitating PCPs was supposed to eliminate their incentive to recommend excessive care and make costly referrals to specialists. But critics complained that capitation went too far in the other direction, giving PCPs a financial incentive for undertreatment. For example, many specialists complained that patients were not receiving appropriate referrals. Critics also complained about the additional paperwork, especially the referral forms required before a patient could see a specialist. Even today, most providers lack the kind of computerized administrative systems that could facilitate these processes. The role of the hassle factor in the managed care backlash cannot be understated.

The reversal of economics only went so far in changing incentives. HMOs did not expect PCP capitation to cover the cost of hospital care, as this would expose the PCP to too much financial risk. Nor could they find a reasonable way to capitate hospitals directly. At first, HMOs paid hospitals either discounted charges or fixed per diem rates, leaving in place the financial incentives for hospitals to provide more care. By the late 1980s, Medicare had demonstrated the viability of the DRG-based prospective payment system and many HMOs adopted this system for themselves.

Not every provider was willing to abide by these rules or grant sufficient discounts to the HMOs. Nor did the HMOs feel obliged to assemble large networks for their enrollees. As a result, most HMO networks consisted of about half of the local physicians and a somewhat higher percentage of the local hospitals. By selectively contracting with just a subset of providers, HMOs paid lower provider prices than the indemnity insurers, but kept many enrollees away from their providers of choice. This was another major contributor to the managed care backlash.

Was "Choice" the Same Thing as "Quality"?

Patients with generous indemnity insurance had little reason to comparison shop among providers, as they would keep virtually none of the savings. Even if they wanted to comparison shop, it would not be easy. They would be confused by the opacity of medical bills and would have to make important choices under duress. In contrast, HMOs had every incentive to shop around—they could keep the savings—and they were much better equipped to do so. They employed accountants to make sense of the medical bills and hired statisticians to analyze reams of data. After all of this work, HMOs had a pretty good idea of which hospitals were most efficient. Motivated and informed, HMOs sat down at the negotiating table with each hospital and coolly hammered out bargain prices. This was good news for the HMOs but even better news for their patients; as long as there was competition among HMOs, most of the savings would ultimately be passed along to enrollees in the form of lower insurance premiums.

It would mean little for HMOs to be good price shoppers if this came at the expense of quality. It is fair to say that through the 1980s, prior to HMOs, quality shopping by payers and patients alike was virtually nonexistent. For patients, quality shopping began with their choice of primary care physician. More often than not, patients judged their PCPs on the basis of personality and location (and the word of mouth of relatively uninformed friends and family). Other than the certificates hanging in the office lobby, patients had little objective quality information to go by. Patients sought out specialists and hospitals for problems that seemed complex and they knew that some hospitals—Mayo, Johns Hopkins, Massachusetts General—were better than others for high-end care. But patients otherwise left it to their PCPs to choose the hospitals and specialists. As with the patients' choices of PCPs, the PCPs choices were more likely to be based on convenience and social factors than on any objective information about quality.

Most patients and physicians thought the system was working. Almost everyone thought they were receiving above average care. This view is reminiscent of humorist Garrison Keillor's fictional Lake Woebegone, where "the men are strong, the women are handsome, and all of the children are above average," and it still persists. I frequently ask groups of physicians if they believe that some specialists and hospitals are better than others. Everyone agrees. But when I ask if any of them have referred a patient to a below average specialist or hospital, I am met with silence. These physicians are suffering from "Lake Woebegone Syndrome." Half of all referrals must go to below average specialists and hospitals. No one admits to making those referrals. Patients are suffering from the same syndrome, of course, and accept the referrals with few if any questions.

Mired in the Marcus Welby mythology, patients were satisfied with this approach to quality "shopping" and reacted with hostility to the restrictions on choice imposed by HMOs. It did not matter that the provider selected by the HMO might offer objectively comparable or even higher quality; the possibility was rarely considered. (As I will discuss later on this chapter, the real world evidence on this is mixed.) Physicians have long held that freedom of choice is sacrosanct to the practice of medicine. Most patients have agreed and often equate quality to freedom of choice.

Containing Costs

The Evidence

Through most of the 1990s, HMO cost-containment strategies seemed to be working. HMO premiums were lower than indemnity insurance and overall healthcare spending was beginning to moderate. Despite continued cost pressure from medical innovation (including stents, artificial limbs, radical improvements in care for extremely low birth weight babies, and PET scans), the rate of healthcare inflation in the mid-1990s was not much higher than the rate of overall inflation in the economy (see table 4.2).

In 1994, Harold Luft and Robert Miller took another look at the research evidence on HMO costs. Reviewing over a dozen recent studies, they found that both prepaid group practices and newer HMOs had lower inpatient utilization, similar or slightly higher outpatient utilization, and slightly lower costs than indemnity plans.[12] Most analysts interpreted their findings as evidence that HMOs did save money, though Luft and Miller still could not rule out that HMOs had healthier patients. Several studies published since 1994 have provided even more convincing evidence of cost savings, for example by showing that states with faster HMO growth experienced lower rates of cost

Table 4.2. Annual Health Spending: 1980–2000

Year	Total health spending ($billion)	Per capita health spending	Real per capita health spending (today's dollars)	Annual inflation in real per capita health spending	Health spending as percent of GDP
1980	$255	$1,110	$2,640	3.9%	9.1%
1990	720	2,820	4,220	4.8	12.4
1993	910	3,470	4,700	3.7	13.7
1997	1,130	4,100	5,000	1.6	13.6
2000	1,350	4,790	5,440	2.9	13.8

Source: CMS.

increases.[13] Other studies find that HMO growth leads to reductions in inpatient utilization, an increase in the number of primary care physicians and fewer specialists.

How Did HMOs Achieve Their Savings?

There is a strong consensus in the academic community that HMOs save money. But the answer to Harold Luft's original question: "How Do HMOs Achieve Their Savings?" is still somewhat of a mystery. At the end of the day, there are only two ways that you can reduce spending on anything: you either pay lower prices or buy less stuff. What were HMOs doing? Were HMOs paying lower provider prices or were HMO patients receiving fewer healthcare services? And which of the HMO strategies was most responsible for the savings: selective contracting, capitation, or utilization review? Casual empiricism coupled with systematic research has provided some answers.

Selective contracting worked exactly as expected. HMOs secured deep discounts from hospitals, sometimes as much as 50 percent of full charges. Enrollees benefited from the discounts, as premiums finally seemed to stabilize, but even this came at a cost. The discounts eliminated the cross-subsidy from private insurance that was an unspoken but crucial aspect of the safety net. Hospitals could no longer shift uncompensated care costs, or the costs of caring for under funded Medicaid patients, onto private insurers. The government was unwilling to expand coverage or boost Medicaid reimbursements, so hospitals were forced to become more efficient. This was easier said than done; many hospitals had to cut staff and reduce services to all of their patients. When all else failed, private hospitals dumped more uninsured patients onto government hospitals. Even this was not enough to keep many safety net hospitals from closing.[14]

Selectively contracting payers have also secured large discounts for outpatient services and prescription drugs. Drug discounts could be as high as 80 percent, especially when there is competition from generics or therapeutically equivalent brand name drugs (e.g., Levitra, Cialis, and Viagra, three drugs that treat erectile dysfunction). For all the rhetoric about how expensive drugs are in the United States compared with Canada, it turns out that private insurers do not pay much more than Canadian provincial governments and they usually pass the savings along to their enrollees. (Americans who do not have a prescription drug plan pay much higher prices, of course.)

Selective contracting has also brought market discipline to healthcare. Discounts are larger in markets with more competitors and, in the case of hospitals, where there is excess capacity. Ironically it is the uninsured who are most likely to be asked to pay full charges, though few end up paying more than a fraction of this amount.

There is also some evidence that HMO patients receive fewer services, most likely because of the reversal of economics. For example, a study by Jason Barro and Nancy Beaulieu found that when physician incomes were no longer directly tied to their billings, their billings decreased by 30 percent.[15] Physicians responded to even more complex incentives. Martin Gaynor and colleagues studied a compensation scheme that was tied to the performance of a physician's group; this diluted the cost-cutting incentives for each member physician.[16] They found that a 20 percent increase in group size was associated with 7 percent higher revenues. Through most of the 1990s, HMOs experimented with various compensation schemes to try to generate just the "right" incentives. They discovered that there was no best scheme, just some inevitable tradeoffs between individual incentives, group monitoring, and group risk sharing.

The evidence on utilization review proved to be less compelling. A 1989 study by Thomas Wickizer, John Wheeler, and Paul Feldstein found that UR reduced inpatient costs by 10 percent.[17] However, it was possible that these savings were offset by increases in outpatient use. It is widely believed that UR agencies ended up approving almost all requests for care, though it is possible that they discouraged requests for unnecessary care. The overall consensus is that UR had only a small effect on the amount of care delivered.

Taken together, the studies of selective contracting, physician incentives, and UR suggest that HMOs reduced both prices and quantities. Recent research by David Cutler, Mark McClellan, and Joseph Newhouse asked which mattered more.[18] They examined medical claims data from a large employer that offered its employees a choice of newer HMOs and a standard indemnity plan. Focusing on the costs of heart disease, they found that medical costs were substantially lower in the HMOs and that nearly the entire cost difference was due to lower prices. This is hard to reconcile with prior studies showing that HMO strategies like capitation reduce quantities. Perhaps doctors treating heart disease did not restrict services based on incentives. I believe that two things are going on at the same time: (1) providers did respond to incentives and (2) providers tended to deliver about the same level of services of care to all of their patients. The result—lower HMO payments lead to slightly lower quantities for all patients, but minimal differences in quantities across different types of insurance. Other studies suggest that HMOs may reduce both prices and quantities for some medical conditions.[19]

Managed Competition and National Health Insurance

Enthoven's Consumer Choice Health Plan

The idea of using HMOs to expand access would be inconceivable to most people. Thirty years ago, Alain Enthoven saw things quite differently. He envisioned expanding access through a national scheme that encouraged competition among HMOs. Enthoven's ideas remain central to today's market-based efforts to expand coverage.

Educated at Stanford, Oxford, and MIT, Enthoven served with distinction in the public sector (he introduced cost benefit analysis to President Kennedy's Department of Defense) and private (he was president of Litton Medical Products.). His interest in HMOs may have begun when he was a schoolboy in Seattle, where his paperboy route included a hospital owned by the Group Health Cooperative. But his interest was piqued in 1971 when he attended a national healthcare conference in Aspen, Colorado, and met Paul Ellwood on the way to the slopes. Two years later he joined the faculty of the Stanford Business School in 1973, where he established a relationship with the Kaiser Permanente Medical Program.

In 1977, Enthoven served as a consultant to President Jimmy Carter. It was in this role that he designed a national health insurance program around two key principles: consumers should have a choice of plans and the tax advantage enjoyed by more expensive plans should be eliminated. Enthoven called his proposal the "Consumer Choice Health Plan (CCHP)."[20] CCHP became the model for what became known as "managed competition" and Enthoven has been dubbed the "father of managed competition." Enthoven's goal was to secure the benefits of competition by overcoming the traditional problems of information and adverse selection. For this to happen, the government would have to create a few basic ground rules for competition and then stay out of the way.

The centerpiece of CCHP was an annual open enrollment period during which plans would have to accept all enrollees who wished to join. Just prior to open enrollment, each plan would disseminate detailed information about coverage, quality, and pricing. To ensure access for all Americans, the government would provide means-based vouchers that would cover the cost of less expensive plans. Patients would have the option of buying more expensive indemnity coverage but would have to make up the additional cost with after-tax dollars. Having leveled the tax playing field, Enthoven believed that HMOs would out compete more expensive indemnity plans.

Enthoven also sought to minimize the incentives for plans to cream skim the healthiest enrollees. He proposed to experience rate payments to plans, i.e., adjust premiums according to enrollees' health needs.[21] Enthoven realized that the success of experience rating hinged on the availability of meaningful risk adjusters. I was his student at the time and he asked me to find out whether available data and methods would permit adequate risk adjustment. What I found was discouraging; it would be difficult for the government to perform meaningful risk adjustments. Insurers would still have opportunities to cream skim. Even today, advocates of market-based health policies decry the lack of broadly available and highly predictive risk adjusters. Enthoven was undeterred, viewing this as an unavoidable minus in a proposal with many plusses.

Enthoven published the framework for CCHP in the *New England Journal of Medicine* and then set to work trying to convince policy makers to turn theory into reality. President Carter invited Enthoven to be the assistant secretary for Planning and Evaluation but Enthoven declined the position when he perceived that Carter was focusing on welfare reform and was disinterested in healthcare policy. Congressmen Richard Gephardt and David Stockman crafted a bill based on CCHP that received some bipartisan support but never came up for a vote during Carter's administration.

When Ronald Reagan took office in 1981, the time seemed right for market-based health reform. Richard Schweiker, the new secretary of Health and Human Services, publicly supported making healthcare more competitive and even took some important steps in that direction. The Reagan administration allowed Medicare recipients to drop out of the traditional indemnity program and switch into private HMOs. It introduced the prospective payment system for hospital reimbursement. But Reagan balked at the idea of government-managed competition and was reluctant to fund the vouchers required to assure universal access. CCHP never came up for a vote in Congress.

Enthoven went back to the drawing board, spending much of the 1980s tinkering with CCHP. He offered a revised version of CCHP to President George H. W. Bush. But Bush's chief of staff, John Sununu, informed Enthoven that "If the American people want health care, they'll vote for Democrats" and that was that for CCHP.[22]

Clinton's Health Security Act

The American people did vote for Democrats in 1992 and the concept of managed competition was revived by President Bill Clinton. Hillary Clinton led a five-hundred-member healthcare task force consisting largely of civil servants and academics. The task force included many notable health policy and health research experts, including Richard Kronick, a political scientist who had worked with Enthoven on revisions to CCHP, Paul Starr, a Princeton University sociologist and author of the seminal book *The Social Transformation of American Medicine*, and David Cutler, a young Harvard economist who had studied under both Joseph Newhouse and future treasury secretary and Harvard University president Lawrence Summers. (Cutler is no slouch himself and is the dean of the College of Arts and Sciences at Harvard, as well as a policy advisor to Barack Obama.) This was a talented group and much was expected from them.

As the task force debated its policy options, many policy analysts speculated that the time had finally come for Congress to enact NHI. There had been similar moments of enthusiasm for previous NHI proposals, always followed by disappointment when the proposal never even came up for a full congressional vote. But the conventional wisdom had it that "this time was different" and that a coalition of consumers, employers, and providers was finally ready to support NHI. Many signs certainly pointed that way. The number of uninsured continued to grow, employers were fed up with rising costs, and the AMA scorned HMOs more than it scorned government intervention. Elected as a "new Democrat," Bill Clinton's proposal promised to be market-based and therefore likely to garner bipartisan support.

In June 1994, the Clinton task force released the text of the Health Security Act. Though based on Enthoven's principles for managed competition, this was MANAGED competition, with a much bigger role for government than Enthoven ever intended. Clinton's 1,700 page proposal had important new rules for seemingly every facet of the health economy. Individuals would be required to enroll in health plans selected by local government councils called "regional health alliances." (Very large employers could opt out of the system.) The alliances could approve all plans or just a few. Under pressure from physicians, Clinton required the alliances to offer all available indemnity plans. At the same time, HMOs would have to offer a "point of service" option that partially covered out-of-network use. All plans were required to offer the same comprehensive benefits at the same copayment levels. This would limit opportunities for Rothschild/Stiglitz-style cream skimming and instead force plans to compete on efficiency and quality. But it also put the government in the position of deciding what would and would not be covered, reminding many of the costs to small employers that resulted from state benefits mandates. A national board would review all new technologies for cost effectiveness. Republicans suggested that this would lead to rationing or suppress innovation altogether.

President Clinton proposed to eliminate the employer as middleman for health benefits, but still relied on employer financing. Employers would make flat contributions toward the costs of health plans, with employees paying the rest. Employees could keep some of the savings if they chose a cheaper plan. Those without access through an employer could purchase an individual plan under the same terms. Low income individuals would receive subsidies.

This mix of market incentives and government controls represented Clinton's desire to accomplish many goals at once: control costs, cover all Americans, keep labor markets functioning smoothly, and limit adverse selection, all without causing any major disruptions to the existing system. Proponents of the plan believed that it represented the best possible compromise between economic theory and political reality. Detractors came from both ends of the political spectrum. Conservatives felt that it was an administrative nightmare waiting to happen; competition hamstrung by overzealous regulators. Some liberals thought that the existing system was an utter failure and should have been blown up entirely, replaced by a simple Canadian-style system. Perhaps most telling was Enthoven's reaction. At a 1994 conference at Northwestern University he remarked, "Of the 1700 pages in the plan, we should throw out 1700 of them."[23]

Why had Clinton diverged so much from Enthoven's vision? Part of the reason was that the task force experts recognized that adverse selection could not be prevented without considerable restrictions on insurance competition. This led to many of the regulatory restrictions that Enthoven decried. President Clinton also believed that he could not win approval for his plan without built-in cost controls. This added to the plan's complexity. Hillary Clinton may have had a simpler reason to regulate insurers, providers, and suppliers. According to one task force insider, Mrs. Clinton believed that the three biggest problems with the healthcare system were "greed, greed, and greed." Only through the enlightened oversight of the government could all that greed be harnessed for the greater good of society.

By the summer of 1994, the Clinton health plan became a lightning rod for opinions about the Clinton presidency and the expanding role of the government. Although the Clinton plan was expected to cause only modest increases in total health expenditures, the Congressional Budget Office projected a massive increase in federal spending (with a partial offset in the private sector), requiring equally massive tax hikes. Republicans savaged the plan during the 1994 election that launched the Gingrich revolution and handed Republicans control of Congress. The plan never came up for a vote.

Even as Clinton was pushing his Health Security Act, a few states considered their own versions of a market-based universal health system. Northwestern University sociologist Steven Shortell helped Iowa and Washington craft programs that would involve managed competition among integrated delivery systems (IDS), in which hospitals owned physician practices and offered their own capitated health plans. Shortell was the nation's leading academic proponent of IDS and he believed that IDS would take a global approach to community health, resulting in lower costs and better outcomes. Many hospitals were starting their own IDS at this time, though the strategy ultimately bogged down due to difficulties that hospitals experienced managing large vertically and horizontally integrated organizations. For a short time during the 1990s, however, IDSs were considered a panacea for the ailing healthcare system.

Iowa and Washington's proposals were complex and required the formation of new IDS. The proposals also required additional revenue sources to cover the uninsured. It is unlikely that they would have succeeded in the 1990s, because the information systems necessary to properly manage IDS were not available. It did not matter, because the proposals met with the same fate as the Clinton proposal. But the Shortell-inspired proposals in Iowa and Washington showed the rest of the nation that states could develop their own highly thoughtful versions of national health insurance.

Despite the failure of the Clinton plan, the federal government did not stand still in its efforts to expand access. The previous chapter described several federal initiatives that have had some success: SCHIP, COBRA, and HIPAA are the most prominent but there is a veritable alphabet soup of such programs. The Family and Medical Leave Act (FMLA) of 1993 guarantees that workers can keep their health insurance coverage for up to twelve weeks if they leave work for illness, birth or adoption of a child, or to care for a seriously ill family member. The Temporary Assistance for Needy Families (TANF) program, created as part of the Welfare Reform Law of 1996, assured Medicaid eligibility for pregnant women and their children while developing a plan for self-sufficiency. The Health Coverage Tax Credit (HCTC) program created in 2002 provides tax credits worth up to 65 percent of the cost of insurance to workers who lose their jobs or take early retirement in industries deemed to have been displaced by foreign trade. These programs reflect the mentality of creeping incrementalism that has captured federal thinking about health reform.

The Backlash Begins

A Loss of Trust

The mid-1990s were heady times for HMO supporters. President Clinton's plan gave them a lot of publicity while the plan's failure assured that they could have free rein to compete as they saw fit. Some government programs directly benefited HMOs. During the 1990s, states moved the majority of Medicaid beneficiaries into HMOs and Medicare changed its rules to encourage HMOs growth, with 16 percent of members opting into a Medicare HMO by 1998. Private sector enrollments also held strong. Never mind that the typical HMO was losing money, most analysts felt that continued enrollment growth would assure long run profitability and provide the nation with a true market-based solution to its health system woes.

Even so, HMO executives were beginning to worry that consumers might rebel against their cost cutting restrictions. They did not have to wait long for the rebellion to gather strength. By the fall of 1996, most of the nation's major newspapers began to run stories about an HMO backlash.[24] Critics of HMOs pulled no punches. A group of 2,000 Massachusetts physicians and nurses calling themselves the Ad Hoc Committee to Defend Health Care published a highly charged editorial in the 1997 *Journal of the American Medical Association*, stating "Canons of commerce are displacing dictates of healing, trampling our profession's most sacred values . . . Physicians and nurses are being prodded by threats and bribes to abdicate allegiance to patients."[25] The *Boston Globe* put it more simply: "The managed care industry has a problem. People hate its guts."[26]

If America's fondness for Marcus Welby medicine was based on trust, then their hostility toward HMOs was based on a lack of it. A Harris survey conducted every year since 1966 reports that in 1970, over 60 percent of Americans had a "great deal" of trust in those running medicine.[27]

Table 4.3. How Well Are Industries Serving Their Customers?

	Percent saying industry doing a "good job"	
Industry	1997	2000
Banks	75	73
Car Manufacturers	70	67
Drugs	79	59
Managed Care	51	29
Tobacco	34	28

Today that figure is down to 30 percent. A more recent series of Harris surveys asks respondents how well different industries served their consumers. In 1997, 51 percent of respondents said that managed care companies were doing a "good job." By 2000, only 29 percent felt the same way. As shown in table 4.3, only tobacco companies ranked lower and only drug companies experienced a comparable decline.

Although it is widely perceived that Americans loathed managed care, most HMO enrollees reported that they were satisfied with their own plans. In a 1997 ABC News survey, 88 percent of HMO enrollees reported that they were satisfied with the quality of care, compared with 92 percent of enrollees in traditional plans. The difference of 4 percent was not statistically meaningful. Surveys also revealed that the vast majority of Americans were satisfied with the care they received from their physicians and in 2000, 67 percent stated they were confident they could pay for a serious illness, an all time high for this question.[28]

Despite these findings, the backlash was no illusion. HMO critics correctly observed that most survey respondents were healthy and might therefore have favorable opinions of their *current* care. But Americans feared what might happen should they become seriously ill; no one wanted to be the next Janet Theriot. The fact that these were isolated anecdotes did not matter. Nor did the absence of systematic evidence about quality. Expectant mothers worried about "drive through deliveries" despite the lack of evidence that early discharges did any harm to mother or child. Patients fumed when HMOs denied claims for emergency room visits even if their "emergencies" turned out to be constipation or food poisoning.

I do not mean to imply that the backlash was all about perceptions (or misperceptions). There was no denying that HMOs could create a bureaucracy that the average patient dreaded. Ironically HMOs were supposed to simplify things and often did. If the HMO patient visited their designated PCP and obtained proper referrals, they received no bills and had no further paperwork. But if patients did not follow the rules, sought care without a referral or without proper preauthorization, or if doctors filed the wrong claim forms, the results could be Kafkaesque. And if HMOs failed to convey the image that customers came first when it came to paperwork, who could blame customers for thinking that the quality of care delivered by HMOs was also wanting?

HMOs also made few friends among physicians. Apart from the obvious reason that physicians preferred the higher reimbursement they received from indemnity insurance, they also objected to the new administrative duties. Physicians also blanched at UR authorization. Some HMO contracts even had "gag rules" limiting what physicians could say about expensive alternatives to authorized treatments.

Patients and physicians wanted the freedom to make referrals to any specialists and hospitals, not just those in the HMO network. In the same vein, HMO enrollees tended to be most dissatisfied when their employers did not give them a choice of plans.[29] Restricted choice, difficulty obtaining referrals, and administrative hassles reinforced by the steady drumbeat of physician complaints, these were the forces behind the managed care backlash.

Effects of Managed Care on Quality

HMOs could not shake the widespread view that they cared more about profits than patients. The administrative hassles were real enough, but so were the cost savings, which could amount to thousands of dollars annually for every enrollee. I suspect that most enrollees would have accepted this tradeoff of hassles for savings. But what if HMOs also provided inferior care? What if they were killing people (as the harshest critics alleged)? Then no amount of cost savings might justify enrolling in one.

In an effort to sort out perception and reality, academic researchers went to work assembling data on the medical side of quality: Were HMO patients receiving more preventive care? Were HMO providers following recommended practices for treating chronically ill patients? Were HMO patients getting healthier? HMO supporters were confident that the plans were a win/win proposition, offering better healthcare at lower costs. That would surely be worth the administrative hassle. Detractors were equally confident that the quality of care was deficient. The results of dozens of research studies would disappoint those on both sides of the debate.

In 1996, Fred Hellinger, an economist at the federal Agency for Healthcare Research and Quality, published a review of the research on HMO quality. He concluded that HMOs had few measurable effects on quality and when HMOs did have an effect, it was as likely to be favorable as not.[30] Robert Miller and Harold Luft reached similar conclusions from their review of thirty-five studies published between 1993 and 1997[31] Miller and Luft sum up their findings as follows: "Fears that HMOs uniformly lead to worse quality of care are not supported by the evidence. . . . Hopes that HMOs would improve overall quality also are not supported."

In a follow-up published in 2002, Miller and Luft reviewed forty-four new studies. Again, the findings were a mixed bag. The studies are almost equally divided between those finding better quality in HMOs, those finding worse quality, and those finding no differences at all.[32] There are some nuances to the findings. HMOs seem to do best when it comes to prevention. Low income patients in Medicaid HMOs and elderly patients with chronic conditions enrolled in Medicare HMOs appear to be a bit worse off, perhaps because Medicaid and Medicare may fail to provide adequate funding.

We rely on trust when we lack facts. The facts about HMO quality suggested that we may have been wrong to distrust them. Privately insured patients could expect about the same quality of care in HMOs as they received in their indemnity plans. They might want to pay more for indemnity insurance in order to have free choice and fewer hassles, but quality of care should not have been a major consideration. By the time the HMO quality studies were published, the reputation of HMOs had gotten so bad that the facts no longer mattered. A remarkable study by

James Reschevsky, J. Lee Hargraves, and Albert Smith suggests that patients may have even invented facts to fit their preconceived notions.[33]

Reschevsky, Hargraves, and Smith asked individuals to rate their satisfaction with their health plans. Individuals who stated that they belonged to an HMO were generally less satisfied than those who said they were in indemnity plans. This would be rather damning evidence against HMOs were it not for the fact that about one-fourth of all respondents misidentified the type of plan they were in! When the researchers reexamined the data but based their analysis on the plans that respondents actually belonged to, rather than the plans they thought they belonged to, they found no difference in quality. It seems that individuals who were unhappy about their healthcare assumed they were in an HMO, regardless of whether they were actually in an HMO. Talk about how hard it is to overcome a bad reputation!

Single-Minded Shopping

Selective contracting cannot succeed unless payers can credibly threaten to exclude some providers from their networks. Credibility requires that some providers are, in fact, occasionally excluded from some networks. Patients justifiably balk at such limits on their freedom to choose. It would be even more disconcerting if HMOs were steering enrollees to low-quality providers.

There is no compelling reason to think that HMOs would systematically exclude the best providers. The reality is that HMOs cannot sell their networks to employers without including at least some of the best providers. Two recent studies suggest that HMO patients are actually *more* likely than average to be admitted to high quality hospitals.[34] There is no comparable evidence, one way or the other, on the quality of contracting physicians. However, there are many outstanding specialists who do enough business with indemnity and Medicare patients that they can afford not to contract with HMOs. But fears that HMOs would shop for price while ignoring quality are surely overstated.

Indeed it would be devastating if HMOs shopped more aggressively for low-cost providers without paying the same attention to quality. My research with Mark Satterthwaite identified the dangers.[35] Providers must be compensated for the time and effort required to maintain high quality. HMO discounts will eat into providers' margins and reduce their incentives to improve quality. If HMOs are lax about quality, then enrollees could be much worse off overall; total spending would fall, but the quality of care would fall by even more. Prior to managed care, patients cared about as much about prices as they knew about quality, this is to say not very much at all. When HMOs injected price competition into the market, there was a real danger that they would focus exclusively on price. The limited available evidence suggests that HMOs paid more than lip service to quality. Even so, the need to balance price and quality shopping remains a paramount concern in the modern health economy.

The Patient Bill of Rights

The backlash reached new heights in March 1997, when President Clinton appointed a commission to write a patient "bill of rights." Clinton wanted to eliminate gag rules that prevented physicians from describing costly treatment alternatives. HMOs argued that the gag rules were necessary to discourage moral hazard and demand inducement. Clinton also wanted to prevent HMOs from financially rewarding doctors who withheld care. This had the potential to cut out the heart of HMO cost-containment efforts, as there was no practical way to remove the financial incentives for overtreatment without simultaneously rewarding undertreatment.

Over the next year, Congress and the nation debated the bill of rights. The Democrats proposed legislation that included the Clinton guidelines and also guaranteed patients the right to choose a provider. This would have spelled the end of managed care cost containment. Of course, this may have been exactly what some of the bill's sponsors wanted. In due time, they could say that market forces had failed, so it was time for the government to step in. They would conveniently leave out that their legislation was responsible for the demise of market forces.

It turned out that the most controversial element of the Democratic version of the bill of rights was a proposal to allow patients to sue their

HMOs for malpractice. Many Republicans were no friends of HMOs, which they saw as a market-place version of socialized medicine. But Republicans were equally wary of relying on the courts to assure quality and backed away from the Democratic proposal in favor of their own stripped down bill of rights. With furious lobbying by medical providers in favor of the Democratic proposal and by insurers and many employers who backed the Republican version or no bill at all, the legislation stalled.[36] It hardly mattered. By the end of the 1990s, HMOs were backing off on some of the tactics targeted by the legislation, and HMO enrollments were shifting to less restrictive Preferred Provider Organizations.

Toward Managed Care "Lite"

The Rise of PPOs

The term managed care first appears in newspapers around 1988. It quickly became a catchall term describing the myriad of tactics that payers used to correct some of the perceived inefficiencies of indemnity insurance. Many people equate managed care to HMOs, and much of the research on managed care focuses exclusively on HMOs. But while HMOs rely heavily on prepayment to contain costs, most managed care organizations (MCOs) nowadays have abandoned prepayment and rely almost exclusively on selective contracting with "preferred providers."

The earliest preferred provider organizations (PPOs) date to the 1970s, when third-party administrators for self-insured employers in Los Angeles began selectively contracting with local hospitals. Self-insured firms were among the first to use selective contracting because state laws prohibited the practice by insurance companies, laws that ERISA-exempt self-insuring firms could ignore. In the 1980s, most states rewrote their insurance laws to permit selective contracting and PPOs proliferated. Many employers viewed PPOs as a less forbidding way station on the path between indemnity insurance and HMOs, and enrollments in PPOs grew steadily. In 1988, the first year for which data is available, PPO enrollments were not that far behind

Table 4.4. Enrollments in MCOs

Year	Percent of Workers Enrolled in Indemnity Insurance	Percent of Workers Enrolled in HMO	Percent of Workers Enrolled in PPO or POS
1988	73	16	11
1990	62	18	25
1993	46	21	47
1996	27	31	59
1998	14	27	62

Source: KFF and author's interpolation for 1990. KFF obtains their data from surveys of employers. Like other survey-derived managed care enrollment data, these are rough estimates at best, in part because respondents do not always know whether their plan is an HMO.

HMO enrollments, as shown in table 4.4. Point of Service plans, which include HMO-like incentives for providers but gave enrollees PPO-like coverage for out-of-network use, appeared in the early 1990s. For the next few years, PPO/POS enrollments grew rapidly, HMO enrollments grew slowly, and traditional indemnity insurance enrollments plummeted. Not coincidentally, healthcare spending began to level out.

Full Retreat

Healthcare spending has renewed its upward climb and now exceeds 16 percent of GDP. (See table 4.5.) In a complete reversal from the 1990s, Medicaid and Medicare spending growth has slowed somewhat and most of the increase has come from growth in private-sector spending. Preliminary data from 2006 suggests that there may have been a modest slowdown in the private sector in 2006, and overall health spending may once again be subsiding a bit.

Perhaps it was too much to expect healthcare costs to remain under control. After all, there was little MCOs could do to hold down technological change and wage inflation, the two biggest contributors to rising costs. The shift to managed care may have put us on a lower cost level,

Table 4.5. Annual Health Spending: 2000–5

Year	Total health spending ($billion)	Per capita spending	Real percapita spending (2005 dollars)	Annual inflation in real per capita spending	Health spending as percent of GDP
2000	1350	$4790	$5440	2.9	13.8
2003	1730	5950	6320	5.1	15.8
2005	1990	6700	6700	3.0	16.0

Source: Catlin, A. et al. 2007. "National Health Spending in 2005: The Slowdown Continues" *Health Affairs* 26, 1: 142–53.

but the upward trend remained intact. We ought not to scoff at the savings. While many predict that healthcare will reach 20 percent of GDP by 2015 or even sooner, imagine what spending would be like if we had already reached that threshold in 2000?

But recent increases may have more to do with the changing face of managed care in the wake of the HMO backlash. We have moved away from an era in which insurers made serious efforts to contain costs into an era of managed care "lite," where the cost cutting tactics favored by MCOs have been watered down or abandoned.

One of the first tools to go was utilization review. The decline of UR was initiated in 1998 by one of its biggest proponents, Aetna. Aetna had the largest nationwide market share among HMOs and was one of the more aggressive cost-cutting insurers, making it a lightning rod for the backlash. According to health policy expert Paul Ginsburg, Aetna's management "seemed almost to take pride in alienating physicians."[37] Aetna felt the full wrath of the medical profession in 1998 when it proposed to acquire Prudential's health insurance business. The AMA protested to the Department of Justice, and soon thereafter launched a campaign against insurer market power that is still ongoing. The DOJ approved the deal in 1999, but not before requiring Aetna to divest some of the Prudential HMO products.

Aetna felt that it needed to repair its relationships with physicians. It sacked its CEO and appointed an outsider, William Donaldson, who, in turn, appointed John Rowe to run its HMO unit. Dr. Rowe was a member of the Institutes of Medicine, founding director of the Division on Aging at Harvard Medical School, and immediately prior to joining Aetna, the head of the Mount Sinai NYU Health Center.[38] His appointment signaled a sea change in Aetna's philosophy. Donaldson and Rowe went to work mending fences with physicians. They built a strategic unit to build physician relationships and then took the unexpected step of scrapping mandatory utilization review.

On the list of things that physicians most despised about managed care, UR was number one with a bullet. Aetna was also skeptical about whether utilization review even worked. It was costly to manage, Aetna was approving 99 percent of requests, and independent research was failing to unearth substantial savings. Aetna initially established an appeals process for denied claims and, shortly thereafter, eliminated mandatory UR altogether. Aetna still performed UR, but its decisions were strictly advisory and there was a greater focus on prevention.

Other HMOs, notably United Healthcare, had the same growing skepticism about UR. United's UR practice cost over $100 million annually to operate and, like Aetna's was approving 99 percent of all requests.[39] United shut it down in 2000. Physicians contacted United to express support for the decision; quite a change from the bitter relationship that had existed. United has begun replacing UR with a new compensation system that links physician pay to measurable health outcomes. As I discuss in chapter 6, such pay-for-performance systems are becoming commonplace.

The shift to PPOs meant even more watering down of managed care. The comparison with old-style HMOs was becoming stark. HMOs capitated physicians; PPOs paid fee for service. HMOs had narrow provider networks with deep discounts; PPOs had broader networks and smaller discounts. Provider networks have expanded further in the past few years as PPOs respond to patient concerns about choice. It is difficult to find systematic time series data about network size, but the conventional wisdom is that PPO networks in the mid-1990s excluded as many as 25 percent of local hospitals whereas nowadays perhaps 10 percent are excluded. Recent research by Katherine Ho partly confirms this; she finds that most plans in large markets now contract with nearly all of the major local hospitals.[40] There is less data available on physician contracting, but again the pattern seems to be that most physicians are now in most PPO networks. HMO networks also appear to have expanded and in many markets, it is difficult to tell the HMO and PPO networks apart. Payers once relied on the threat of exclusion to obtain provider discounts. As that threat began to ring hollow, providers were able to raise their prices.

Co-Conspirators

All of these responses to the MCO backlash—the end of UR, the shift from HMO to PPO, and the expansion of networks—have contributed to rising healthcare costs. Employers are once again complaining, but we must remember that employees bear the most of the cost increases. Macroeconomic data confirms this. During the 1990s, employer-provided health insurance costs leveled out and workers enjoyed one of the longest and largest periods of real wage growth in history. In the past five years, insurance costs have risen rapidly and real wages for the median worker are essentially flat.[41] The full story behind these trends is much more complex, of course, but the inverse relationship between health costs and wages cannot be ignored.

Perhaps the HMO backlash would have been weaker if employers and employees were better economists. Employers would have realized that their employees shouldered most of the burden of rising costs and employees would have been a bit less upset about having to join HMOs. The HMOs themselves played an important role in their own demise through their occasional heavy handed tactics. They may have overestimated the desire for cost cutting, failing to realize that the market would ultimately be dominated by the concerns of employees more than employers.

I would be remiss if I did not mention the important role played by providers in forging the path to managed care lite. Not only have providers given HMOs a worse name than they deserved, they did their best to assure that selective contracting would not succeed. Many large markets, including Boston, Cleveland, Milwaukee, and Sacramento, are now dominated by a small number of healthcare systems. Consolidation in smaller cities such as Dubuque and Joplin has left local healthcare plans to negotiate with a single dominant provider. You can't rely on competition to save money if no one is competing.

The Federal Trade Commission—the antitrust agency with jurisdiction over most healthcare matters—challenged several hospital mergers during the 1990s but lost every case as suspicious judges doubted whether higher prices would result. The FTC took a brief hiatus from hospital antitrust in order to lick its wounds. When researchers began demonstrating that many mergers were causing substantial increases in provider prices, the FTC went back to work.[42] It developed new pricing models that captured the important role played by selective contracting and subpoenaed pricing data from hospitals that had recently consolidated. The FTC filed a challenge to a consummated merger between Evanston Hospital and Highland Park Hospital in suburban Chicago. A federal district court judge sided with the FTC and ordered Evanston and Highland Park Hospitals to split up. In a complex decision, the commissioners of the FTC have sided with the district court judge but will allow the hospitals to remain together, provided that they set prices independently. The hospitals are considering an appeal.

Providers correctly point out that payers have been consolidating as well. Some of the highest profile mergers, including the recent Wellpoint/Anthem consolidation, involve geographic diversification and do not increase market concentration dominance in any one particular location. But attrition and consolidation have left many markets with a small number of insurers. The AMA estimates that a single health insurer has at least a 30 percent market share, and the top two insurers have at least 50 percent combined share, in nearly every metropolitan area.[43] In some areas, concentration is far higher. These are not definitive findings because they do not account for self-funded plans and the ease of entry in some markets, but they represent an unprecedented degree of insurer concentration.

The AMA, provider groups, and the FTC have been engaged in heated discussions over whether insurer consolidation is threatening the health economy. Provider groups complain that large payers can command even lower fees from their members while, at the same time, driving up premiums. They feel that provider market power is therefore necessary to counterbalance payer market power. This is likely to be the next battleground in the critical realm of healthcare antitrust.

The Current Cost Crisis

What Are We Spending So Much Money On?

Annual U.S. health spending now exceeds two trillion dollars and accounts for over 16 percent of GDP. Data from the Center for Medicare and Medicaid Services (CMS) allow us to sort out where the extra dollars have been going. Table 4.6 breaks down spending into six major categories: hospital, physician and clinical services, long-term care (nursing homes and home healthcare), drugs and other supplies (including drug industry profits), government administration and the net cost of private health insurance (including insurance industry profits), and other (including dental care, other professional services, and research).

The figures may surprise some people. Hospitals remain the cornerstone of the U.S. healthcare system, accounting for over 30 percent of total spending (or about 5 percent of the total U.S. GDP.) Physician

Table 4.6. Health Spending 2000 and 2005, by Category

Category	Spending 2000 ($billions)	% of 2000 spending	Spending 2005 ($billions)	% of 2004 spending
Hospitals	$417	30.9%	$612	30.8%
MD/clinic	289	21.4	421	21.2
Long-term care	126	9.3	169	8.5
Drugs/supplies[1]	170	12.6	259	13.0
Admin/health insurance	81	6.0	143	7.2
Other	267	19.8	386	19.4
Total	1,350	100%	1990	100%

Source: Catlin, A. et al. 2007.

[1] Does not include drugs and supplies dispensed in hospitals or other institutions and included as part of their costs.

and clinical services are next, account for about 21 percent of total spending (over 3 percent of GDP). Despite the constant media focus, spending on drugs ranks fourth, after "other."

Table 4.7 offers a different way of looking at recent healthcare cost inflation. It reports the rate of growth of spending by category and indicates how much these increases have contributed to total healthcare spending growth. It is probably no surprise that the fastest growing categories of spending are drugs/supplies and administration/net cost of health insurance. Even so, because spending in these categories remains relatively small, the increases account for less than 24 percent of total spending growth. If drugs/supplies and net health insurance costs had grown at the average rate for the entire health economy (47.4 percent), then total spending in 2005 would have been $1.932 trillion instead of $1.990 trillion. (This assumes, rather optimistically, that there are no offsetting increases in other categories of spending.)[44] The savings of $58 billion would be welcome, but we would probably be every bit as concerned about healthcare spending growth.

If we cannot pin the blame for health spending growth on drug and insurance costs, then what is to blame? The move to managed care lite

Table 4.7. Change in Health Spending 2000–5, by Category

Category	Change 2000–5 (billions)	Change 2000–5 (percent)	Percent of overall spending change 2000–5
Hospitals	$195	46.8%	30.5%
MD/clinic	132	40.9	20.6
Long-term care	43	25.4	6.7
Drugs/supplies	89	52.3	13.9
Admin/health insurance	62	69.1	9.7
Other	119	44.6	18.6
Total	$640	47.4%	100%

Source: Catlin, A. et al. 2007. The percentages in the second column of data are computed by dividing the first column of data in table 4.7 by the first column of data in table 4.6. The percentages in the third column are computed by dividing the first column by $649 (the total change in spending).

has certainly played a role, as has market consolidation. Technological change is inevitable and should be welcomed, even if it means higher costs. Despite all the attention paid to medical technology, healthcare is a labor intensive business and labor costs continue to increase as providers scramble to fill positions in the teeth of long-standing labor shortages. Between 2000 and 2004, for example, real nursing wages increased by 16 percent, continuing a trend that dates back at least to 1980.[45] Other allied health professionals have enjoyed similar increases.

So what can be done to lower costs? Purchase only older drugs and technologies? That would save money, but the cost in terms of lives and quality of life would be excessive. Pay lower wages? That would intensify current shortages. Cap insurer and drug industry profits? Such populist policies would help, but only a little. (We could sharply reduce administrative costs by moving to a single payer system, an option I take up in chapter 8.) Ultimately we must figure out how to buy less stuff or pay less for it. If we do the latter, we had better hope that providers can become more efficient or we will force them to reduce quality or leave the market altogether. And somehow, we need to figure out how to achieve these goals without ignoring the uninsured.

Whither Access and Quality?

Unfortunately access seems to have deteriorated even as spending has increased. According to U.S. census data, the number of uninsured in the United States increased from roughly forty million in 2000 to forty-seven million in 2006, or about 16 percent of the population. There is considerable variation in rates of uninsurance across the states. Just 8.5 percent of Minnesotans lack insurance versus 18.4 percent in California, 18.5 percent in Florida, and 25.1 percent in Texas. If we focus on the nonelderly (remembering that nearly all elderly are on Medicare), then uninsurance rates exceed 20 percent in California and Florida and top 28 percent in Texas. There is considerable variation in children's uninsurance rates as well. Texas "leads" the nation with over 20 percent uninsured, but there are fifteen states where the rate has fallen below 8 percent (versus just eight states in the late 1990s).

The stereotypical uninsured American is unemployed or works part time for minimum wage. But fully one-third of the increase in the uninsured was in households making at least twice the federal poverty level. One reason for the sharp rise in the uninsured has been a dramatic decline in employer sponsored coverage—the percentage of employers offering insurance dropped from 69 percent in 2000 to 60 percent in 2005.[46] Some of the affected employees have purchased individual coverage. Others are eligible for Medicaid and the SCHIP program has been particularly effective in extending coverage to children.

The recent decline in employer-sponsored coverage accelerates a trend that began in the 1980s. Behind the trend is a shift in U.S. labor markets from large, unionized, industrial firms that offered insurance to virtually every employee to smaller, nonunion, service firms, nearly half of which offer no insurance at all. An increase in the percentage of part-time and seasonal workers further contributes to the decline.

If the decline in employer sponsorship is a major cause for concern, an even bigger concern may be the decline in the rate at which employees "take up" the insurance that they are offered. A 2003 study by Jonathan Gruber and Ebonya Washington finds that one quarter of the uninsured had access to employer-sponsored insurance but declined to pay their share of the premium, even though this was usually much less than half the total.[47] Gruber now estimates that a recent decline in the take-up rate is the most important reason why the ranks of the uninsured are swelling.[48]

A big factor behind the decline in take up is the dramatic increase in the amount that employers ask employees to contribute. In the 1980s, employers usually paid the entire cost of insurance. Today, the average employee is asked to pay $2,000 to $3,000 toward the premium. It is not entirely clear why the employee cost-share has risen so rapidly. If anything, tax laws favor the employer paying the full premium. Perhaps employers hope that some of their employees will decline to take up the offer of insurance. If so, the strategy of raising the cost-share seems to be working. But while some employees who decline take up can obtain coverage through their spouse, many others are choosing to go without any coverage.

It is difficult to say what has happened to quality of care. Indicators such as life expectancy and infant mortality show steady improvement, but this may be due to technological progress. There is no way to know if providers are doing their jobs more effectively and the extent, if any, to which this reflects changes in health system financing. The Institutes of Medicine reports on problems with the quality of care in the U.S. healthcare system, *To Err Is Human* and *Crossing the Quality Chasm*, published in 2000 and 2001 respectively, suggest that we have a long way to go.[49]

So this is the sorry state in which we find ourselves: The managed care revolution came and went, temporarily leaving a vacuum of ideas about how to reduce costs and boost quality. Markets, like nature, abhor a vacuum and we are now seeing a new wave of ideas such as consumer-driven healthcare and quality report cards. On the access front, federal efforts to broaden coverage have slowed to a crawl, but a few states, led by Massachusetts, are marching forward with bold initiatives of their own. The second half of the book takes a closer look at these new ideas, which could be our last, best chance of reviving the U.S. healthcare system.

2

Searching for Cures

Self-Help

The concept of Health Savings

Accounts is not conservative or

liberal . . . It should appeal to

everyone who suspects that

impersonal bureaucracies care less

about us than we care about

ourselves.

—JOHN GOODMAN, president,
National Center for Policy Analysis[1]

The Shopping Problem Revisited

It is difficult to be a good healthcare consumer. We must make decisions with very limited information and often under considerable stress. We want to be protected against financial risk, but insurance insulates us from considerations of costs. These are universal concerns and the resulting problems that I have described in earlier chapters cannot be wished away with a magic wand. The evolution of our healthcare system can be seen as a series of efforts to solve these problems.

For most of our lifetimes, the most comforting solution has been "Marcus Welby medicine." But health services researchers showed that this comfort comes at an enormous cost, namely the inefficiencies of moral hazard, demand inducement, practice variations and the medical arms race. Nor does it guarantee quality. The 1970s saw planners try and fail to make things better. By the 1990s, Marcus Welby medicine and health planning were replaced by managed care. Systematic research on cost and quality puts managed care in a fairly favorable light but patients do not agree. Most people's minds are now closed about HMOs. Enrollments have plummeted and most of today's health insurance plans are best described as managed care "lite."

We have tried a doctor-centered system and an insurer/employer-centered system. We are still looking for solutions to the shopping problem. To some, it is time for a patient-centered system. This requires us to reject the fundamental premise behind Marcus Welby and MCOs, namely, that patients are incapable of being effective shoppers. Supporters of the new approach aim to empower patients with information about quality and costs and give them strong financial incentives to act on that information. If they achieve these goals, then we may yet realize the full benefits of the marketplace, with lower costs, higher quality, and, equally important, the full support of consumers.

These ideas are embodied by new insurance products known as Consumer Directed Health Plans (CDHPs) and new financial instruments known as Health Savings Accounts (HSAs). CDHPs and HSAs are the talk of the industry. Having only recently arrived on the scene, they are rapidly gaining market share in the wake of the managed care backlash and President Bush has made them central to his health policy agenda. Even so, there are reasons to be skeptical about the future of CDHPs, making me believe that we have not seen the end of managed care.

Consumer Directed Health Plans

Origins of the Idea

Jesse Hixson, an economist working at the Social Security Administration in 1974, is widely credited with developing the idea of "health banks." These were to be bank accounts financed by employers, owned by employees, and created specifically to pay for health services.[2] In

1978, Paul Worthington, an economist at Slippery Rock State College and one-time coauthor of Hixson's, published the framework for health banks in the health research and policy journal *Inquiry*.[3] Citing the twin problems of moral hazard and the absence of price shopping, Worthington proposed a simple solution. Employers would form credit unions and open an account for each of their employees. Rather than purchase insurance, employers would deposit the amount of the premium into each employee's account. Workers could draw down their accounts over their lifetimes to pay for healthcare services. They could even borrow against future deposits if needed as a way of obtaining catastrophic protection. Upon retirement, workers could keep the funds for their own personal use.

Worthington's proposal contains many of the essential features of today's CDHPs: Individuals would have their own private accounts to pay for first-dollar expenses; true insurance protection would be limited to last-dollar (catastrophic) coverage; and consumers who avoided costly healthcare services could even use their accounts to supplement their retirements. Worthington also seems to suggest that the funds deposited into the health bank would be exempt from income taxation.

Despite the prescience of his proposal, Worthington drops out of the story line after this publication. Hixson's influence grows, however. He becomes chief economist at the American Medical Association, overseeing what was for many years one of the nation's most productive groups of health economists. (In the category of "it's a small world," Hixson edited a 1980 report that found numerous flaws in the research on physician-induced demand.[4]) Hixson's growing influence in policy circles would pay off in the late 1980s when he shared his ideas with John Goodman, the founder and president of the National Center for Policy Analysis (NCPA). Goodman would prove to be an effective champion of CDHPs in the policy community.

Goodman was always interested in politics, first as an undergraduate at the University of Texas where he served in student government and then as an economics doctoral student at Columbia University where his dissertation emphasized how government decision making could be a poor substitute for individual choices in the private sector. After a few academic jobs, Goodman founded the NCPA in 1983 with the goal of advancing ideas about how to weaken the economic power of the government. From its inception, the NCPA has taken traditional conservative positions on policy issues, favoring lower taxes, school vouchers, and privatizing social security. After Goodman's encounter with Hixson, the NCPA became a force in the health policy arena. In 1992, Goodman and fellow economist Gerald Musgrave published *Patient Power*, which endorsed and expanded on Hixson and Worthington's health bank proposal.[5] The book became a surprising best seller, launching Goodman and Musgrave on a nationwide series of lectures about their ideas for healthcare reform.

In the audience at one of Musgrave's lectures was Pat Rooney, president of Golden Rule Insurance Company. Golden Rule was a small health insurer specializing in the individual and small group markets. Golden Rule was small enough that Rooney could involve himself in day-to-day employee relations issues. Seeking to reduce healthcare costs and increase worker satisfaction at Golden Rule, he was captivated by the concept of health banks, which by then were renamed Medical Savings Accounts (MSAs). In May 1993, Golden Rule offered its own employees high deductible insurance with MSAs. At this time, the MSAs were not tax deductible.

It wasn't long before Rooney marketed MSAs to other companies. Rooney also began lobbying state and federal legislators to exempt MSA contributions from income taxes. Rooney joined Goodman in suggesting that tax-exempt MSAs could be the centerpiece of market-based national health reform.

I learned about Golden Rule's experiences first hand when Rooney spoke about MSAs at a conference in 1993 sponsored by the American Enterprise Institute, a conservative think tank. Economist Mark Pauly served as Rooney's discussant that day. Pauly remarked that MSAs seemed like a complicated solution to the inequities created by the IRS tax code. He did not mean this in a pejorative sense. Pauly lauded the effort to level the tax playing field and make high deductible plans competitive with indemnity insurance. But Pauly recognized that once you stripped away the tax considerations, MSAs were essentially forced savings plans in which individuals set money aside at the start of the year to fund any subsequent spending that would fall under their annual deductible. Pauly called MSAs a "Christmas Club" for healthcare.[6] If it were not for tax considerations, it would be much simpler to allow individuals to pay their deductible as they incurred medical expenses throughout the year. Surely there would be better ways to address the tax issues. The economists in the room agreed. In chapter 8, I describe some of these better ways.

I had another reason to be skeptical of Rooney's proposal. I had met Rooney a few years earlier when I was a professor at the University of Chicago. The deans at the University of Chicago Graduate School of Business had gathered a group of faculty and business leaders to discuss health policy. Toward the end of the meeting, the deans invited the faculty to ask the business executives more practical management questions. I described a hypothetical situation: A young, healthy Golden Rule enrollee is hit by a car, incurs heavy medical expenses, and then fully recovers. From a strict insurance standpoint, that individual was a good actuarial risk and should have no trouble with renewing coverage. When I asked Mr. Rooney what Golden Rule would do, he reminded me that Golden Rule was in the business to make money; having already lost money on this individual, he would have no interest in renewing the policy.[7]

I was nonplussed to say the least. I have asked the same question to other insurance executives. They indicated that they would be happy to reenroll the individual without any special rate increase. (Perhaps they were being politically correct, but that is the correct profit maximizing choice.) A few also volunteered that Golden Rule might simply be trying to cream skim the healthiest enrollees.

Therein lays the dark side of CDHPs. High deductible insurance plans with a savings option make economic sense—they will limit the inefficiency of moral hazard. This will translate into a better value insurance product that should do well in the market. But the same plans will appeal most to healthy individuals who can expect to bank their savings. This will segment the risk pool. Healthy enrollees will opt into CDHPs and CDHP carriers will reap handsome profits (at least until competition from other CDHP plans forces their premiums down.) Less healthy enrollees will remain with more generous plans, which will have to raise their premiums to cope with this unfavorable selection. We will lose the principle of cross-subsidization that is fundamental to the distinctly American approach to health insurance. The policy debate about the today's CDHPs boils down to whether the benefits of efficiency will more than offset the perils of selection.

Old Wine in New Bottles

None of the protagonists in the development of CDHPs invented moral hazard. Mark Pauly drew economists' attention to it in the late 1960s and the RAND study publicized its perils to a wider audience in the early 1980s. The RAND conclusions were definitive and remain unchallenged: absent tax considerations, optimal health insurance ought to include substantial deductibles and copayments. The fact that far more generous insurance policies have dominated the market is prima facie evidence of the distortions created by tax policy. Ironically in a nation where tens of millions of people lack any health insurance, those who have it are usually overinsured.

Many economists have long advocated a solution to this problem that is far simpler than CDHPs: eliminate the tax deductibility of health insurance. Tax deductibility is, after all, a vestige of a World War II policy to get around wage controls. But like so many government policies, it has lived on long after the reasons for it have disappeared. Eliminating the deduction for health insurance would not only drive efficiencies in the healthcare system, it would generate huge revenues for the government. The foregone taxes on employer sponsored health insurance approach $200 billion annually. This tax subsidy is more than ample to cover all of the nation's uninsured.

Any proposal to completely eliminate the tax deductibility of health insurance would likely be political suicide—akin to a $200 billion middle-class tax increase. In his Consumer Choice Health Plan, Enthoven proposed capping the tax deduction so that those buying more expensive plans would have to pay only the difference in cost. But no one in Congress wanted to risk their political capital on HMO-friendly legislation, so Enthoven's idea languished.

Goodman et al. put a new spin on Enthoven's solution. They also want to level the tax playing field. But they adopt an "if you can't beat 'em, join 'em" mentality. Instead of eliminating the tax advantages enjoyed by generous health insurance policies, they propose extending comparable tax advantages to CDHPs!

The Ground Rules for CDHP

Even before Congress began serious consideration of CDHPs, Rooney and Goodman's lobbying efforts were paying off. By the mid-1990s, nineteen states had exempted deposits into MSAs from state income taxes. But federal tax exemption was still the big Kahuna.

Congress took the first legislative steps toward federal income tax exemption when it authorized a pilot program creating MSAs as part of the 1996 HIPAA legislation. The program rules should sound familiar. High deductible health plans could be coupled with MSAs, personal accounts to be funded by employer and employee contributions. The MSAs would be exempt from federal income taxes and could be used to pay for any uncovered healthcare costs. MSA funds spent on nonhealthcare goods and services were subject to income taxes and a steep penalty (the penalty was waived once the individual reached age sixty-five.) Unspent MSA funds rolled over and could be used by the employee for future healthcare spending needs.

The HIPAA-MSA experiment was limited to small firms and individuals and expired in December 2000. The experiment also suffered because the rules made it unclear as to whether individuals could keep their MSA if they changed jobs. (Many people I spoke with who sold MSA policies were unsure themselves.) Perhaps because of these restrictions, fewer than 100,000 enrollees signed up for a HIPAA-MSA. Even so, policy makers and politicians, especially Republicans looking for a market-based health reform initiative, remained enthusiastic about the concept.

In 2003, Congress created new rules for HSAs (which are rechristened MSAs) as part of the Medicare Modernization Act. The basic rules for HSAs are now as follows:

- Employers and employees can contribute tax deductible funds to an HSA; the current annual limits are $2,700 for an individual and $5,450 for a family.[8]

- The accompanying insurance plan—the CDHP—must have a deductible of at least $1,000 for an individual and $2,000 for a family. Some deductibles are much higher, higher even than the annual HSA contribution. This is supposed to encourage enrollees to bank their HSA to cover future deductibles.
- Interest on the HSA is tax free.
- The individual can use the HSA to cover deductibles, copayments, and various uncovered medical expenses including over-the-counter drugs and long-term care insurance.
- The HSA is portable and can be passed on to one's estate.
- Upon retirement, the individual can withdraw funds to be used for any purpose. If the funds are used for healthcare (for example to pay Medicare copayments), they are subject to traditional income taxes. If used for any other spending, they are subject to an additional 10 percent tax. Thus, the HSA is like a restricted individual retirement account (IRA).

Under these rules, the HSA unambiguously belongs to the worker. The money invested in the HSA receives the same tax benefits as money spent on more costly health insurance plans. The playing field may actually be tilted slightly in the favor of CDHPs by offering a unique opportunity for millions of American workers who max out on their annual IRA contributions to further increase their retirement nest egg.

While these rules give high deductible CDHPs the same tax advantages as more expensive health plans, they tilt the tax playing field even more against HMOs. HMOs have few friends on Capitol Hill these days, so it is no surprise that they have come out on the short end of the tax fairness stick. Expect HMO enrollments to drop almost as rapidly as CDHP enrollments rise.

Empowering Patients to be Make Medical Decisions

Consumers comparing CDHPs with traditional PPO or indemnity plans will find that they have a lot more to offer than just big deductibles and HSAs. Many CDHPs offer a Web-based information management portal designed to help patients diagnose symptoms and identify treatment options. Whenever I attend public forums on CDHP, the Web-based health management tools come up for the greatest criticism. CDHP supporters claim that patients will finally be able to make medical decisions for themselves. Whom are they kidding? It takes four years of medical school and another four to six years of postgraduate residency training before doctors start their practices. And they are not called practices for nothing. A newly minted physician is almost invariably a very bad doctor. It takes years of experience for real doctors to hone diagnostic and treatment skills. Patients using the Internet to play at doctor risk learning just enough to be dangerous, leading to false-positive and false-negative diagnoses, delayed treatments, and unproductive arguments with frustrated providers over the proper course of treatment.

This is not just a criticism of CDHPs. Anyone can access Internet health information sites like WebMD or Mayoclinic.com. These sites can help us ascertain the importance of seeking out proper medical help, ask better questions of our doctors, and more fully understand the importance of compliance. But no one should be fooled into thinking that they can rely on the Internet to make diagnoses and chart a course of treatment. The best Web sites already state this, but many consumers ignore this advice. To paraphrase an old saw, anyone who diagnoses and treats their own illness has a fool for a doctor. I do not think most people want to be their own doctors anyway. CDHPs will have to prove their worth in other ways.

Other CDHP Features

CDHP Web sites also allow patients to manage their own medical records, creating the type of electronic record that is currently scattered across multiple providers, if it exists at all. This could be a big boon to patients and providers, assuming that the record is accurate, complete, and up-to-date. But these sites currently require patients to enter their own diagnostic and clinical information; this can be challenging for the lay person. And as with Web-based medical information sites, patients do not need to purchase a CDHP to enjoy these benefits. Many companies provide similar personal medical records products without tying them to CDHPs.

CDHPs not only give patients a financial incentive to shop around, they are trying to make it easier for them to do so, by providing comparative price and quality information. But the plans have been frustrated thus far by a lack of pricing transparency, a topic I will address later in this chapter. Moreover CDHP quality information is not much different than that provided by other Web sites, a subject I will discuss in the next chapter. Clearly CDHPs have a long way to go if they are to provide unique opportunities for enrollees to become superior consumers.

It seems that the only Web-based information that is truly novel to the CDHP is the tool to manage the HSA. This is obviously important, but consumers seem to be frustrated with this tool as well, and the value-added above what is currently available to consumers who have traditional insurance is questionable.[9]

Revisiting Moral Hazard

For all the bells and whistles, the key feature of CDHPs is the big deductible. This may be why the RAND study has become a sort of bible for many CDHP proponents. Recall the key result of the RAND study—enrollees in the "free care" plans spent 30 to 40 percent more than enrollees in cost sharing plans. If CDHPs afford similar savings, then shifting all Americans into these plans could save us several hundred billion dollars annually!

There are many reasons to expect the actual savings to be much lower. One is that the baseline RAND plan against which all cost savings were calculated provided complete indemnity coverage. The baseline for comparison today should be PPOs or HMOs, which are far less costly than indemnity plans. Thus the opportunities for savings are far lower.

If we dig deeper into the RAND study, we will discover more reasons to dampen some of the optimism about CDHP cost savings. Recall that the RAND cost sharing plans did not provide catastrophic coverage until patients had made very high out-of-pocket annual contributions. In today's dollars, the RAND deductibles would be well over $10,000 for a family of four. Today's CDHPs have much lower ceilings, closer to $5,000. It might be unrealistic to expect anything higher, because few enrollees want to be exposed to substantial financial risk. Lower deductibles mean lower cost savings.

The RAND study also reminds us that the old 80/20 rule applies in health economics (in this case it is the 80/15 rule): 80 percent of health spending is accounted for by about 15 percent of enrollees. These big spenders—those with diabetes, asthma, cancer, heart disease, mental illness, and other significant chronic and acute problems—will predictably exhaust their deductible every year. As a result, they will have no incentive at any time during the year to curtail their spending or shop around for the lowest cost providers. Their annual healthcare spending will exactly equal the amount of their deductible no matter how much they spend or how much they have accumulated in their HSA. In fact, any patient who enters a hospital for even a minor problem is likely to top $5,000 in annual spending. CDHPs may encourage the 85 percent of us who are healthy to spend less money on healthcare, but the resulting savings will be minimal. CDHPs will do little to alleviate moral hazard among the chronically ill or encourage hospital patients to shop around for the lowest prices.

Recent studies based on the RAND data predict that total savings from CDHP/HSA arrangements will be somewhere between 2.5 and 7.5 percent, assuming everyone enrolls.[10] This ain't chicken feed—$50 billion annually or more is serious money—but it is far from the lofty savings initially suggested by the RAND study. Interestingly if health plans had high deductibles but dropped the HSAs, the savings could double, because the "use it or lose part of it" feature of HSAs encourages enrollees to spend down their HSAs.

Some supporters of the consumer movement, such as the prominent law professors Mark Hall and Clark Havighurst, believe that CDHPs should adopt MCO-style cost-containment strategies for those individuals who have exhausted their deductibles.[11] There are no rules preventing MCOs from adding deductibles and HSAs; nor does anything prevent CDHPs from adopting MCO strategies such as limited provider networks. In fact, most CDHPs are better described as CDHP/PPO hybrids combining deductibles with networks. Despite the rhetoric, it seems that the market has not abandoned some aspects of managed care. There do not appear to be any CDHP/HMO hybrids to date, perhaps because large deductibles are redundant to the physician-centered cost-containment strategies already used by HMOs.

The most ardent supporters of consumerism would probably dismiss my complaints as nitpicking. The true believers argue that we are on the verge of a paradigm shift that will put the patient center stage in the healthcare marketplace. Replacing the Marcus Welby mentality will not happen overnight of course. Indeed a major reason given by employers for offering CDHPs is to introduce consumerism *for long-term change.*[12]

We can speculate as to how exactly this transformation is supposed to occur. Perhaps once patients worry about the price of low-cost services they have to pay for, they will instinctively worry about the price of more costly services that they do not pay for. I suppose the exact opposite might happen; once patients have exhausted their deductible and someone else is paying the bill for high-cost care, they might want to spend as much as they can. They may even equate higher prices with higher quality and visit the most costly providers. Perhaps cost consciousness will spring up organically from a new-found understanding of how much medical care costs. But I think most patients already know that medical care is frightfully expensive. Perhaps patients will cut back on their own spending for the good of the healthcare system. Perhaps not. So when I hear about the paradigm shift that is going to take place, I do not hold my breath waiting for it.

Delving further into the RAND evidence points to a related limitation of CDHPs. Once RAND enrollees initiated a visit to a provider, their spending was largely independent of their deductible and co-payment. Even patients with the highest deductibles appeared to delegate all medical decision making to their providers. Thus *virtually all of the RAND cost savings resulted from individuals who elected not to visit their providers.* I am not comfortable making this the basis for major reductions in healthcare spending. CDHPs seem to be aware of this problem, particularly when it comes to prevention, and many CDHPs provide complete coverage for prevention. But this seems to contradict the most fundamental tenet of consumerism, namely that patients should be entrusted to make their own cost-effective medical decisions. If we cannot trust patients to make economic decisions about such simple things as prostate exams and Pap smears, how can we trust them to know whether it is worth visiting their physician when they have heartburn or whether they should purchase a costly PET scan or drug eluting stent?

A lot has changed since Arrow first articulated the benefits of a physician-centered healthcare system. Healthcare is more expensive. The Internet brings information to the masses. But human nature endures. We can alter financial incentives and provide more information than ever before, but at the end of the day, patients will still want to rely on Doctor Welby. CDHPs can only go so far to change this.

The Market Reaction

Off to a Fast Start

CDHPs became widely available to employers and employees in 2004. They received lavish attention from the media after President Bush embraced HSAs during his reelection campaign. According to Lexis-Nexus, over five hundred articles in major newspapers mentioned HSAs in 2004, often citing them as a new strategy for cost containment. (CDHPs and HSAs have become synonymous, even though one can, in principle offer big deductibles without the HSA.) Start-up companies like Definity Health and Lumenos became the darlings of Wall Street. In November 2004, United Healthcare paid $300 million to acquire Definity, allowing United to quickly enter what everyone expected would be a rapidly growing market. In 2005, WellPoint paid almost $200 million to acquire Lumenos.

By most accounts, the market for CDHPs is growing, though it is hard to pin down the numbers, in part because different groups use different definitions and in part because of differences in survey methods. For example, the industry trade group America's Health Insurance Plans states that enrollments in HSA-eligible plans increased from under 500,000 in September 2004 to over three million in January 2006.[13] In contrast, only 1 percent of respondents to a September 2006 Commonwealth Fund survey of 3,000 consumers were reported to be in a CDHP, a figure that had not changed much since a similar 2005 survey.[14] If we extrapolate the Commonwealth survey results to the entire population, this would peg CDHP enrollments at less than two million.[15] A Kaiser Family Foundation survey suggests that enrollments through work reached 3.8 million in 2007, up from 2.7 million in 2006.[16] At the high end of the spectrum, the U.S. Government Accountability Office reviewed sources of data on CDHP enrollments and estimated that over five million Americans were in CDHPs by early 2006, up from three million the previous year.[17] In any event, the consensus is that several million Americans are enrolled in a CDHP and that figure is growing.

CDHPs are especially popular in the individual and small group markets, accounting for more than half the total enrollments. Given the failure of traditional insurance to adequately serve these markets, this is welcome news. Still there are reasons to temper one's optimism. Enrollments remain well below 5 percent of the market and at least one survey suggests that the rate at which employers introduce CDHPs is for the first time leveling off.[18] This means that continued rapid growth will have to come from employees agreeing to join, rather than employers agreeing to offer. I expect CDHP enrollments could top ten million by 2010 and would not be surprised if they surpassed HMO enrollments shortly thereafter. A bit of caution is warranted, of course. Just one decade ago, HMO enrollments were soaring, in part because plans were low-balling premiums and taking big losses in the process. I suspect that something similar may explain some of the current growth in CDHP enrollments.

Even so, most of the growth of CDHPs is due to their simple value creation proposition: high deductible/low premium plans offer a favorable mix of modest cost savings and substantial risk protection when compared to more expensive plans. By leveling the tax playing field through HSAs, the market will take its natural course. Many individuals seeking to save on health insurance will find CDHPs an attractive tax-advantaged alternative to HMOs.

If anything is holding back CDHPs, it is the newness of the thing. Patients now have three potential ways to pay providers (insurance, their own out-of-pocket payments, and the new HSAs.) To reduce some of the confusion, some CDHPs are giving patients something akin to debit cards to pay for care covered by the HSA. Not every provider will be equipped to take them and many enrollees do not understand how to use them. Patients who do not use the debit cards may find it a hassle to do the paperwork required to manage their HSA. As with any new product, we should expect most of these kinks to be worked out over time. They had better. CDHPs sell themselves as consumer-friendly health plans. It would be ironic if they failed because consumers could not figure out how to use them.

If CDHPs continue to gain share, investors will be thrilled. I wish I could say the same for policy makers. The 80/15 rule and other RAND evidence suggests that cost savings will be no more than a few percentage points. I have a nagging feeling that the business position of most CDHPs is not so much to provide a cost-savings alternative for all potential enrollees, but is instead to sign up the healthiest ones. If so, you can throw the 80/15 rule out the window. Try the 95/50 rule— half of the population accounts for 95 percent of the cost. If CDHPs are enrolling the other half, then any hope for substantial cost savings will be lost.

Is It Selection or Efficiency?

Unfortunately the early evidence supports such skepticism. In a recent study appearing in *Health Affairs,* a team of RAND researchers reviews the evidence on selection into first generation CDHPs.[19] Through 2005, seven published studies had measured selection based on health status, income, and/or age. The studies found that when compared with other plans, CDHP enrollees were healthier, wealthier, and with one exception, younger. The differences ranged from not too big (one study found that CDHP enrollees were one year younger on average than enrollees in other plans) to staggering (another study found that 18 percent of CDHP enrollees reported themselves to be in poor/fair/good health versus 39 percent in other plans.) The evidence of favorable selection into HMOs was never this striking. A senior executive with one large CDHP plan has told me that the evidence of selection in second generation plans is not as striking, but thus far there is no published evidence of this.

Even small differences in enrollee health can have big consequences for the market. PPOs and other "traditional" plans will have to raise their premiums to account for their adverse risk selection. This would likely drive more good risks into CDHPs, possibly triggering a death spiral for the PPOs. It is not clear whether the favorable selection enjoyed by CDHPs is due to their inherent attractiveness to healthy, wealthy, and Internet savvy individuals or whether the plans themselves are selectively marketing to these segments. It hardly matters for relatively healthy individuals who do not want to sign up for a CDHP. They will find it increasingly difficult to find alternative insurance at actuarially fair rates.

This could be tolerated if CDHPs made the healthcare system more efficient. There are a few studies claiming that CDHPs are lowering costs, but are they believable? For example, the UnitedHealth Group reports that enrollees in CDHPs seek more preventive care than enrollees in PPOs and that CDHP enrollees experience reductions in inpatient utilization whereas PPO enrollee utilization has increased.[20] Unfortunately favorable selection into CDHPs can also explain these patterns. The RAND *Health Affairs* review singles out a few studies that try to control for selection by accounting for differences in enrollee characteristics and finds that "higher deductibles reduce total health care use and spending."[21] Again this is a reassuring finding, but none of these studies uses the kind of sophisticated statistical techniques required to fully rule out selection.[22]

What Happens to Doctor Welby?

Robert Berenson, a physician and health policy expert at the Urban Institute, recently wrote a compelling essay about CDHP in which he reminds us of Arrow's important insights into the physician-patient relationship.[23] Berenson worries that the consumer movement will strain if not destroy that relationship, inadvertently turning medical care into a commodity, to be bought and sold like big screen televisions.

I am not convinced that CDHPs will necessarily weaken the physician-patient relationship so much as change what it is that binds the two together. Even if patients are forced to seriously consider costs, this does not turn medical care into a commodity or diminish the importance of quality. If anything, it gives patients that much more to worry about. A few patients might find all the answers they need on the Internet, but many others will be more confused than ever. This might create opportunities to strengthen the role of the physician, who can help patients decide whether services are cost effective. This would be a new role for physicians, but one that should be welcome by all. Dr. Welby was all about creating value for his patients. When costs count, Dr. Welby's opinions become more valuable, not less.

Nor will CDHPs replace managed care. Virtually all CDHPs rely on selective contracting to secure discounts. Most rely on disease management to control costs of chronic illness. There may even be a day when HSAs are incorporated into HMOs, if only for the tax benefits and the attraction of retirement savings. I don't think CDHPs are as revolutionary as their ardent backers would have you believe.

There is more to today's consumer movement than CDHPs. Advocates of consumerism such as Princeton's Uwe Reinhart and Harvard's Michael Porter, argue that a truly competitive healthcare market will require pricing transparency. How else could we expect patients to comparison shop? This is such as simple idea that one wonders why no one thought of it before Porter. The reality is that lots of folks have thought of it. The problem is not in articulating the theory, but in putting into practice. And this is where big thinking goes face to face with reality . . . and loses.

Pricing Transparency

From Transparent to Translucent

Facing market prices, we should expect CHDP enrollees to comparison shop on the basis of price. Market forces should then encourage providers to reduce prices and become more efficient. This is strictly conjecture, of course. The RAND study did not examine comparison shopping and involved such a small fraction of the population that providers probably ignored it. Providers did cut costs in response to the growth of managed care, but MCOs have massive data bases and highly skilled analysts that make it easy for them to determine which providers offer the best prices. Individual patients have no such advantages. When we try to comparison shop on the basis of price, we are likely to be left scratching our heads. And if we do, market forces will lie dormant.

Imagine trying to find out a hospital's price for an expensive procedure like hip replacement surgery.[24] You might call a hospital and ask for their price, but it is doubtful if anyone in the accounting or billing office would know. It may sound unbelievable, but hospitals do not price the procedures they sell. A hospital could tell you the price for one day in the intensive care unit (ICU) or one hour of physical therapy, but this is hardly enough information. How many days will you be in the ICU? How many hours of therapy will you require? The hospital could not tell you. Factor in drugs, supplies, radiology, lab tests, and dozens of other services and the confusion quickly mounts. The hospital might be able to tell you prices, but you still need to know the quantities.

Let us suppose (and this is a big leap), that you could find out the number of ICU days, therapy hours, etc., for a hospital's average hip replacement patient. With the help of a spreadsheet, you could compute the hospital's average total price. But will that be the price for your surgery? Not unless you are an average patient. Nor could you reliably comparison shop. A "high price" hospital might simply have admitted patients with more significant health problems. Unless you risk adjust the data, you could not be sure which hospital would offer the best price for *your* surgery.

By now you have probably given up hope of finding out about hospital prices and simply go to the local community hospital for your surgery. A few days after leaving the hospital, you would receive your bill. There is a good chance that the bill will be several pages long and itemize the charges for every service that you received. When you get to the end of the bill and see the bottom line charge, sticker shock is sure to ensue. For a typical hospital, the total charge for hip replacement surgery would be about $30,000 and it could easily surpass $50,000. Unbelievably even this is not the price of your surgery. For virtually all patients, the bottom line charge is meaningless fiction. The hospital will never see anywhere near this amount.

If you are covered by Medicare, the payment to the hospital is fixed according to the rules of the Prospective Payment System. For hip replacement patients, that amount is about $20,000, regardless of the number of days in ICU, minutes in surgery, or physical therapy treatments. Private insurers and Medicaid pay either a fixed rate for the entire stay, a fixed rate per day, or "discounted charges," which is usually a fixed percentage of the bottom line on the bill. The total payment for hip replacement surgery is also likely to be about $20,000, though this could vary substantially from one patient to the next depending on their specific medical needs. It can also vary a lot from one insurer to the next. For example, Medicaid would probably pay your provider about $15,000 for that new hip.

So we see that there really is no such thing as the hospital's "price for hip replacement surgery." How can you make something transparent when it is so murky? Never mind transparency. Translucence is a more reasonable goal.

From Translucent to Opaque

The quest for transparency only gets worse. Even if you knew in advance the price you would have to pay the hospital for your surgery, you would still have to gather a lot more pricing information before you knew the total outlay for your care. While you are in the hospital, you will be poked and prodded by any number of doctors who will be submitting their own bills. For hip replacement surgery, these "professional fees" can add half again to the hospital's price. And the stay in the hospital is just part of the treatment. You may require weeks or months of physical therapy and follow-up diagnostic tests. You will probably have to pay for a few trips in an ambulance. The area around your hip joint may become infected, requiring further expensive treatment. Not only do you need to determine the prices of all of these individual services, you need to anticipate how much of each you will need. And consider that a skillful surgeon or therapist might allow you to shorten the recovery period; in this case, a high professional fee might translate into a low total price.

It is perhaps unfair to use hip replacement surgery as a prototypical example. Even in a CDHP, hip replacement patients will probably end up paying the same amount (their deductible) regardless of who provides the care. As a result, we should not expect any price shopping for hip replacement surgery or any other costly procedure, whether prices are transparent or opaque. If CDHP is to promote price shopping, it will have to be for less costly services.

Suppose you want to comparison shop for something a little simpler, like the treatment of your child's ear infection. You would think that it would be easy for your pediatrician to quote a price for a simple office consultation. Think again. Current billing practices allow for five different office consultation codes, with five different prices that depend on the extent of the medical history and other work done by the physician. You might be able to get the prices for all five codes, but you would also want to know which code the pediatrician would be likely to bill. Not all physicians will provide the same level of care for your child, and a few might even "upcode" by assigning the visit to a more remunerative code regardless of the level of care they provide.

Your comparison shopping does not end there. Your child's pediatrician may want to do a culture to test for the infection. You need to know the price of the culture, the probability that the pediatrician will order one, and the probability that this would be an "induced" test. Then there is the question of medication—what drug is the doctor likely to prescribe and how much does it cost? Add in the price of any follow-up visits in case the infection does not go away or if the pediatrician recommends follow-up visits just to keep the schedule full. This may not be nearly as daunting as pricing out hip replacement surgery, but it is hard enough. And if your child is crying and needs immediate attention, are you really going to bother?

Reasons for Opacity

Sellers of other goods and services could make our lives just as difficult if they wanted to. Imagine if McDonald's followed the example of hospitals, charging separately for each unit of meat (25 cents per ounce), ketchup (5 cents per packet), and service (reducing price by

20 cents for each minute of waiting). If McDonalds really wanted to copy hospitals, it could wait until you have committed to buying the hamburger and then tell you how much ketchup you have to buy. This would be absurd. You pay McDonalds a flat fee and you get what you want, with no charge for extra ketchup. So why can't medical providers do the same thing?

This was exactly the question posed by Medicare when it established the PPS. Prior to PPS, Medicare payments were based on the services provided and varied from patient to patient and hospital to hospital with little rhyme or reason. Medicare now pays hospitals an all-inclusive fee for inpatient care. There is a different fee for each of the approximately 590 DRGs, but otherwise there are only a few mechanical adjustments to the price. Many private insurers also pay hospitals a flat DRG-based price per admission. In principle, hospitals could move to DRG pricing for all of their patients, including those who pay for their own care. That would enormously simplify pricing. If you know your DRG, you could look up your bottom line price and quickly compare across hospitals. Thus far, hospitals are refusing to go along and this is perpetuating some of the pricing opacity.

Hospitals may be worried that such flat pricing could expose them to a kind of adverse selection. There is considerable variation in medical needs from patient to patient, even after accounting for the DRG. Take DRG 544—Major Joint Replacement (including hip replacement). It costs the typical hospital about $20,000 to provide all needed inpatient services to an average patient in DRG 544. But there is considerable variation in this amount, with perhaps 20 percent of patients incurring costs of more than $30,000. That $20,000 DRG payment is just enough to cover a hospital's costs on average; the hospital uses the profits it makes on relatively "easy" hip replacement patients to cross-subsidize those who are more expensive to treat. Hospitals don't mind this cross-subsidy for a given Medicare or privately insured patient because they expect the law of averages to hold. Moreover Medicare and some private insurers have "outlier" provisions that pay the hospital extra for the small percentage of patients who prove to be extremely costly.[25]

Hospitals that set a flat fee for individual patients may be worried that they may fail to admit a cross-section of patients and would be unable to cross-subsidize the care of the sickest patients. They would also lose their "outlier" protection against patients with extraordinary needs. Hospitals are currently unwilling to take on these risks. There are several methods available to refine the existing DRG categories to provide hospitals with better predictability; adopting these could encourage some hospitals to provide greater pricing transparency.

Episode of Illness Payments

In the unlikely event that hospitals set inclusive fees for inpatient care, patients would still need to account for the costs of physician and ancillary services. The solution is for providers to set an all inclusive fee for the entire *episode of illness*. In the case of hip replacement surgery, a single fee of perhaps $50,000 could cover everything from the first ambulance trip to the last physical therapy treatment. This would make it very easy to shop on the basis of price. But sellers would still have a few concerns. They would still be worried about whether they would get a representative cross-section of patients. Will $50,000 be enough to cover their particular patients, whose medical needs may exceed the norm? Sellers would also have to figure out how to divide up the money.

These problems were encountered in the 1990s by integrated providers known as "physician-hospital organizations" (PHOs). PHOs were established to do business with MCOs eager to push financial responsibility for cost containment onto the backs of providers. PHOs accepted a monthly capitated fee for each enrollee and agreed to provide virtually all necessary medical care. Although the capitated fee was not restricted to a single episode of illness, the problems encountered by PHOs indicate the kinds of problems that would be encountered with episode-of-illness pricing.

Before there were PHOs, the MCOs had to figure out how much to pay hospitals and doctors and how to hold the line on utilization. These became the responsibilities of the PHOs. Ironically they turned to the same strategies that the MCOs had been using. PHOs capitated the payments to primary care physicians, set fees for specialists and the hospital, and intervened to limit excess utilization. Not only did PHOs internalize the MCOs' cost-containment strategies, they internalized all of the associated problems. The capitated primary care physicians viewed aggressive surgeons as a drain on their income, while surgeons objected to penurious PCPs placing restrictions on referrals. Meanwhile PHO managers lacked the information to determine which physicians were making economically rational decisions and which were draining away the profits. By 2000, patients had grown skeptical of capitation and PHOs were caught up in the general backlash against managed care. The PHO movement all but ended.

Any effort to introduce episode-of-illness payments for specific treatments like total hip replacement will have to come to terms with the same set of problems. They will require sophisticated information systems to set prices, track utilization throughout the illness episode, and assure that all providers are paid. More importantly, physicians must accept limitations on their own profits in order to serve the greater good. They refused to do so when they were parts of PHOs; I am not optimistic that such parochial infighting can be resolved by a shift to episode-of-illness payment.

Pricing Exposed

There is no need to throw in the towel on price competition. In fact, we already have a great deal of price competition in healthcare, thanks to selective contracting by MCOs. MCOs do not shop on the basis of list charges. They instead analyze aggregate data to determine which providers offer the best bottom-line prices, net of discounts. The best insurers—United Healthcare and some of the Blues come to mind—even account for the total costs of an illness episode and try to reward providers who have done the best job of holding down the aggregate bottom line.

This raises an interesting possibility. If insurers have the data to figure out which providers offer the best deals, couldn't they share it with their enrollees? As an example, United Healthcare of Illinois knows whether a hip replacement at Northwestern Memorial Hospital (NMH) is likely to cost more than a hip replacement at University of Illinois Medical Center (UIMC). United could not tell any individual enrollee exactly how much the procedure would end up costing at NMH and UIMC, but it could tell all of its enrollees which hospital tends to offer a better deal, and the approximate price difference. United would not have to go through the hassle of posting prices for each and every service. United would instead merely have to post average *total* prices for entire episodes, with proper risk adjustments—something like "NMH's all in-clusive price for the typical patient is $20,000, whereas UIMC's price is $22,000."

There are no technical obstacles to making such information avail-able, but there are strategic obstacles. In particular, United might give other insurers a sense of the discounts it has realized from hospitals. Don't hold your breath waiting for United to do this. Even announce-ments like "NMH is 10 percent more costly than UIMC" might reveal sensitive competitive information. This raises another possibility. A third party—perhaps a company that aggregates administrative data provided by employers—could identify the lowest priced providers. Consulting firms that already work with claims data could help em-ployers and employees do just this sort of pricing comparison.

I am not sure if such pricing transparency is really necessary to reap the benefits of price competition. Consider the Medicare PPS. Medicare beneficiaries have essentially zero incentive to find low priced providers. Nonetheless hospitals have incentives to lower their costs of treating Medicare patients, because under the rules of the PPS, hospitals get to pocket the savings. Moreover the rules are set up so that any aggregate cost reductions will result in lower payment rates in future years, with the savings returned to the taxpayers. Economist Andre Shleifer called this "yardstick competition" and the effects are comparable to free market competition.[26] From the patients' perspec-tive, all of this takes place in a world of nearly complete pricing opacity.

A similar sort of thing happens when insurance companies selec-tively contract payment rates with providers. Insurers know every provider's prices and utilization patterns and can risk adjust to deter-mine if a provider has low costs because it has taken care of relatively healthy patients. All of these factors enter into the price negotiations. Hospitals offering genuine efficiencies are rewarded, and the benefits of competition are again realized. Although patients are again left in the dark about prices, the payers are very well informed and act accordingly.

Transparency zealots should get their story straight. The debate is not about whether we should encourage competition and efficiency. Thanks to Medicare and selective contracting, this is already occurring. Instead the debate is whether the motivation should come from payers or patients. The backlash against managed care suggests that many patients resent it when their payers do the shopping for them, largely because when payers secure discounts, they must necessarily limit network access and freedom of choice.

In an ideal world, transparency would encourage price competition and drive efficiency without restricting choice. This is what CDHP supporters are aiming for. But I doubt whether patients will be nearly as successful in driving price competition as their MCOs. For one thing, if only a few patients shop around, providers will have little reason to reduce their prices for anyone. Second, and equally important, patients in CDHPs will have little incentive to shop for the big ticket items because they will have exhausted their deductibles. If you remove selective contracting from the equation, there will be no price shopping at all.

There is one more reason to be suspicious of full transparency. It may be that patients do not know about each provider's prices, but it is also true that providers do not know each other's prices. Any antitrust economist can tell you that if prices become fully transparent, it will be easier for providers to gravitate toward *higher* prices.

Final Thoughts about Pricing

I have made three simple points about pricing. First, it is nearly impossible to achieve pricing transparency when individuals buy their own healthcare services. Second, payers have the kind of aggregate data necessary to sort out which providers are more or less costly, and already use this information to stimulate price competition through selective contracting. Third, if we want to rely on patients to impose pricing discipline, then payers will still have to be involved. Either payers provide their enrollees with the information necessary to comparison shop or they continue to selectively contract to obtain discounts on big ticket items. It is hard to see how consumer-driven markets can realize the benefits of price competition without the active involvement of payers.

Let me close with three additional points. First, no amount of price sensitivity on the part of patients or payers will do any good unless there is competition among the providers. I have already described how provider consolidation contributed to the rise of managed care "lite" and rising healthcare costs. If we see a continued shift to CDHPs, there will be even more of a need to maintain provider competition. Second, one of the complaints lodged against MCOs was that they focused too much on price and not enough on quality. This concern will only be amplified by CDHPs. If we give patients incentives to find the best prices and the information to do so, but we fail to give them the information necessary to shop on the basis of quality, the market outcome will be predictable—low price providers will win out and quality will suffer. Fortunately there is a powerful ongoing movement to measure and reward quality that I will describe in the next chapter.

Finally I do not mean to imply from all of this skepticism that I am down on consumer driven healthcare. From a business perspective, CDHPs are probably the next big thing, with the potential to achieve market shares of 10 to 20 percent or even higher. They may even allow some small percentage of the currently uninsured to buy an affordable plan. But even if CDHPs are successful in the market, they are unlikely to put much of a dent in the major policy problems facing this country. If CDHPs swept the nation, healthcare costs would still be rising, efficiency and quality would still be in doubt, and tens of millions of Americans would still be uninsured.

The Quality Revolution

Thousands of studies . . . have shown that the level of quality care provided to the average person leaves a great deal to be desired and, perhaps more importantly, the variation in quality of care by physician or by hospital is immense.

—ROBERT BROOK, RAND Corporation[1]

ROBERT BROOK may rightly be considered the "father" of the health-care quality movement.[2] After receiving his M.D. and Sc.D. degrees from Johns Hopkins, Brook joined the RAND Corporation in the 1970s where he was a key member of the Health Insurance Experiment research team. He showed that the RAND enrollees who received free care did not experience any systematic improvement in health relative to those facing large copayments, despite the marked difference in utilization.[3] Brook continued to make profound contributions to the research literature on quality measurement and in 2005, the Institutes of Medicine awarded Brook the Lienhard Award, citing him "as the individual who, more than any other, developed the science of measuring the quality of care and focused U.S. policymakers' attention on quality of care issues."[4]

Brook stirred up a tempest of sorts when he published a 1998 editorial in the *Journal of the American Medical Association* with the provocative title, "Managed care is not the Problem, Quality Is."[5] A quote from this editorial prefaces this chapter. When Brook's editorial appeared, the HMO backlash was is full swing. Thanks to research by Harold Luft and Robert Miller, among others, we now know HMO quality was never as bad as its detractors claimed. But Brook was not defending HMO quality so much as he was criticizing quality of care across the board. It did not matter whether patients were in HMOs, indemnity plans, Medicare, or whatever. As Brook stated, the level of quality care received by all patients left "a great deal to be desired."

Brook was not alone in his concerns about healthcare quality. The 1999 Institutes of Medicine study *To Err Is Human* found "at least 44,000 people, and perhaps as many as 98,000 people, die in hospitals each year as a result of medical errors."[6] Many of these deaths were attributed to medication errors. (To put things in perspective, there are about thirty-five million hospital admissions in the United States every year, so 98,000 deaths represents 0.28 percent of all admissions; too big for sure, but only part of the quality equation.) The next year, the IOM released *Crossing the Quality Chasm*, stating "during the last decade alone, more than seventy publications in leading peer-reviewed journals have documented *serious quality shortcomings* (emphasis added).[7]

The momentum to improve quality has since picked up steam. The ongoing emphasis on quality is exemplified by the proliferation of provider "report cards." Prior to 2000, there were only a handful of attempts to quantify and rank provider quality. Most report cards were generated by state governments and tended to focus on inpatient mortality rates for selected heart procedures. In just a few years, we have gone from famine to feast, with report cards produced by all kinds of organizations and covering all sorts of maladies.

Many Americans are familiar with the *US News and World Reports* annual rankings of "America's Top Hospitals," which list the top fifty hospitals in sixteen specialty areas. Healthgrades.com, which ranks all of the nation's hospitals (and many doctors) in dozens of clinical areas, claims an on-line readership of over one million consumers.[8] The U.S. Department of Health and Human Services has just launched "Hospital Compare" and "Nursing Home Compare" Web sites that offer dozens of metrics on the nation's providers.[9] These are just the tip of the iceberg. As of July 2005, there were over fifty Web sites reporting hospital quality and many other sites reporting quality for doctors and other providers.[10] I would guess that the number of report card Web sites has doubled since then. As report cards continue to metastasize, patients who want to find the best providers (or shun the worst) will have no shortage of places to look for advice.

Every healthcare stakeholder group has become an active participant in the quality movement. Government agencies, employer alliances, provider organizations, and independent magazines and Web sites all produce report cards. Private insurers have even begun a "pay for performance" movement, giving direct financial rewards to providers who meet or exceed quality standards. But I am seeing a bit too much back patting by report card zealots and not quite enough introspection. The zealots think they are on the road to quality nirvana. I am worried that they may be on a dead end street.

If we are going to understand the promise and potential limits of report cards, we must answer a few important questions:

- Why is it important to generate report cards?
- What data are required to generate useful measures?
- Is it sufficient to publicly report the measures, or must there be a direct link between pay and performance?
- Will providers respond by gaming the system, rather than seeking to genuinely improve quality?

Not all the answers are comforting. If the quality movement were to stop where it is today, I could make a good argument that we would be better off without it. Fortunately I think it is early days for the quality movement. We are still moving down the learning curve of how to collect, report, and use quality data. The future of a competitive-based healthcare system depends on our ability to get this right.

Why Do We Need Quality Report Cards?

It seems rather obvious why should worry about healthcare quality. But there are alternative ways to assure quality; report cards are only the latest quality assurance initiative and might prove to add little to what is already done. For the better part of the past century we relied on our physician-agents to assure quality. Not only did we trust in Marcus Welby medicine to make sure we received appropriate high quality care, the medical profession took very seriously its responsibility for quality assurance. Medical societies established licensure standards, created the rules for specialty certification and (on rare occasion) disciplined doctors who provided substandard quality. Hospital medical staffs conducted peer review. To this day, you are probably better off asking physicians to identify the best specialists and hospitals than you are relying on report cards, provided that the physicians will tell you the truth and not try to protect their referral networks. That is a big proviso.

The legal system could also promote quality by putting providers on notice that they will pay the price for delivering substandard care. But research suggests that the likelihood of a negligent physician being sued is small.[11] Moreover most physicians pay community-rated malpractice premiums that do not increase even if they are shown to have been negligent.

While most Americans thought that Marcus Welby medicine was delivering quality care of the highest order, researchers were discovering otherwise. Wennberg's evidence on practice variations showed that costs might be excessive in some regions but also suggested that quality might be inadequate in others. The PSROs that grew out of 1972 federal health planning legislation were supposed to assure that physicians would follow prescribed care guidelines. PSROs morphed into PROs in the 1980s, which begat private Utilization Review agencies in the 1990s. UR agencies refined treatment guidelines and threatened to withhold payments from providers who failed to abide by them. Third-party development of treatment guidelines and disease management programs has continued apace, but insurers are now replacing the stick of UR payment denial with the carrot of pay-for-performance rewards.

The 1999 and 2000 IOM reports came at a crossroads in the history of our healthcare system. Everyone agreed (well, everyone except for organized medicine) that the institutions of Marcus Welby medicine did not do enough to assure quality. Even its most ardent supporters could not claim that managed care was improving quality. It was time to find another approach.

The problem of quality assurance is not unique to healthcare. There are lots of goods and services for which quality is important yet difficult to measure. By examining how other markets identify and reward quality, it might be possible to find new ways to assure healthcare quality. One common approach is to ask friends and family for referrals. We do this when we are looking for a plumber or an auto mechanic and when we want a restaurant recommendation. This is a perfectly sensible way to shop for quality. Our friends and family have lots of experience to draw on and they can do a pretty good job of evaluating the quality of a plumber or a restaurant. While this approach might make sense if your drains are clogged, it might not be a particularly valuable way to find someone to treat clogged arteries. You probably have very few friends who have faced such a serious health problem and those who did may be unable to accurately discern the quality of care they received.

There are other ways to assure quality. Consumer electronics customers often rely on brand name. Brand is much less important in medical care and aside from the great teaching institutions like Mayo and Johns Hopkins, there are few brands that scream out "quality." Consumer electronics customers also rely on the recommendations of salespeople. Patients do something akin to this when they ask their primary care physicians for referrals to specialists and hospitals. But PCPs partly base referrals on factors that have nothing to do with quality, such as location and social linkages. Quality should be first on the list. Even when physicians think about quality, they usually suffer from Lake Woebegone syndrome, comfortable in the feeling that the specialists and hospitals in their referral networks are all above average. Half the time they are wrong.

In many markets where consumers cannot rely on friends and family, brand name, or the opinions of salespeople, they do have one other place to turn for quality information—third-party report cards.

The importance of *Consumer Reports* and other third-party quality rankings should not be underestimated. Just ask Japanese and U.S. car makers. A few decades ago *Consumer Reports* began ranking Japanese cars tops for quality. U.S. car buyers responded by purchasing Hondas, Toyotas, and Nissans in record numbers. The auto industry has never been the same.

Advocates of healthcare provider report cards hope to have a similar impact. If patients flock to the top ranked providers, it could revolutionize the healthcare industry. Patients will visit the best providers, and all providers will redouble their efforts to give better care. But we are hardly there; after two decades of publicly available data, and nearly a decade after the IOM reports, few patients seem to be responding to report cards and many critics believe they do more harm than good. Before we examine how well (or poorly) report cards are doing in practice, it is essential to understand how report cards get constructed. In that way, we can better determine what needs to be done if they are to fulfill their promise.

Constructing Provider Report Cards

What Should Report Cards Report?

If you asked one thousand people to define healthcare quality, you would get one thousand definitions. Fortunately there is a unifying framework that greatly simplifies the task of defining this elusive concept. The framework was developed several decades ago by public health expert Avedis Donabedian. A physician by training, Donabedian began his career at American University of Beirut where he ran the student health service in the 1940s. Eager to learn more about running a clinic, he enrolled in the Harvard School of Public Health. He later joined the faculty of the School of Public Health at the University of Michigan, where he held the Nathan Sinai Distinguished Professorship. (Nathan Sinai was a member of the Committee for the Costs of Medical Care.) It was during the 1960s and 1970s at Michigan that Donabedian developed and refined his paradigm for quality measurement. For this work, Donabedian was an original inductee into the

Institutes of Medicine of the National Academy of Science and received the George Welch Medal from the American Medical Association.

Donabedian classified quality measures into three broad categories: structural (or input) quality, process quality, and outcomes quality.[12] Measures of structural quality for hospitals include number and training of personnel and availability of sophisticated medical equipment. A popular structural measure used by today's report card advocates is whether the hospital uses computerized physician order entry (CPOE) of drug prescriptions.

Measures of a hospital's process quality vary according to the treatment. For example, Medicare's Hospital Compare report card includes the following eight process measures for heart attack care:

- Percent of Patients Given ACE (angiotensin converting enzyme) Inhibitors
- Percent of Patients Given Aspirin at Arrival
- Percent of Patients Given Aspirin at Discharge
- Percent of Patients Given Beta Blocker at Arrival
- Percent of Patients Given Beta Blocker at Discharge
- Percent of Patients Given PCI (percutaneous coronary interventions) with 120 minutes of arrival
- Percent of Patients Given Smoking Cessation Advice/Counseling
- Percent of Patients Given Thrombolytic Medication Within 30 Minutes of Arrival

Process measures for physicians might include frequency of cancer screening and vaccination rates. Outcome measures include mortality, morbidity, and patient satisfaction. One can even measure overall quality of life using the Quality Adjusted Life Year (QALY) scale. QALY scales are routinely used to assess the cost effectiveness of new drugs and could be used to assess the well-being of an entire population. I will have more to say about them in chapter 8.

Subsequent to Donabedian's work, researchers have found substantial evidence linking quality to a provider's *experience*. For example, many studies document that surgeons with higher volumes have better patient outcomes.[13] What is less clear is whether this is due to a learning curve or if it is simply that better doctors receive more referrals.[14] It makes no matter to patients trying to choose a surgeon.

Whether because of selective referrals or learning, high volume providers are more likely to be high quality providers. It is no wonder that the influential Leapfrog Group, a national consortium of major employers concerned about healthcare quality, reports surgical volume as an indicator of quality. This is a sensible and simple measure.

Although report cards may include any of the four broad categories of quality—structure, process, outcomes, and experience—we should not fool ourselves about what ought to matter most. No one visits a healthcare provider to admire the efficiency with which they administer beta blockers or ogle their CPOE system. We visit our providers to get well and keep well. Outcomes are all that matter; everything else is just a means to that end.

If outcomes are all that matter, then mortality is what matters most. The Health Care Financing Administration (now CMS) published the first widely disseminated mortality report cards in 1986. HCFA reported DRG-specific mortality rates for hospitalized Medicare patients. The mortality rates were expressed as the percentage of total patients who died either during the hospital stay or within a well-defined interval thereafter (often 90 days or 180 days). For open heart surgery, the typical inpatient and 180-day hospital mortality rates were less than 5 percent. For other DRGs, the mortality rates were usually much lower.

Some of the very best hospitals have very high mortality rates, because they attract the sickest patients. If HCFA reported mortality rates without adjusting for patient severity, the resulting report card rankings would be very misleading. Instead of relying on the "raw" mortality rates, HCFA assessed how patient characteristics affect the probability of mortality and used statistical methods to compute each hospital's "risk adjusted mortality," which is the mortality rate that would be expected if the hospital treated patients of average severity. If the data is good and the statistical methods are valid, then a patient can be reasonably confident that hospitals with low risk-adjusted mortality rates are likely to offer high-quality care.

Having good data and valid statistics should not be taken for granted. HCFA statisticians had to rely on administrative claims data (i.e., the information submitted by providers seeking payment from Medicare), which contain fairly limited medical information. Many critics felt that the resulting risk adjustments were inadequate. As a result, some of the hospitals with the best reputations for quality had high risk-adjusted mortality rates. HCFA refined its methods over time but providers remained suspicious about the validity of the rankings. HCFA discontinued reporting hospital mortality rates in 1992. Many states and private organizations have picked up where HCFA left off. As of 2005, there were at least twenty-seven Web-based mortality report cards, including Healthgrades.com, which uses Medicare administrative claims data to produce risk-adjusted mortality rates (and other quality metrics) for a wide range of conditions for all U.S. hospitals. In June 2007, CMS reentered the hospital mortality report card business. It computed risk adjusted mortality scores for heart failure and heart attacks and identified those hospitals with scores that were significantly above or below average.

Constructing Mortality Report Cards

If report cards are accurate and reliable, then providers who deliver the best care should expect to rank near the top and patients who visit top-ranked providers should expect better outcomes. That is all good, but report cards can only be as accurate and reliable as the data and methods permit. If you look at available data, you soon discover that the most accurate and comprehensively measured outcome is mortality. Information about mortality comes from administrative claims data and Social Security death records. Most hospitals also identify patients who have postsurgical infections and this has become another common report card metric.

The biggest obstacle to constructing mortality report cards occurs when statisticians try to do risk adjustment. Administrative claims data contain very few useful risk adjusters: age, sex, possibly race, and a few diagnostic codes. The resulting statistical models do a poor job of predicting which patients are likely to live or die.

Statistical models can be useful even if they do not give accurate predictions for every patient. Statisticians sometimes invoke the "law of large numbers" to defend models that study large populations. But the law of large numbers does not work in the case of procedure-specific hospital mortality rates. One reason is that for any given procedure, most hospitals treat only a few hundred patients annually. With mortality rates of just a few percentage points, the number of deaths can be very small. At best we can invoke the "law of small numbers," which is not much of a law at all. Another reason for concern is that the limited risk adjustments in administrative claims data may not reveal which hospitals treat the sickest patients. If so, the statistical model and resulting rankings are biased, regardless of the sample size. If the bias is too large, then the report card rankings could be inversely related to actual quality. Fortunately I doubt this is the case even for the worst of the current report cards.

In a recent survey, 79 percent of physicians agreed that report card rankings do not adequately adjust for severity.[15] Providers who fare poorly in the rankings inevitably complain that they treat the sickest patients but do not receive an appropriate risk adjustment. The former medical director at Anthem Blue Cross & Blue Shield, Joseph Berman, described this complaint as "the Holy Writ" and many providers discourage patients from relying on report cards.[16] I question whether this is grounds for dismissing report cards. As long as rankings are positively correlated with actual quality, then patients can expect better outcomes if they visit the top-ranked providers. At the same time, providers can expect to improve their rankings if they boost their quality. These goals are far too important to be derailed by complaints that report cards are occasionally unfair. Fairness to providers should take a backseat to improving patient outcomes.

I am more concerned about the "law of small numbers" that I alluded to earlier. When one or two extra deaths in a year can cause a hospital to drop precipitously in the rankings, providers may think twice before treating a patient whose chances of survival are low. I will say a lot more about this possibility later in this chapter. The "law of small numbers" also presents an important statistical problem. Statisticians cannot always reject the possibility that differences in rankings are merely due to random chance. This can make things very confusing for the patient trying to find the best hospital.

Consider a cardiac surgery patient in New York State choosing among the forty hospitals in the state that perform the procedure. New York generates perhaps the best cardiac surgery report cards in the nation, augmenting administrative claims data with risk adjusters culled from medical records. Even though the risk adjusted cardiac surgery mortality of the 10th best hospital is less than half the mortality rate of the 30th best hospital, the difference is not statistically meaningful, because it reflects a difference of just a handful of deaths, which could have been due to random chance. Thus there is no way to know for sure if a hospital ranked near the top is really better than one ranked near the bottom. And this is for a report card that uses state-of-the-art risk adjustment! The current CMS report cards have a similar shortcoming; fully ninety-seven percent of the hospitals evaluated for heart failure or heart attack were reported to have average quality. It is even more difficult to obtain statistically meaningful differences for physicians, for whom the "law of very small numbers" is very weak indeed, or when risk adjustment is limited to administrative claims data. We should not blame the statisticians for failing to report meaningful statistical differences in quality; this is an artifact of the available data.

Good News and Bad about Mortality Report Cards

One of the main goals of report cards is to encourage providers to improve their quality. My own research, with Mark Satterthwaite, suggests that the resulting benefits can be huge.[17] I hear many anecdotes about hospitals with high reported risk adjusted mortality scores making genuine efforts to get better, even as they invoke the "holy writ." They are replacing their department heads, kicking out the worst doctors, upgrading equipment, and retraining support staff. Much of the impetus for this seems to come from hospital board members who may be worried that poor report cards will translate into fewer patients, or may simply want their hospitals to be better for the sake of being better. I hear fewer anecdotes about board members expressing concern when their hospitals receive average rankings. Perhaps report cards can discourage bad care but do not do such a good job of promoting excellence.

There is also some systematic evidence that risk adjusted mortality in report card states such as New York is falling much faster than the rest of the nation.[18] This is very good news as it suggests that the changes in hospital policy are translating into real improvements in the quality of care. But this evidence must be received with a measure of caution. This is exactly what we would expect to find if hospitals chose some of the less desirable options for boosting their report card scores, as I now discuss.

Hospitals can easily boost their rankings by reporting more diagnoses and more severe diagnoses (either because they had previously been lax in reporting this information, or because they are now being excessive). Through such "upcoding," hospitals can make their patients look sicker. This causes reductions in reported risk adjusted mortality rates, even if actual quality is unchanged. Could this explain some of the good news from New York?

Upcoding is merely a record keeping issue and one that does not directly affect patient care. Hospitals have a far more troubling option for improving their report card scores without improving their quality. They can choose to treat only the "right" patients, those that give them the best chance of boosting their scores. To understand how this can happen, it is important to realize that providers can observe a lot more about a patient's condition than can be observed by our beleaguered statisticians. The "right" patients are those whose chances of surviving surgery based on what the provider can observe are better than the survival chances based on what the statistician can observe. Conversely the "wrong" patients are those whom the provider can tell are unlikely to survive surgery, even if the statisticians' risk adjusters say otherwise. Providers who treat the "right" patients and avoid the "wrong" patients should experience very low mortality rates, even though the statistician predicts they should have high mortality. Their risk-adjusted mortality rates will be terrific. Only their patients (and competing providers who do not play the game) will suffer.

There is considerable evidence that such gaming is going on. For example, it appears that heart surgery patients in report card states have gotten "sicker" over time based on the diagnostic codes used for risk adjustment. This is exactly what we would expect if providers were manipulating the coding. There is also systematic evidence that providers have been "selecting" patients so as to boost their scores. Daniel Kessler, Mark McClellan, Mark Satterthwaite, and I studied the initial provider responses to the New York and Pennsylvania cardiac surgery report cards.[19] (These were first released in the early 1990s.) We examined a measure of patient severity that was observable to providers but not included among the risk adjusters—prior hospitalization. We found that after the introduction of report cards, providers tended to select slightly healthier patients (i.e., those without recent hospitalizations). Patient outcomes were overall slightly worse and costs were slightly higher.

These findings suggest that some providers are placing their own rankings above the health of their patients. This is to be expected from any report card scheme and does not mean that we should abandon the effort. The harmful effects documented in my study are not particularly large. If providers were to boost their overall quality even as a few were gaming the system, the positive benefits would likely outweigh these negatives. I am pretty confident that this has been the case.

Racher Werner's study of gaming based on race is more disturbing.[20] Werner examines how the New York report card affected surgical rates for blacks and Hispanics. Race is a predictor of outcomes but is not used by the statisticians in New York.[21] Prior to the report cards, there were race-based disparities in surgical rates—whites were 1 to 2 percentage points more likely to get heart surgery than blacks or Hispanics, even after adjusting for other demographic factors. After the report cards, the size of the race-based gap doubled.

So what can be done? One way to address the problems that I uncovered in my research is to generate report cards based on diagnoses rather than treatments. This would eliminate incentives to choose surgical patients with one eye on the report card. This is what CMS has done by reporting outcomes for heart failure and heart attack rather than for heart surgery. Another way to limit patient selection is to use more sophisticated risk adjusters from clinical records. This is what New York has done and their risk adjustment model is second to none, yet this is where researchers are documenting gaming. (This is not New York's fault; their report card came out first so it has received the most attention.) New York's report card still omits many factors that predict mortality, including some such as race and prior hospitalization that are available in administrative claims data. New York should include these additional factors, even if there are not clinically linked to outcomes.

Some report card enthusiasts, such as Bruce Boissonault, the president of the Niagara Business Coalition on Health, which produces its own report cards for New York hospitals, are adamantly opposed to using clinical risk adjusters on the grounds that they are too easy to manipulate. But the report cards that rely on administrative claims data are so noisy and subject to patient selection as to render them almost meaningless as a basis for comparing providers. Almost meaningless might still be better than nothing: if patients take these noisy report cards to heart, they still might encourage providers to improve their quality. Even with the worst report cards, providers who save lives will move up in the rankings.

Process Report Cards

Outcomes report cards have many limitations. Clinical risk adjusters are highly desirable but hard to obtain. Outcomes report cards also invite potentially pernicious gaming. But the biggest drawback may be identified by taking a look at the report cards that receive the most attention. There is an overabundance of mortality report cards on cardiac surgery mortality. There is not much else. What about report cards for diabetes, asthma, or cancer? Where do patients turn for rankings of providers of joint replacement surgery, maternity services, and mental healthcare? The reason these report cards are few and far between is that it is difficult to gather the relevant outcomes data. Mortality may be easy to measure, but sometimes there are other outcomes that matter even more.

Suppose you were a prostate cancer patient trying to choose a surgeon for a prostatectomy. (If you are a woman, suppose you are helping a loved one make this choice.) You will care about mortality for sure, but you may be even more concerned about other outcomes. If the surgery is not entirely successful, you may face a lifetime of pain, incontinence, and impotence. Wouldn't you like to know your surgeon's record on these outcomes? Unfortunately there is no way for you to find out, let alone do any kind of systematic comparison. Information about these outcomes is not collected systematically. Urologists and primary care providers may keep hand-written notes, but only a smattering has transitioned to electronic medical records (EMRs) and even these may be of little use unless they can be linked electronically to surgeons' and hospitals' EMRs.

For the time being, such all-encompassing EMRs are a pipe dream. (I discuss how to turn the dream into reality in chapter 8.) As a result, there is no way that statisticians can construct meaningful outcomes report cards for prostatectomies. The same is true for diabetes, asthma, and the rest of the medical conditions that consume the vast majority of our healthcare dollars but for which mortality is hardly the only outcome of interest. This leaves us with two alternatives for constructing report cards. We could measure more outcomes and create all-encompassing EMRs, but this will not happen overnight. Alternatively we could base report cards on process measures that proxy for the outcome measures that we really care about. Thus far, report card advocates have taken the latter route.

There is ample evidence that process measures are correlated with outcomes. The Harvard Medical Practice Study of hospital care in New York State, for example, found that substandard processes were responsible for more than one-fourth of all adverse inpatient events.[22] Another study of care in Veterans Hospitals found that patients suffered fewer inpatient complications (the outcome) when their physicians followed protocols for diagnosis and treatment (the process).[23] The IOM reports highlighted a direct inverse link between CPOE (process) and adverse drug complications (outcome). In the first study that broadly examines the relationship between process report cards and outcomes, Racher Werner and Eric Bradlow show that Medicare's Hospital Compare measures are favorably correlated with mortality rates.[24] The correlation is very small, however, and Werner and Bradlow call for more refined process measures. Process report cards may have the virtue of ease of construction, but if they do not adequately promote better outcomes, they are of little independent value.

Are Patients Paying Attention?

Thousands of individuals work full time to prepare dozens of provider report cards. I sometimes wonder if they are despairing of their efforts.

If they are like me, they rarely meet anyone who has seen a provider report card. Even those who have might be baffled by what they see. Suppose you lived in my neck of the woods, Lake County, Illinois, and you wanted to find the best hospital for heart care. If you go to Medicare's Hospital Compare Web site, www.hospitalcompare.hhs .gov, it will take you six mouse clicks to generate a heart attack report card for local hospitals. The report card consists of eight bar charts—one for each of the eight process measures listed earlier in this chapter—with scores for each hospital in the county plus state and nationwide averages. It is almost impossible to make sense of all of these charts; for one thing, it is necessary to repeatedly scroll down the screen to see successive charts.

If you search hard enough, you one can find a link that displays all the information on a single table, as shown in table 6.1. But what should you make of all this data? Some information is missing, some hospitals score very well on some measures but poorly on others. There are lots of footnotes, there is no guidance as to which of the eight measures matters most. There is no overall score. No wonder that many people find report cards confusing.

The Leapfrog Hospital Survey at www.leapfroggroup.org/cp is easier to use.[25] I needed only three clicks to find the report for my local hospitals. Surprisingly only one hospital appears in both the Leapfrog and Medicare reports. The Leapfrog report card, also shown in figure 6.1, features scores for structure, process, and outcomes measures. The scores consist of simple circles filled in completely for the hospitals with the best rankings. This *Consumer Reports*-style rating system is a lot easier to use than the raw statistics reported at Medicare's Hospital Compare Web site. Unfortunately it is difficult to figure out just what Leapfrog is scoring. What are the "Leaps?" Even after clicking on the hyperlinks, I am baffled as to why CPOE and critical care training for certain ICU staff appear to be the most important "Leaps" and it is all but impossible to figure out what to make of Leaps 3 and 4. (It turns out that Leap 3 measures volumes of six unidentified high-risk treatments; you have to follow the links and read a technical file to figure out what they are. Another link to another technical file reveals that Leap 4 measures compliance with thirty "safe practice" processes developed by the National Quality Forum.) I suppose that most

Table 6.1. Heart Attack Report Card for Lake County

Heart Attack Care Quality Measures—*Higher Percentages Are Better*				
Quality Measure *Click on a measure name* *to compare all hospitals* *in a graph*	*Percentage for Advocate Good Shepherd Hospital*	*Percentage for Condell Medical Center*	*Percentage for Lake Forest Hospital*	*Percentage for Waukegan Illinois Hospital Company LLC*
Percent of Heart Attack Patients Given ACE Inhibitor or ARB for Left Ventricular Systolic Dysfunction (LVSD) if appropriate*	86% of 37 patients	56% of 63 patients	50% of 4 patients[1]	100% of 1 patients[1,3]
Percent of Heart Attack Patients Given Aspirin at Arrival if appropriate*	95% of 166 patients	88% of 205 patients	100% of 32 patients	94% of 17 patients[1,3]
Percent of Heart Attack Patients Given Aspirin at Discharge if appropriate*	96% of 166 patients	90% of 259 patients	100% of 7 patients[1]	100% of 2 patients[1,3]
Percent of Heart Attack Patients Given Beta Blocker at Arrival if appropriate*	98% of 117 patients	77% of 200 patients	87% of 30 patients	81% of 16 patients[1,3]
Percent of Heart Attack Patients Given Beta Blocker at Discharge if appropriate*	97% of 196 patients	88% of 259 patients	89% of 9 patients[1]	100% of 3 patients[1,3]
Percent of Heart Attack Patients Given PCI Within 120 Minutes Of Arrival if appropriate*	86% of 21 patients[1]	52% of 61 patients	0 patients[†]	0 patients[3,†]
Percent of Heart Attack Patients Given Smoking Cessation Advice/ Counseling if appropriate*	82% of 56 patients	67% of 84 patients	0 patients[†]	0 patients[3,†]
Percent of Heart Attack Patients Given Thrombolytic Medication Within 30 Minutes Of Arrival if appropriate*	0 patients[†]	0 patients[†]	0 patients[†]	100% of 1 patients[1,3]

Figure 6.1. Leapfrog Hospital Survey

Click to Compare	Hospital Name	Leap1 CPOE	Leap2 ICU	Leap3 High Risk Treatments								Leap4 Safe Practices Score	Survey Results Submitted
				CABG	PCT	AAA	Esoph.	Panc.	Bariatric	Aortic Valves	NICU		
☐	GLENBROOK HOSPITAL	◯	◯	(NA)	◯	◔	◔	◔	◔	(NA)	(NA)	◯	6/14/2007
☐	HIGHLAND PARK HOSPITAL	◯	◯	◐	◕	◔	◕	◔	◔	◔	(NA)	◯	6/15/2007
☐	LAKE FOREST HOSPITAL	◔	◔	(NA)	(NA)	(NA)	(NA)	(NA)	(NA)	(NA)	◑	◑	6/08/2007

Leapfrog users will just take their word for it that these are important quality measures.

Combine the highly technical nature of process measures with the opacity of statistical risk adjustment and it is no wonder that currently available report cards leave most patients baffled. This may be why many report cards continue to report patient satisfaction scores (usually based on a simple survey question such as "Rate your satisfaction with this provider on a 1–5 scale"). This is the one concept that most patients understand. Unfortunately the reason we have report cards is that subjective patient satisfaction is too often at odds with objective quality measures like mortality. The objectivists need to do a much better job of marketing their quality metrics.

Getting patients to pay attention to report cards is literally a matter of life and death. Mortality rates can differ across providers by several percentage points and patients who do not shop for the best quality are, for all intents and purposes, playing Russian roulette. This is why it is so disheartening that very few patients read report card rankings before choosing providers. Fortunately such findings do not provide compelling evidence of failure. It is sufficient for referring doctors to read and react to the report cards, or for a few patients to read them and then share what they learn with others.

There is more encouraging news about report cards emerging from systematic studies of how provider market shares move in response to report cards. Early research was pessimistic. A 1997 study found that hospital market shares in the early 1990s were completely unmoved by HCFA mortality rankings.[26] Indeed market shares were much more susceptible to newspaper reports of single unexpected deaths than to

HCFA reports of systematic mortality differences. Other studies from the 1990s reached similar conclusions.

Researchers are becoming more sophisticated in how they think about the potential impact of report cards, and their methods and findings are evolving as a result. One reason why patients may seem to ignore report cards could be that the top-ranked hospitals were already regarded as the best. If this is true, then it is not so much that report cards have failed to move market share as it is that report cards are redundant. If so, we will have managed to solve the shopping problem quite nicely without them, and there is no need to be discouraged. But before we leave report cards and declare victory, it might be helpful to ask whether report cards move market shares when they provide genuine "news," that is, when the rankings differs markedly from patients' preconceptions. Two recent studies suggest that patients do respond to news.[27] For example, Andrew Sfekas and I find that New York hospitals that receive very good news in their cardiac surgery rankings (i.e., they rank near the top in the state) get about 25 percent more patients than hospitals that receive very bad news. This can represent a difference of a million dollars or more in annual revenue, more than enough to attract the attention of hospital management and doctors.

Despite findings such as these, many payers doubt that report cards can have enough impact to create a true quality-driven market. So they are taking quality incentives into their own hands, directly rewarding providers who offer the best quality. Before I discuss these pay-for-performance schemes, I want to briefly address a question that no one wants to answer: what happens if report cards really work, and patients choose their providers largely on the basis of the rankings?

Matching

I recently had an opportunity to discuss report cards with CEOs from many of the nation's biggest and best-known hospitals. These executives were enthusiastic about report cards because they were convinced their hospitals would come out on top, while also encouraging all hospitals to get better. But they had one concern that has largely gone unnoticed amidst all the hoopla. Hospitals like Massachusetts General or the Cleveland Clinic may be among the best, but they have no interest in treating every patient who seeks admission. The fact is these hospitals lack the capacity to treat everyone. Access to them must be rationed.

Historically rationing of care at the best hospitals has occurred through a system of triage whereby doctors single out the toughest cases for referral. This is as it should be; it is the most seriously ill patients who gain the most from visiting a top hospital. But if report cards succeed, this could all change. As patients discover that not all hospitals are created equal and come to realize the stakes involved, many more may seek treatment at the top ranked facilities. How then will rationing occur? The top hospitals will have to perform more triage themselves, embittering patients whom they are forced to turn away. Some hospitals may choose to raise prices in the same way that top quality providers of other products use price as a rationing device. At the same time, they may shun Medicaid or even Medicare patients for whom prices are fixed. I am not sure if the advocates of report cards are ready for the type of two-tiered system that one would expect if report cards succeed and market forces run their course.

This scenario is unlikely to unfold any time soon. If anything, report card enthusiasts are concerned that patients are paying too little attention to them. If the purpose of report cards is to provide financial incentives to boost quality, then there is an alternative to relying on patients. Payers can directly link pay to report card scores. This is the basic motivation behind the pay-for-performance movement.

P4P

After Milton Roemer posited that "a bed built is a bed filled" and the subsequent research on demand inducement, most payers were convinced that fee-for-service medicine led to unnecessary overtreatment.[28] When payers countered with prepayment and capitation, there was a backlash amidst claims of undertreatment. The seesawing of sentiment merely confirms the First Axiom of Incentives in Medical Care that I described in chapter 2, namely, if you pay providers to do more X, they will do more X. The same payers who used to invoke this axiom as a way to reduce costs are now using it in the name of quality. Rather than wait for patients to respond to report cards, payers are paying providers to do the X's that will lead to better quality. This is what the pay-for-performance (P4P) movement is all about. Physicians who meet P4P goals can see their compensation increase by 10 percent or more.

Thus far, the list of X's is long and growing. Here are some examples from ongoing P4P programs:

- Comprehensive diabetes testing
- Controlling high blood pressure
- Use of appropriate medications for people with asthma
- Pneumonia vaccination status
- Childhood immunization status
- Beta blocker treatment after heart attack
- Cholesterol management after acute cardiovascular event
- Breast/colorectal/cervical cancer screening
- Call answer timeliness
- Ability to schedule appointments on short notice
- Ease of communication with nurse/physician

Outcomes measures are few and far between. P4P is mostly about process, not outcomes.

There is nothing new about tying physician compensation to specific process goals. Payers tried this once before under the rubric of utilization review. There was a furious backlash to UR and it was abandoned. Today's P4P has several advantages over yesterday's UR programs. In the years since the backlash, the IOM reports and many other studies have confirmed that unfettered physician decision making does not always lead to the best outcomes. The subsequent outpouring of quality research now gives payers a stronger empirical basis for their recommendations. And by replacing the stick of fee withholds with the carrot of performance bonuses, payers hope that their recommendations will go down gently, even if the total compensation to providers is unaffected.

Most P4P process goals seem obviously worthwhile. If physicians are failing to meet them, it is not for lack of understanding their importance. For some of the goals, it is probably not for lack of incentives either. On an hourly basis, physicians get paid more to provide vaccinations and order tests than for just about anything else they can do. Yet data show that physicians often fall short in these areas. If additional financial incentives can improve performance, what is the harm?

What Is the Harm?

Some of the P4P goals depend on patient compliance. This is dangerous, because it rewards physicians both for doing the right thing and for selecting the "right patients." Here is an example. Everyone agrees that it is important for children to get vaccinated on schedule. But single parents with several small children can find it difficult to keep medical appointments; this can be costly to the physician who appears to have been negligent in meeting vaccination deadlines. Patient compliance with cholesterol reducing regimens and even something as essential as Beta Blocker therapy also varies enormously.[29]

Compliance may be linked to socioeconomic factors such as income and education. But current P4P systems do not "risk adjust" performance based on demographics. As a result, physicians who treat the "wrong kind" of patients—i.e., those who tend to be noncompliant—may see lower income as a result. It is a simple matter to risk adjust cases based on demographics, but this might invite politically incorrect conclusions about the demand for medical care among different socioeconomic groups.

There are also problems with P4P goals that involve meeting deadlines. For example, some P4P programs punish emergency rooms that fail to start patients on IV drip with thirty minutes. ERs now make thirty minutes the target for every patient, even though some patients require quicker administration of IV and others can wait longer than thirty minutes. To take another example, one of the P4P goals in England is whether patients can schedule appointments on short notice. To meet this goal, some physicians refuse to schedule appointments more than two or three days in advance.[30] Strict deadlines invite creative but unwanted responses.

These problems fall into the category of "games providers play." Any incentive system invites some gaming and most payers are aware of them. But there remains one final problem that has scarcely been acknowledged yet may prove far bigger and far less tractable. This one stems from the "Second Axiom of Physician Incentives":

If you pay providers to do more X, they will do less Y

The problem of "multitasking," as economists call it, can bring down even the best-intentioned incentive systems.[31]

Multitasking

When we delegate others to act on our behalf, we cannot always be sure they will do what is best for us. Economists describe this problem in the context of the relationship between a principal (the person who owns the productive assets and stands to benefit if the assets are put to good use) and an agent (the person who makes decisions about how to use the assets.) Agents often have to engage in several tasks on behalf of the principal, but invariably have limited time and money to do them all. This poses a dilemma: How can the principal get the agent to perform the tasks that most benefit the principal? This is known as the *multitasking* problem and is regarded as perhaps the thorniest of all the problems that arise in agency relationships.

Medicine is a quintessential example of agency and the evolution of the healthcare system has largely been about assuring that physician/agents do the right thing for their patient/principals. The rise of consumerism has not fundamentally altered the agency relationship; at its best, it empowers patients to be more effective principals. Medicine is also one of the most important examples of multitasking. Physicians have many options for how to spend their limited time with patients. By the same token, hospitals have many options for how to spend their limited financial resources. In the past, providers had complete discretion in these matters but we have come to conclude that they did not always act in the name of efficiency or quality. The new world of P4P aims to correct these mistakes and assure that our physician/agents make the right choices.

It sounds good on paper. If it is important that physicians perform retinal exams or spend time lecturing patients on the hazards of smoking, then by all means reward the physicians who do these things. But this ignores the second axiom. Once the reward scheme is in place, patients will get more retinal exams and learn yet again about lung cancer, but they may also get fewer blood tests and fewer discussions about diet and exercise. Unless we are sure about what matters most, patients may be worse off than if providers had been left to use their own discretion.

Bengt Holmstrom and Paul Milgrom, economists who may one day join Kenneth Arrow as Nobel Prize winners, have done an in-depth analysis of multitasking and the problems that may result.[32] In research published in 1991, they offer this succinct explanation of the multitasking problem:[33] "When there are multiple tasks, incentive pay serves not only . . . to motivate hard work, it also serves to direct the allocation of the agents' attention *among* their various duties." They also remind us to think carefully about the variety of tasks that we assign to our agents, stating: "Job design is an important instrument for the control of incentives." This means that if you are providing someone with incentives to do one task, you should ask whether you also want that person to be responsible for other tasks, knowing that they might give them less than their full attention.

Let's consider how these principles apply to provider report cards and P4P. The IOM report *To Err Is Human* found that tens of thousands of deaths could be avoided every year if hospitals eliminated medication errors, and the IOM recommended that hospitals adopt CPOE. CPOE can also reduce hospital costs by cutting lengths of stay. Before jumping to the conclusion that every P4P program should require hospitals to adopt CPOE, we need to consider the multitasking problem.

The cost of adopting CPOE ranges from $3 million to $10 million, depending on hospital size and current information technology capabilities.[34] Taking depreciation and interest into account, this can easily amount to $750,000 or more annually. It costs another $500,000 annually to maintain CPOE, for a total annual expense in excess of $1.25 million. An argument can be made that CPOE will pay for itself through cost reductions.[35] But if this were true, hospitals would adopt

CPOE without P4P or report cards. Apparently many hospitals do not believe that CPOE will pay for itself. Payers are using P4P to further motivate its adoption.

The financial incentives could make a big difference. No hospital has unlimited financial wherewithal and modest subsidies to purchase CPOE could help a lot. But the hospital will still have to pay for nearly all of the system, and if it spends upward of $1.25 million annually on CPOE, *it must spend $1.25 million less on something else.* What if that "something else" is nursing staff, something that every hospital is scrambling to enhance? For $1.25 million, a hospital could hire about twenty-five additional full-time registered nurses. According to a widely cited study of hospital quality and nursing staffing, this extra staff would lead to reduced rates of infections, hospital acquired pneumonia, and cardiac arrest.[36] It is impossible to do an exact benefit-cost comparison of CPOE versus extra nurses; the data is too imprecise and the results would vary by hospital. But we must acknowledge that hospitals have alternative uses for CPOE spending that could be just as effective. The report card/P4P folks who reward CPOE but ignore staffing had better be right when they decide that CPOE is the way to go.

Perhaps payers should reward hospitals both for CPOE and staffing. Of course, this would mean either diluting the incentives for each or increasing the total bonus payment. Perhaps more importantly, it will force hospitals to take resources away from still other activities, such as staff training, hiring allied medical personnel, and subsidizing care to the uninsured. There is always another "Y." Payers could add these to the list as well, but if payers are keen on such micromanagement, then they might as well acquire the hospitals and manage them themselves.

Some payers are encouraging physicians to use their discretion by combining a prescribed list of P4P tasks with rewards for overall patient outcomes. But this may not be that much better than ignoring outcomes altogether, as suggested by this additional observation by Holmstrom and Milgrom: If "individuals spend part of their efforts on individual projects and part on team production, and assuming that individual contributions to team effort are difficult to assess, it would be dangerous to provide incentives for good performance on the individual projects." In the case of P4P, the specific process-linked P4P metrics, such as "gives smoking cessation advice" correspond to the "individual projects" and overall patient outcomes such as mortality correspond to "team production." Because the link between physician effort and overall patient outcomes is usually indirect and murky, physicians will focus on the process metrics. Payers may say "outcomes" matter with these mixed reward systems, but due to the multitasking problem only process will matter.

P4P in Action

Because P4P is relatively new, there is not a lot of systematic research on how it is doing. The limited available evidence is consistent with the two axioms of incentives while documenting the potential for multitasking. In other words, P4P generally does lead to desirable changes in measured performance but may also lead to unintended changes in unmeasured performance.

(As an aside, there is a similar ongoing P4P movement in education, for which the evidence to date is also mixed. Teachers do respond to P4P incentives, but there is considerable gaming of these programs, referred to generally as "teaching to the test," and it is not obvious if students are better off as a result.[37])

A 2006 review article appearing in the *Annals of Internal Medicine* identified seventeen published studies of P4P programs.[38] Most of the programs rewarded prevention and thirteen of the seventeen studies report positive effects. However, in three cases the results may have reflected superior documentation rather than changes in performance, and one study of a P4P program for substance abuse treatment found that providers shunned more severe patients in order to improve their P4P scores.[39] Most studies have failed to look for such unintended consequences, so it is difficult to state if they are widespread.

A lot of attention is being given to an ongoing Medicare experiment with P4P.[40] More than 270 hospitals are participating in a three-year demonstration project that focuses on five clinical areas including heart care and pneumonia. Medicare will pay a 1 to 2 percent bonus for hospitals that rank in the top 20 percent on composite quality scores that include both specific processes and outcomes. This is a meager incentive and hospitals with high baseline quality stand to earn the bonus even if their quality fails to improve, while low initial quality hospitals may find it difficult to earn the bonus even with substantial improvements. Even so, the initial returns are encouraging, with average measured performance in each of the five clinical areas increasing by 2.6 to 4.1 percent relative to trend.[41] Thus far, we do not know if this reflects superior performance, superior measurement, or whether there have been unintended consequences.

The United Kingdom is completing the third year of its Quality and Outcomes Framework (QOF) P4P program.[42] Physicians in the United Kingdom are scored on nearly 150 quality indicators and can augment their salary by as much as 30 percent if they comply with program guidelines. The first-year results were impressive—general practitioners greatly exceeded projections with a 91 percent compliance rate. The results were so good that payments to providers were $700 million over budget.

A closer look at the data suggested that the program may have been less successful than the numbers indicate. A few years earlier, the United Kingdom launched an initiative to establish treatment guidelines. Though largely informational it was enormously successful and quality of care was rising sharply prior to the introduction of QOF. The new numbers may simply reflect a continuation of this trend.

There are a number of other indications that the QOF system has brought about exactly the kinds of problems that P4P skeptics have identified. Much of the improved performance appears to be due to better physician record keeping rather than actual changes to clinical practice. Along these lines, the United Kingdom allows for "exception reporting," which enables physicians to depart from guidelines for patients where circumstances dictate exceptional care. Unfortunately the United Kingdom has not yet automated data collection on exception reporting and does not know the extent to which the 9 percent of cases that did not meet guidelines were approved exceptions. The QOF program does not risk adjust and some physicians have found it easier to meet standards for certain population groups. Thus far, however, there is no evidence that physicians are refusing to care for certain groups of patients. Finally while QOF administrators are aware of the potential for multitasking, they have yet to determine whether it is occurring.

There is very little research anywhere else about multitasking. The main reason is that P4P payers tend to only measure those physician activities that they are paying for. This makes it impossible to find out what is happening to things that they are not paying for. In November 2006, Kathleen Mullen, Richard Frank, and Meredith Rosenthal of Harvard University released the first systematic study of multitasking in response to P4P.[43] They studied physician activities before and after the introduction of P4P by PacifiCare HMO. P4P did induce physicians to score better on some dimensions that were rewarded by the program, most of which were related to diagnostic and preventive testing. However, physicians did not improve their performance on other P4P dimensions. More troubling is that physicians significantly cut back on other dimensions of quality that were not rewarded, most of which dealt with prescription and management of medications. Mullen et al. do provide some cause for optimism about P4P. In addition to rewarding specific behaviors, PacifiCare rewarded physicians who improved on outcomes such as reducing hospital readmissions. These outcomes showed significant improvements relative to trend. Even this finding must be tempered by the realization that outcome measures can be gamed, but they suggest that outcome-based P4P may hold more promise than one might expect after reading Holmstrom and Milgrom.

Finally my doctoral student, Susan Feng Lu, is finding in her dissertation research that nursing homes are cutting back on some unreported aspects of quality in response to the publication of process quality measures at Medicare's Nursing Home Compare Web site.[44]

The Bottom Line

Price competition without quality competition is probably worse than no competition at all. The tremendous enthusiasm with which payers have implemented report cards and P4P is therefore welcome, even necessary. But we must temper this enthusiasm with the reality that our measures of quality are incomplete and our implementation of report cards and P4P metrics has failed to catch on with the American public or come face to face with the realities of agency theory. We can solve these problems, but only if consumers and doctors are willing to leave Lake Woebegone and if we can obtain better data. I hope that Robert Brook, the IOM, and others continue to do their part to wake Americans from their reverie. For my part, I will describe how we can generate the required data in chapter 8.

Mending
the Safety Net

*The next Congress must rise above
partisanship and embrace
compromise if we are going to fix
our troubled health care system.
The alternative is to continue to
watch the inevitable, as the health
care system of the United States—
long thought of as the envy of the
world—slips further into a
fractured state of the haves and
have-nots."*

—Risa Lavizzo-Mourey, president
of the Robert Wood Johnson
Foundation[1]

When it comes to health insurance, the United States has about forty-seven million "have-nots." This is not for a lack of ideas about how to cover the uninsured. Politicians and policy analysts from across the political spectrum have offered numerous proposals. The liberal

Physicians for Responsible National Health Insurance recommends a Canadian-style system in which the federal government takes over the financing of healthcare while leaving the provision of care largely in the private sector. Conservatives object that this would lead to more inefficiency, rationing, and the end of innovation. The conservative Heritage Foundation recommends that the government provides tax credits that would enable those of limited means to purchase private sector health insurance. Liberals object that market-based approaches perpetuate administrative waste without guaranteeing equal access for all. Each side blocks the other's agenda in a game of political chicken, while the uninsured wait in vain for a end to the status quo.

Congress has not been totally inactive. Medicaid expansions, SCHIP, and other programs cover millions of Americans, although research suggests that many of the recipients previously had private health insurance. Medicare Part D expands prescription drug coverage for seniors, and the initial response from seniors has bested all but the most optimistic forecasts.[2] But since the inglorious end of Clintoncare, there has been no serious movement toward comprehensive national health insurance. And there is no reason to think that Congress will put aside partisan politics any time in the future. The day may come when one political party controls the White House, has veto-proof majorities in both chambers of Congress, and is willing to spend its political capital on what would be the most important social legislation since the 1935 Social Security Act. Then, and only then, would there be a chance for comprehensive national health insurance.

If you want to find serious efforts to expand coverage, you need to look to the states. Many states have created insurance pools for small employers and individuals who may have been priced out of the private insurance markets. A few states have expanded Medicaid eligibility well beyond the limits envisioned by Congress. And three states have implemented programs and policies designed to dramatically reduce the ranks of the uninsured, with more states waiting in the wings. Many of these initiatives are abject failures, but a few are working and some of the newest, boldest programs have a decent chance of real success. These successes (and failures) may offer us the best hope for finding a politically viable way to cover the uninsured.

Purchasing Pools

A Questionable Idea

There are few certainties in healthcare politics. Who would have imagined that in the past fifteen years, a Democratic president would propose a market-based national healthcare system or that a Republican president would add prescription drug coverage to Medicare? One thing we can be certain of is that most of the candidates in the 2008 presidential election will promise an increased role for health insurance "purchasing pools." They will all give the same simple and compelling rationale: purchasing pools give individuals and small employers "clout" in the health insurance marketplace. The rhetoric of "clout" is appealing but there is a huge gap between rhetoric and economic reality. The economic reality is that there already are dozens of purchasing pools and they are not working. Small employers may need help, but purchasing pools as currently conceived are not the answer.

There is no question that small employers are at a disadvantage in the healthcare marketplace. There is no lack of options—most health insurers sell directly to small firms and small firms can also obtain coverage through a purchasing group or "Association Health Plan (AHP)," which is usually sponsored by a trade association, professional society, or local chamber of commerce.[3] Despite these options, 40 percent of firms with fewer than two hundred workers do not offer insurance to their employees.[4] This compares with just 2 percent of larger firms.

There are many reasons why small firms may be reluctant to offer insurance. Small firms are less likely to be unionized, pay lower wages, and often struggle to cover their operating costs. If they bought insurance for their workers, they may have to slash wages or risk going out of business. All of these factors make health insurance a luxury that many small companies and their workers would prefer to go without. There is one other important factor to consider—small firms must pay higher premiums, perhaps 10 to 20 percent more than what large firms pay for comparable coverage. Jonathan Gruber and Michael Lettau estimate that if premiums at small firms were to drop by 10 percent, then offer rates would increase from 60 to near 65 percent.[5] This seems like a modest increase, but we are still talking about millions of Americans.

The political argument in support of purchasing pools is that the difference in premiums is due entirely to clout—large employers have it and small employers do not. But what exactly is clout and do small companies really lack it? To answer these questions, it helps to think about how employers go about purchasing insurance. Like most large firms, my employer, Northwestern University offers self-insured PPO coverage and contracts with a major insurance carrier—currently Blue Cross of Illinois—to administer the plan. Every major insurer in Illinois has a PPO network and has at one time or another bid aggressively for Northwestern's business. This has forced Blue Cross to hold the line on its administrative services fees.

A small company in the same market cannot afford the risk of self-insuring so it must purchase insurance from one of several dozen small group carriers in Illinois. The small firm may go through an insurance broker or go it alone. Either way, it will bear "purchasing costs"—either through the broker's fee or the time the business owner invests in exploring insurance options and negotiating rates. On a per employee basis, these purchasing costs will greatly exceed what Northwestern must pay. By the same token, insurers incur higher selling expenses per employee. Insurers also perform costly medical underwriting and add an adverse selection "plus factor" because they know that some small employers tend to go in and out of the health insurance market according to the medical needs of their workers. On top of these costs, the insurance coverage for the small firm will have to cover all fifty of Illinois's state-mandated benefits; Northwestern's self-funded plan is ERISA exempt. Insurers also factor in a profit margin, but the small group market in Illinois remains fairly competitive, so this margin may be comparable to that paid by Northwestern to Blue Cross.

Add up all these costs and we find that the small employer has to pay much higher premiums to cover its workers—perhaps 10 to 20 percent higher than Northwestern.[6] What about clout? With more than a dozen carriers to choose from, there is ample competition in the Illinois small group market to keep profit margins largely in check.[7] Though it makes for a good campaign sound bite, the affordability problem for small employers has a lot to do with costs and little to do with clout.

Just because politicians are bad at explaining economics does not mean that purchasing pools are useless. Even if we dismiss the importance of clout, purchasing pools could succeed, provided they can reduce the costs of buying and selling insurance. State governments could help by exempting AHPs and other purchasing groups from costly benefit mandates. Even a modest 5 percent reduction in premiums would increase small firm insurance take-up rates by 2 to 3 percent (based on the Gruber-Lettau estimates), thereby expanding coverage to perhaps one million more Americans.

Unfortunately the elimination of mandates is sometimes tied to legislation creating purchasing pools. Because the latter often requires new taxes, the legislation often stalls. A number of states have eliminated mandates, however, allowing small firms to purchase "bare bones" insurance plans. A federal law exempting AHPs from mandates would also be welcome. Not only would this lead to a modest expansion in insurance coverage, it would help level the playing field with larger self-insured firms that already enjoy ERISA-exemption.

Advocates of purchasing pools claim that they also reduce insurer selling costs. There is some merit to this claim—the insurer need only negotiate with one entity and can let the purchasing pool assume the burden of identifying the needs of its members and educate them about their options. But this is more of a cost-shift than a cost-reduction; the purchasing pool still has to bear the expense of negotiating with and educating its members. Purchasing pools do not cut out the middleman so much as replace one middleman with another.

Advocates also contend that risk pools mitigate adverse selection. Again there is a ring of truth to the claim, but only if the risk pool is stable; that is, the same firms participate in the purchasing pool year after year. If not, then insurers will be forced to continue medical underwriting and maintaining the plus factor for adverse selection. Unfortunately decades of experience indicate that purchasing pools are anything but stable. The wonder is not that most purchasing pools have failed, but rather that they continue to be hyped with so much fanfare.

Purchasing Pools in Practice I: Voluntary Risk Pools

Purchasing pools come in two flavors. There are voluntary pools created and run by private sector organizations, usually large firms bringing smaller firms under their insurance umbrella. There are also government run pools, operated and subsidized by state governments. While neither flavor has proven to be especially successful, there are a few exceptions, especially in the private sector.

Cleveland's Council of Small Enterprises (COSE) is the nation's oldest and most successful purchasing pool. In the early 1970s, Cleveland was recovering from a crippling truckers strike. The city's small businesses were unhappy with the way their business trade group had looked out for their special needs during the strike and lobbied to form a semiautonomous body. In July 1972, COSE was born. COSE had several goals, including advocacy, training of entrepreneurs, and establishing benefits for member employees. In its early years, COSE had some success meeting the first two goals, but did not turn its attention to health benefits until 1978. By that time, its membership was stable and cohesive, an essential ingredient for any risk pool.

COSE created a company to manage health benefits and spent several months convincing Blue Cross of Northeast Ohio to treat it as a single business entity. After a turnover of leadership at the Blue Cross plan, a deal was struck to sell insurance to COSE at group rates. Today COSE has 16,000 member companies and secures insurance for over 225,000 covered employees and families throughout Northeast Ohio. Blue Cross (now called Medical Mutual of Ohio) still accounts for nearly all of the COSE enrollments, offering both PPO and Health Savings Account plans. COSE employees also have two HMO options offered by competing insurers.

COSE is a purely voluntary group formed by small employers. Other successful small employer purchasing pools in New York, Denver, Madison, Milwaukee, and Minneapolis began as voluntary efforts by *large* employers who were hoping to bring down the cost of healthcare. In a typical scenario, the coalition of large employers created its own self-insured PPO, either by negotiating with existing insurers or, in Minneapolis, directly negotiating with providers. In time, small employers are given the option of purchasing coverage from the coalition's PPO. The large employers cite several reasons for this "generosity," including obtaining greater negotiating leverage through expanded enrollments, a desire to ease political pressure on the market-based healthcare system, and to fulfill a sense of corporate responsibility.[8]

Several voluntary purchasing cooperatives started with a push from local governments. The Health Insurance Plan of California was created in 1992 to make health insurance more affordable for small firms. The state required HIPC to privatize in 1999, when the Pacific Business Group on Health assumed responsibility for running the plan. PBGH already purchased health insurance for 500,000 employees and family members. It soon added another 140,000 lives through the HIPC product, which it dubbed PacAdvantage. Beginning in 2000, New York City contracted with the New York Business Group on Health to create HealthPass, which is in the same mold as HIPC. There are similar ventures in other states.

For all of the fanfare surrounding these efforts, they have had little impact on the uninsured. Only COSE and HIPC have managed to attract over 100,000 enrollees from small companies, and HIPC enrollments represent a drop in California's ocean. Enrollments in New York City's HealthPass surpassed 10,000 in March 2007, but this is a tiny fraction of the pool of uninsured. Enrollments in other programs remain mired in the thousands. The death knell for voluntary purchasing pools may have sounded in August 2006 when Blue Shield of California announced that it was losing money on its PacAdvantage product and would no longer offer insurance through the program. Left with only two reluctant carriers to serve PacAdvantage, HIPC disbanded.

The failure of PacAdvantage was due to two related factors. First, PPOs and HMOs in California were offering competitive rates to small employers and Kaiser's rates were lower still. As a result, most small employers in California thought they could get a better deal on their own. In fact, premiums for PacAdvantage plans were slightly *higher* than market rates, driving away many employers.[9] Second, it was not just any employers who were shunning PacAdvantage; it was those with young and healthy workers. These employers benefited from the medical underwriting that HIPC had eschewed. Their departure left PacAdvantage with more than its share of bad risks. PacAdvantage plans increased rates as much as the law allowed, driving away even more of the good risks without fully covering the costs of those who remained. Ultimately PacAdvantage succumbed to a good old-fashioned adverse selection "death spiral," in which raising premiums to cope with the cost of high risk enrollees drives out the low risks, requiring further premium hikes until there is no way to salvage the risk pool.

Any economist who had studied the Rothschild-Stiglitz insurance model that I described in chapter 2 would have predicted such a death spiral.[10] The point to remember is that purchasing pools are just as much at risk for adverse selection as are private insurers, perhaps even more so because purchasing pools are reluctant to experience rate. This makes insurance affordable for high risks, but also makes for an unstable risk pool.

In the final analysis, the question is not why so many voluntary purchasing pools have failed, but rather why COSE has succeeded so well. Voluntary purchasing pools can only work if members resist the temptation to opt out when they have a chance to obtain lower rates in the individual market. The fact that COSE was providing services to members for six years before it offered health insurance may have contributed to the cohesiveness of the group. This reminds me of the classic game theory problem of the prisoner's dilemma, in which participants who seek short-term gains almost always end up worse off in the long run; only those players who learn to trust one another win in the end. Cleveland's small businesses have learned to trust in COSE and each other. There is no ready formula to build such trust in other markets, and this more than anything else may explain why voluntary risk pools are not a panacea for helping to cover the uninsured. Indeed Steve Millard, the executive director of COSE, questions whether another purchasing group can replicate the unique history and business model that makes COSE such a success.[11]

Purchasing Pools in Practice II: State Purchasing Pools

Even as voluntary purchasing pools flounder, most states (thirty-one by the latest count) have created pools of their own. Supporters trot out the same time-worn "clout" argument, as exemplified by a 2006 report prepared for President Bush which stated that these pools would "strengthen the buying power of America's small businesses."[12]

For all of the boosterism, state risk pools have been utter failures. As of December 2004 (the latest year for which data were available), nationwide enrollments in state risk pools stood at about 180,000.[13] If we assume 50 percent crowd out, that implies that the risk pools have provided protection to an additional 90,000 individuals out of a total of forty-seven million uninsured. That is a mere 0.19 percent of the uninsured! Minnesota, the state with the smallest number of uninsured in percentage terms, has the biggest risk pool, with about 33,000 enrollees.[14] Ironically Texas, which has the most uninsured, has the second biggest pool, with 27,000 enrollees. The remaining twenty-nine state risk pools enroll a total of 120,000 individuals, or fewer than 4,200 per state. Accounting for crowd out, this yields a miniscule 2,100 new enrollees per state.

State-sponsored health insurance risk pools have failed for the same reason that most state-sponsored business initiatives fail. If they made business sense, someone in the private sector would have tried them. Advocates act as if they have invented the concept of pooling small business risk. But commercial insurers have been pooling the risks of small businesses for decades. This is what insurers do—they pool risks. Nor is there anything new to giving small business "access to buying power." Most of the buying power that matters is when insurers negotiate discounts from providers, not when firms negotiate with insurers. These provider discounts, which can be 10 to 50 percent or more off of charges, are usually passed along to all of an insurer's customers, including its small business customers. Any clout with the insurers themselves is likely to be minimal because there just isn't much of a margin to play with. State risk pools do almost nothing that private insurers are not already doing, and most small firms that did not purchase private sector insurance are hardly likely to jump at a state's offerings.

A few state risk pools look more like private sector voluntary pools and might have a slightly better chance for success. West Virginia's new Small Business Plan is a prototypical example. Under this plan, insurers who sell to small employers can access the same low rates already offered to state employees through the state Public Employees

Insurance Agency (PEIA). It is not certain whether this will have an impact; the West Virginia small group market was already fairly competitive with over thirty carriers, none of which had more than a 40 percent share. PEIA may offer a better network than some of them, but how much better? It is also difficult to imagine how PEIA will avoid the same problems of adverse selection that have plagued voluntary plans.

One important difference between state pools and private insurers is that the former do not experience rate. This puts state pools are at substantial risk for adverse selection. States end up subsidizing the pools just enough to hold on to high risk employers but not enough to entice the lower risks back in. If states could muster the political will to provide even bigger subsidies, these pools could survive, though the state would quickly replace the private sector as a major supplier of insurance. States might instead consider taking the tax dollars that would have gone to subsidize the state risk pools and use them to help stabilize private sector risk pools. The next section describes this and several other ways that states can increase coverage in the private sector.

Other State Programs

Reinsurance

It may seem surprising but most "insurance" companies make money by avoiding risk. The do this is by pooling the risks of their enrollees and taking advantage of the law of large numbers to assure themselves predictable expenses. One exception is property/casualty insurance, where nature's fury can cause thousands of policy holders to simultaneously suffer enormous damage and wreak havoc on the bottom line of insurers. Property/casualty insurers minimize their losses from such catastrophic events by purchasing *reinsurance*. If they have a larger than expected number of costly claims, the reinsurance company defrays some of the expense. Firms like General Re, Chubb, and Aon can afford to reinsure the property/casualty insurers because they pool the risks of different insurance companies and different types of insurance. In effect, the reinsurers insure the insurers.

Health insurers are much more worried about huge individual claims from individual enrollees than they are about correlated risks among enrollees. In fact, most health risks are not correlated; if one enrollee develops cancer or heart disease, this has no effect on the odds that other enrollees will develop cancer or heart disease.[15] So instead of purchasing reinsurance, health insurers minimize their risk by experience rating individuals or denying them coverage altogether. This makes business sense, but it creates a policy dilemma that can be solved by reinsurance. If health insurers are reinsured against the costs of high-risk patients they will be able to reduce high-risk premiums. More insurers will offer coverage to high-risk enrollees, and more high-risk enrollees will purchase coverage and contribute at least some money to the healthcare system.

At least seven states currently provide some form of healthcare reinsurance.[16] The Healthy New York Program is one of the largest, with nearly 100,000 enrollees. (As with crowd out, it is likely that some of these individuals would have insurance even without the program.) The program is available to small businesses and individuals who pay a nominal fee to participate (the state helps subsidize the plan). In exchange, the state reimburses health plans for 90 percent of any claims paid between $5,000 and $75,000. Reinsurance is also an essential component of Massachusetts's new effort to reinvigorate the state-run risk pool. I will say more about this initiative later in the chapter.

Mark Pauly has suggested an even stronger form of reinsurance. Specifically he has proposed a special federal insurance program for select chronically ill populations, much as Medicare currently offers for renal dialysis. This would go a long way toward encouraging private insurers to enroll all comers.

There is an important downside to reinsurance. If reinsurance is generous enough—and New York's 90 percent reinsurance is *very* generous—then the insurance companies have little incentive to hold the line on costs. Ironically Healthy New York targets HMOs, which are required to offer the plan to qualifying enrollees. As a result, HMOs become little more than claims processors for high-risk patients, stripped of their incentives to hold the line on costs. This returns us to the days of unrestricted fee-for-service medicine and it does so for exactly the wrong patients—those responsible for the bulk of our healthcare costs. New York should reduce the reinsurance rate so as to strike a better balance between incentives for coverage and incentives for cost containment.

Community Rating and Guaranteed Renewability

If high-risk enrollees are shut out of insurance markets due to experience rating, then it stands to reason that restrictions on experience rating would help keep high risks in the market. This might also reduce everyone's insurance costs by limiting medical underwriting expenses. Based on this thinking, most states require insurers to community rate premiums; that is, insurers must set premiums according to an enrollee's risk class, but not that enrollee's particular medical history. Of course, insurers might respond by refusing to sell to high risks, so most states also require that insurers offer to renew coverage for all customers and cap the allowable premium increase. Taken together, these policies are sometimes referred to as "guaranteed renewability."

Mark Pauly has articulated the benefits of guaranteed renewability.[17] Imagine choosing an insurance policy when you are young. You do not know whether you are likely to have significant medical problems as you grow older, so you are happy to purchase an insurance policy priced for the average risk. Guaranteed renewability allows you to purchase that same insurance policy indefinitely while always paying the premium for an average risk. The alternative—buying a new policy every year and facing premium fluctuations according to your health needs—exposes you to unwanted risk and the possibility of getting shut out of the insurance market altogether.

Guaranteed renewability holds to the fundamental principle of insurance—it protects against fluctuations in wealth arising from fluctuations in health. But guaranteed renewability has been almost nonexistent in unregulated health insurance markets. Insurers know that a guaranteed renewable insurance pool is an unstable pool. Healthy, young enrollees may remain in the pool because they want the benefits of guaranteed coverage as they age. But healthy, older individuals may drop out in favor of an insurance plan that charges lower premiums more in keeping with their better-than-expected health status. This destroys the risk pool. Ever fearful of the potential for such adverse selection, insurers are reluctant to offer the lifetime policy.

With the free market failing to provide guaranteed renewability, state governments have stepped in. By the 1990s, most states guaranteed renewability and community rating. These laws protect high risk enrollees from paying high premiums but they also increase the extent of cross-subsidization. This may have helped open the door to CDHPs, whose features would naturally attract younger, healthier enrollees, who, in turn, would no longer be asked to subsidize their older, sicker coworkers.

HIPAA rules do not apply to individuals who are purchasing insurance for the first time or have let their insurance lapse. All states require guaranteed issue, which requires insurers to write policies for new customers, but only a handful of states also require community rating for new enrollees. In a recent study, Mark Pauly and Bradley Herring examined how the individual insurance markets were functioning in those states.[18] They found that these laws had little effect on the total number of uninsured. The number of high risks with insurance slightly increased, but this is a bit more than offset by reduced numbers of insured low risks.

These laws have proven to be very popular among politicians because they require only indirect oversight of insurance markets and do not impose new taxes or additional burdens on employers. The main opponents to these laws are insurers who focus on the small group and individual markets.[19] Although the laws make some economic sense, they have done little to reduce the number of uninsured, so some states are expanding coverage in the one insurance program they directly control, Medicaid.

Medicaid Expansions

The federal government has always given states considerable leeway in setting Medicaid (and SCHIP) eligibility requirements as well as the rules for reimbursing provider services. During the 1980s and 1990s, most states obtained waivers from the federal government enabling them to place Medicaid enrollees into managed care plans. More than half of all Medicaid enrollees are now in managed care.[20] In the past few years, states have been even more interested in waivers to expand enrollments. Sometimes the waivers allow states to expand Medicaid and SCHIP eligibility. Sometimes the waivers allow states to reallocate existing Medicaid and SCHIP funds to other state insurance programs. In a few cases, the waivers come with additional federal funding.

At least thirty states now have Medicaid and/or SCHIP waivers. Most waivers cover the full Medicaid spectrum of services but target narrow populations—usually childless adults (who would not normally fit into a Medicaid eligibility category) or children in families that earn above the traditional Medicaid income threshold. A few states have received broader waivers. Arkansas, New Mexico, and Oklahoma plan to enroll a combined 140,000 workers with incomes under 200 percent of the FPL.

Because the federal government only pays for about half of Medicaid (the exact cost-sharing percentage varies by state), the states must come up with the remaining dollars. Elected officials often use a variety of smokescreens to pretend to voters that the expansions are either costless or are funded by "good" money such as sin taxes or the tobacco industry lawsuit settlements. But government monies are fungible, so any funds derived from taxes or settlements necessarily come at the expense of other state programs or in lieu of tax reductions. Spending money on Medicaid is still a good deal for states—thanks to federal matching they get approximately $2 in local healthcare spending for every $1 taken from the state budget.

One of the most closely watched Medicaid expansions is Illinois's All Kids program. The goal of the program is to "provide affordable, comprehensive health insurance for every child." Governor Blagojevich recently proposed a more sweeping program to cover most of the one million Illinois adults who lack insurance. If enacted (the current prospects appear dim), Illinois will join several states that have implemented sweeping programs that promise to create a safety net for the entire population. Think of them as "mini-national health insurance systems." They may be our best bet for achieving near universal coverage.

Mini-National Health Insurance Systems

While the federal government muddles along, a few states have taken bolder steps to expand coverage. Their mini-national health insurance systems are intended to assure near universal coverage. While it seems that most of these efforts are unlikely to reach their lofty goals, they will serve as valuable laboratories from which we can learn the best (and worst) strategies for covering the uninsured.

Hawaii's Plan

If any state might be expected to have high numbers of uninsured, it would be Hawaii. Small businesses employ over 57 percent of the state's nonfarm workers, versus 50 percent nationwide.[21] A disproportionate number of Hawaii's workers also hold seasonal jobs. Despite these risk factors, only 10 percent of Hawaiians are uninsured. This is partly due to a modest expansion of Medicaid. But the main reason why Hawaii has limited the number of uninsured is that the state regulates the heck out of the private insurance market. Since 1974, nearly all employers have been mandated to offer health coverage to employees who work at least twenty hours per week.[22] Employers must also pay at least half of the premium. The state requires guaranteed issue and disallows preexisting condition exclusions. Insurers may not cancel coverage for individuals who get sick and insurers who sell to any small employer must make the same policies available to all small employers.

Shortly after Hawaii imposed the employer coverage mandate, the uninsurance rate in Hawaii plummeted to 2 percent. Though this rate has risen five-fold, it is still well below national norms. About one in five uninsured Hawaiians are children, most of whom are eligible for Medicaid but have not been enrolled. The Hawaii Uninsured Project has identified these uninsured eligibles and the state is attempting to enroll them.

Nearly 30 percent of Hawaii's uninsured work full time. Many of them work for larger firms that appear to be skirting the law and do not offer insurance. Other uninsured workers decline to pay their share of the premium. They are likely to remain uninsured unless the state provides larger subsidies or requires them to buy insurance. There several other loopholes in the system. The plan does not cover the state's many seasonal workers and many companies hire workers for less than twenty hours per week so as to avoid the obligation to buy insurance. Despite these problems, Hawaii's simple employer mandate has gone a long way to make sure that Hawaii outperforms the nation in terms of coverage.

Hawaii's experiment has shown that employer mandates can substantially reduce the number of uninsured. Such regulations always invite gamesmanship by the regulated and it is up to Hawaiian regulators to close some of the loopholes. They could leave well-enough alone, although this means that 10 percent of the state will remain uninsured. They might instead subsidize insurance for low-income workers or develop programs to cover part-time workers, but these could drive up taxes and further alienate insurers. No one knows whether these steps would be sufficient; only through trial and error will we know for sure. Through their ongoing experiment with employer mandates, Hawaii is showing the rest of the nation one possible path for covering more of the uninsured.

Flirting with History

When Bill Clinton became president in 1992, he was not the only politician taking aim at the access problem. Governors in Kentucky, Colorado, Massachusetts, Oregon, and Florida pushed their own health reform agendas, which usually included a pay-or-play mandate requiring employers to either provide insurance or pay a tax to subsidize a state insurance pool. Washington State offered one of the most complex initiatives. The Washington Health Services Act of 1993 combined an employer pay-or-play mandate with Enthoven's principles of managed competition among organized delivery systems (vertically integrated systems). Hillary Clinton stated that the "features of the Washington plan will . . . be the features of any plan that comes out of Congress."[23]

As the political fortunes of Clinton-care rose in 1993 and fell in 1994, so, too, did the fortunes of these state initiatives. Initiatives in Kentucky, Colorado, and Florida were pulled from the legislature. Employer mandates in Massachusetts and Oregon were enacted but lapsed prior to implementation. The Washington Health Services Act was repealed in 1995. It would be nearly a decade before any more states would take major steps toward covering the uninsured.

Maine's Dirigo Health

In 2003, about 10 percent of Mainers—135,000 individuals—lacked health insurance. Though far below the national average, Governor John Baldacci offered a program that promised to cover all residents within five years while also holding the line on costs. The state legislature approved the governor's plan, known as Dirigo Health, in June 2003.[24]

There are two distinct programs to expand access under Dirigo Health. MaineCare expands Medicaid coverage to families earning up to 200 percent of the FPL, or about $40,000 for a family of four. Dirigo Choice heavily subsidizes health insurance for small businesses, the self-employed, and individuals earning up to 300 percent of the FPL. To limit the potential for adverse selection, participating employers who opt for Dirigo Choice must cover all of their employees. Maine will subsidize 40 percent of the cost of Dirigo Choice as a way to entice employers with low-risk profiles into the Dirigo risk pool.

The initial experience has been mixed. Prior to Dirigo, Maine's Medicaid program was already one of the nation's largest, covering 20 percent of state residents. Much of this increase occurred in 2002, when enrollments in a new program to cover "childless adults" were three times higher than expected. Medicaid enrollments have continued to increase and Medicaid now covers more than 25 percent of state residents, the highest percentage in the nation. Most of the increase has resulted from vigorous efforts to enroll all individuals eligible for traditional Medicaid. Only about 5,000 Medicaid enrollees are covered under MaineCare.

Dirigo Choice has experienced anemic growth. As of early 2007, enrollments stood at 13,500, compared with over 150,000 individuals enrolled in private individual and small group plans.[25] Even this overstates Dirigo Choice's accomplishments—according to a survey conducted by the University of Southern Maine, only 22 percent of the first 7,000 Dirigo Choice enrollees were previously uninsured.[26] If we extrapolate this percentage to the total enrollment, then Dirigo Choice has managed to enroll about 3,000 out of 135,000 uninsured residents. The size of the crowd-out problem should come as no surprise given that Maine is subsidizing so much of the premium, but there might be no other way to avoid adverse selection. Surprise or not, such massive crowd out is a real political problem. Those who continue to purchase insurance must also pay taxes to cover those who do not, and Governor Baldacci has recently asked for new tax revenues to support Dirigo. It becomes a fundamental matter of fairness whether the state should have a heavily subsidized insurance program for those who would have purchased coverage in the private sector had Dirigo never existed.

The fact that so few uninsured have taken up the Dirigo Choice is another concern. Perhaps the subsidy needs to be even higher, especially for those earning below the FPL. The program's complexity may also be part of the problem. Dirigo Choice has six different eligibility categories based on income and household status. Employers and employees cannot easily determine how much they will have to pay for insurance without first going through a lengthy application process. Regardless of the problem, the Dirigo experience will afford researchers and policy makers a closer look at the factors that limit insurance take-up by small businesses and the uninsured.[27] The rest of the nation can learn from any mistakes that Maine is making.

Dirigo Health contains cost-cutting initiatives including a brief moratorium on all capital spending and bed expansion as well as voluntary caps on hospital costs and hospital and insurer profit margins. These are more than just window dressings. Dirigo is supposed to be funded by employers, employees, and the federal share of Medicaid, with any shortfall derived from assessments of insurers. These assessments are based on the savings that private insurers supposedly realize from the cost-cutting initiatives.

Calculating the savings took on added importance when it was discovered that the shortfall in the first nine months was nearly $20 million, or more than $4,000 per enrollee! Dirigo seems to have suffered from adverse selection after all. To recoup its losses, Maine reported that its cost-cutting initiatives saved $44 million in the first year and imposed a $44 million levy on private insurers. Most of the calculated savings were based on reductions from past spending trends, without regard to current trends in other states (healthcare cost growth in the past two years has slowed nationwide, not just in Maine.) Insurers protested the state's methodology but their challenge was denied by the state court.

We should be clear about who bears the burden of the $44 million levy. Insurers will surely pass this tax along to enrollees.[28] If Maine's cost-cutting initiatives really did save $44 million, as the state claims, then enrollees will be no better off than before. But if the state has overstated the savings, then enrollees will be paying out more than the initiatives saved them. There is nothing inherently wrong with this, except for the fact that Maine's political leaders are pretending that it costs nothing for taxpayers to subsidize health insurance for the uninsured when, as always, there is no free lunch.

Unfortunately this lunch may prove to be exceedingly costly. Dirigo's administrators have an incentive to report the largest possible savings, which will translate into the largest possible insurance premium increases. Moreover, there will be no effort to determine whether the purported savings represent genuine elimination of waste or cutbacks in staffing and services. In the final analysis, the Dirigo program to expand access for uninsured Mainers may be funded through reductions in access for everyone else.

At a minimum, Dirigo is enduring significant growing pains. Maine's voters had an opportunity to express their opinion in the fall 2006 gubernatorial election, in which Dirigo was a central issue. Governor Baldacci ran against four opponents, including a conservative Republican party candidate. Baldacci won reelection, but his 38 percent vote total hardly represented a ringing endorsement of Dirigo.

It is too soon to ring the death knell for Dirigo. Although I have my doubts, this experiment with individual subsidies is providing valuable lessons to other states looking for solutions. I hope voters in

Maine give the program a few more years to mature before final judgment is passed.

The Massachusetts Health Plan

The nation's de facto system for covering the uninsured has always been cross-subsidization. Nonprofit hospitals used their tax exempt status, charitable contributions, and profits from the privately insured to cover the costs of the uninsured. Privately insured patients may not realize it, but they have been paying for the uninsured all along. (Ignorance may have been the biggest political virtue of this system.) In recent years, hospitals have had fewer resources available for treating the uninsured, thanks to cutbacks in reinbursements from Medicare, Medicaid, and managed care. Massachusetts responded to this trend by creating a $500 million annual fund to pay for the hospital care of the uninsured. The money came from a tax on employer-sponsored health insurance augmented by federal Medicaid funds through a special agreement with CMS.

The program worked reasonably well, encouraging hospitals in Massachusetts to welcome the uninsured even as nonprofit hospitals in other states received stinging criticism for turning them away, or treating them and hounding them for payment. But the program had obvious limitations. There was not enough money to cover all the costs of hospital care for the uninsured. Many of the uninsured lacked the financial means to pay for other medical care. Residents who had insurance complained about having to pay their own premiums and a tax to subsidize care for others. (Once cross-subsidization was out in the open, a lot of taxpayers were unhappy about it.) Large employers were upset because they felt the program made it easier for small employers to drop coverage. Insurers did not like the program because it encouraged crowd out, which reduced the demand for their policies.

In response to these concerns, in April 1996 Massachusetts created the first state program intended to assure that every resident has insurance. The lynchpin of the plan is a play-or-pay mandate to employers (who must pay about $300 per employee annually if they do not offer them insurance) coupled with a carrot and stick approach with individuals (who are required to buy insurance but will also receive means-tested subsidies). These ideas are not new, but Massachusetts is the first state to try them all at once.

The true innovation in the Massachusetts Health Plan is the creation of a market-based insurance intermediary called the "Connector." The Connector brings together enrollees and private insurance sellers much in the same way that Amazon.com brings buyers to its affiliated sellers. Insurers who wish to participate must provide coverage and premium details to the state. With some important exceptions (described below), insurers are free to offer any type of plan—a high deductible plan, a tightly managed HMO, or a run-of-the-mill broad network PPO. State residents who do not get coverage from their employers must either buy insurance on their own or purchase it through the Connector. Those who opt for the latter may choose among all participating plans. Enrollees who use the Connector can keep their insurance even if they change employers or drop out of the work force; the Connector will always remain a conduit for insurance for those not covered by their employers.

Though novel in its execution, the Connector harkens back to a central provision in Enthoven's Consumer Choice Health Plan, in which individual employees would be free to choose among any of the plans available in the market, and not just the one or two offered by their employer. The same idea of an insurance clearinghouse was resurrected in the late 1990s, only this time it was being promoted by entrepreneurs who wanted to create a private sector "Connector" that would link a dozen or more insurers with hundreds of small employers in each local market. Employees would be free to select their preferred insurer, and the Connector company would affect an electronic transfer of premiums from the employer to the plan.

About ten years ago, I advised a venture capital firm that had been approached by a start-up company seeking to create a Connector-like brokerage service. The fate of the venture seemed to hinge on risk adjustment. In particular, the company needed a way to protect insurers against adverse selection by enrollees and cream skimming by opportunistic competitors. The VC firm concluded that while risk adjustment had come a long way since I was Enthoven's graduate student, it had not come far enough. Other VC firms apparently agreed and private sector Connectors never materialized. It may soon be possible to do a much better job of risk adjustment with publicly available data, as I describe in the next chapter.

Several factors may allow the Massachusetts Connector to succeed where the private sector has failed. The first is the carrot-and-stick approach to both employer and employee participation. According to MIT economist Jonathan Gruber, who was a key player in crafting the plan, a big issue is whether the $500 million that has been redirected from the uncompensated care pool will provide enough carrots to ensure the scale and broad participation necessary for a stable risk pool. Massachusetts is fortunate that it already had this money in hand. It can fund the insurance subsidies by redirecting current spending, rather than imposing new taxes. But Gruber admits that there is no way to know how large the subsidy will need to be in order to limit selection and wonders whether taxpayers will foot the bill if more money is needed. His fears seem to be justified, as there are already rumblings about the need to raise taxes further to support the plan.

The Massachusetts Health Plan has taken other steps to make the Connector work. It follows the model of Clinton-care by establishing a set of benefits that all plans must offer, thereby limiting opportunities for cream skimming. For individuals earning up to 100 percent of the federal poverty level, plans must cover inpatient care, outpatient and preventive services, prescription drugs, mental health and substance abuse care, and dental and vision care. No more, no less. Moreover for individuals earning up to 300 percent of the FPL, plans may not impose deductibles and must have fairly broad networks.

These restrictions upset some free marketers. The Heritage Foundation, which generally supports the Massachusetts plan, wonders how consumers would feel if the state dictated the features of other products such as automobiles. There is obviously much to be gained when consumers have a wide choice of car features, but that misses the point. When it comes to cars, consumers have different preferences over a lot of factors, including roominess, sportiness, and reliability. Variety is important. When it comes to health insurance, variety in coverage options does not meet consumer needs so much as it facilitates cream skimming and adverse selection. The main benefit of competition, both in automobile and insurance markets, is to encourage sellers to find innovative ways to reduce costs while meeting consumer needs. Restricting plan design does nothing to stand in the way.

The Massachusetts Health Plan takes a number of other steps to limit adverse selection and cream skimming. Individuals earning between 200 and 300 percent of the FPL who select a low premium/high copayment plan will keep only half the savings. At the same time, the state will provide insurers with 50 percent reinsurance for all enrollees whose costs exceed 105 percent of the expected amount and also collect a 50 percent "rebate" from insurers for all enrollees whose costs are below 95 percent of that amount. Finally participating plans must pay an additional 1.2 percent tax that goes to reimburse full expenses for individuals incurring more than $150,000 in costs for the year.

The Massachusetts Health Plan seems to solve most of the problems with the state's old way of doing business. The uninsured will now contribute toward their healthcare costs and have coverage for more than just hospital care. It will be easier for participants to keep their insurance even if they quit or change jobs. Private insurers will continue to pay a tax but they will also enjoy higher enrollments. Employers will have to contribute toward insurance costs even if they do not provide it themselves. The program will rely on subsidies and reinsurance to limit cream skimming and adverse selection.

Despite these promising changes, many challenges remain. Will the subsidies be large enough to encourage individuals to buy insurance and if not, will taxpayers be willing to open their wallets wider? Will reinsurance reduce efforts to cut costs? And will it be sufficient to limit selection? Does the state need to risk adjust premiums and not just act as a reinsurer. Will employers cease offering insurance and pay the "tax" instead, causing crowd out?

Given that key provisions of the plan did not kick in until July 2007, it is too soon to know the answers to these questions. However, many policy analysts are optimistic. Policy guru Paul Ginsburg of the nonpartisan Center for Studying Health System Change stated "This is probably as close as you can get to universal."[29] Perhaps surprisingly, the plan has been enthusiastically endorsed by many conservative thinkers, such as Robert Moffit of the Heritage Foundation.[30] Though not everyone likes the plan. Sally Pipes, president of the conservative

Pacific Research Institute and ardent supporter of consumer-driven healthcare thinks that the end result of the Massachusetts Health Plan will be a "total government takeover of health care," while Steffie Woolhandler and David Himmelstein, equally ardent supporters of a Canadian-style universal health system, label the plan "Massachusetts's Mistake."[31]

No one knows for sure how employers will respond to the pay-or-play mandate or how high subsidies must rise to assure that everyone participates. While Pipes and Woolhandler and Himmelstein assume their roles in the tired debate about markets versus state control, Massachusetts is doing more than paying lip service to the problem. It is conducting an experiment and, like Hawaii and Maine, serving as a guinea pig for the rest of the nation. The fact that the Massachusetts plan is criticized by those on the extreme ends of the policy spectrum while receiving hopeful reviews from those in the middle makes me think that the experiment just might work.

All Kids in Illinois

Another smaller experiment is taking place in Illinois. As its name suggests, the goal of Illinois's All Kids program is to provide insurance coverage to all of the state's children. When Governor Blagojevich's program was enacted in 2005, the state had about 250,000 uninsured children. All Kids hopes to enroll nearly 125,000 children who are eligible for Medicaid or SCHIP but not yet signed up. The rest will be covered through a means-tested subsidized expansion of Medicaid for families earning too much to qualify for existing programs. The rules for All Kids are much simpler than those for Dirigo Health or the Massachusetts Health Plan, and All Kids got off to a fast start, enrolling 50,000 children in the first month. However, nearly all of them were already enrolled in other state programs. There is also considerable concern about crowd out. Thus far, net new enrollments appear to be minimal.

One aspect of All Kids that has raised some eyebrows is the funding mechanism. Governor Blagojevich claims that All Kids will be funded by a shift to managed care in other state insurance programs including

Medicaid. Thus the program seems to have no impact on the budget. This may be true from an accounting standpoint, but is otherwise grossly misleading. The shift to managed care could have been done without All Kids, freeing up funds for any number of other uses. The money that is now earmarked for All Kids could have been used to make up shortfalls in provider payments, increase spending on education, or even reduce taxes in a state that has chronic budget shortfalls. There is nothing inherently wrong with the state choosing to use the money instead for All Kids, but if we are to evaluate the program fairly, it is important to know its true cost.

Other Initiatives[32]

As many as half the states are developing plans that will greatly expand coverage.[33] A few are exploring the "play or pay" feature that is at the heart of the Hawaii and Massachusetts plans. Maryland and New York City require large retailers to provide health insurance to their employees or pay a health insurance "tax." The Maryland law has been challenged in the courts on the grounds that it targets a single firm—Wal-Mart. San Francisco's Healthcare Access Program began in January 2007 and hopes to enroll at least 15,000 of the city's estimated 80,000 uninsured residents. It will be funded by a tax on employers who do not currently provide insurance.

Governor Schwarzenegger's recent proposal for California has received considerable attention. Firms with more than ten employees would be required to provide coverage or pay a 4 percent payroll tax. Smaller firms would be exempt. Workers who do not have employer-sponsored insurance would be required to obtain coverage either on their own or from a state pool. Low income individuals would receive subsidies to be funded by a 2 percent tax on doctors and a 4 percent tax on hospitals. Rules concerning guaranteed issue and guaranteed renewability of insurance would be toughened as well. There will also be caps on insurance company profits, though this might be difficult to enforce given the potential for national insurers to finesse their accounting data. The proposal is languishing, as state legislators try to deal with short-term budget needs.

These "pay or play" initiatives allow governments to expand access without raising taxes. Employers and their employees would have to bear the burden, of course, but this burden is already being borne by society in other ways. It is no wonder that several candidates for president have endorsed some form of pay-or-play proposal. Pay-or-play initiatives do not guarantee universal coverage, of course. Individuals who are not covered by their employers must still obtain coverage on their own. Here is where there are major differences across plans. The Massachusetts plan provides cash incentives for individuals to purchase private insurance. Senator Barrack Obama's proposes something along similar lines. No one yet knows the size of the incentive (and the associated tax increase) necessary to realize near universal coverage; some individuals may refuse to buy insurance unless it is completely costless. In Senator Hillary Clinton's pay-or-play proposal, individuals who cannot obtain coverage from their employers would be enrolled in Medicaid or a similar program. Again, the requisite tax levy is unknown.

Some states have explored even more ambitious proposals for covering the uninsured. A 2001 proposal in Connecticut to create a Canadian-style single payer scheme did not get out of committee. In 2004, California voters rejected a ballot initiative ("Prop. 72") requiring the state to cover all residents who lack employer-sponsored coverage. Similar proposals have been made every other year by single-payer advocates in New Mexico, with no success.

Wisconsin is considering legislation that revives Enthoven's Consumer Choice Health Plan. Enthoven's ideas had already played out successfully in Wisconsin in 1984, when the state capped the amount it would contribute toward its own employees' health insurance and required state workers to pick up any extra expense. This forced health plans to compete directly for the business of state employees. The effect was most pronounced in Madison, Wisconsin, the state capitol and home of the state's flagship university. In short order, most of Madison's state employees enrolled into HMOs and, as reported by Stephen Hill and Barbara Wolfe, the result was a dramatic reduction in their healthcare costs.[34]

The current legislative initiative is the brainchild of David Riemer, the director of the nonprofit Wisconsin Health Project. Enthoven heard about the Project's efforts to rely on competition to expand access while containing costs and has become their spiritual guru. The resulting Wisconsin Health Plan would cover virtually all Wisconsin residents under age sixty-five, including those currently covered by Medicaid and the uninsured. Enrollees would select among any licensed health plan in the state, which would be placed into one of three tiers based on cost and quality measures. (The purpose of the tiers is to simplify choices while encouraging competition.) The state will provide means-tested tax credits funded through payroll taxes to enable all residents to purchase a Tier 1 plan. The amount of the credit (and the plan premium) would be risk adjusted. Enrollees would have to use their own money to purchase a plan in Tier 2 or 3. There is no provision for reinsurance, as in Massachusetts.

Like most other proposals to expand access, the Wisconsin Health Plan would impose substantial new taxes. One version of the plan would give Wisconsin the highest state income tax rates in the nation. As legislators ponder the Wisconsin Health Plan, they will come to realize what all policy makers must ultimately understand. There is no way in the near term that we can assure near universal coverage without raising taxes.

The political reality may be that we have to integrate efforts to expand access with efforts to find the most cost-effective ways of delivering care. State experimentation once again provides a valuable lens on the opportunities available to us. Recall the 1970's state experiments with price setting that led to the prospective payment system for hospitals. In the 1980s, Tennessee led a movement by the states to enroll Medicaid recipients in HMOs. Today's most daring experiment is ongoing in Oregon, which is using cost-effectiveness criteria to rationalize the Medicaid program. Supporters say it is the best way to rationalize a chaotic healthcare system. Naysayers describe it as blatant rationing.

Getting More Bang for the Healthcare Buck: Oregon's Medicaid Plan

If any policy makers have experience trying to get the most out of limited tax revenues, it is the directors of state Medicaid programs. Lacking a powerful voting constituency, state Medicaid programs always seem to face tight budgets. Some states stretch their Medicaid dollars by refusing to pay for certain high-cost treatments. This type of rationing received national attention twenty years ago when a boy covered by Oregon's Medicaid program was denied access to a bone marrow transplant that might have saved his life. When news of his death made the national media, the legislature appointed a commission to examine rationing in the state.

The commission approved a methodology based on cost-effectiveness analysis. It ranked about eight hundred medical interventions from most to least cost-effective and recommended against paying for about two hundred low-ranked treatments, including life support for extremely low birth weight babies and medical therapy for end-stage HIV. President of the Oregon Senate, John Kitzhaber (a physician by training), defended the plan. He noted that Oregon was already rationing medical care and that the new program would bring it out into the open.[35] By rationalizing rationing, the state could free up money to cover more low-income residents and even add additional services to the coverage package.

Despite objections from many quarters, the plan moved forward and, after several revisions, was implemented in 1994. Oregon's rationing scheme is still in place. The state has expanded coverage to include dental care, preventive services, and organ transplants, and enrolled 100,000 previously uninsured residents. Most Oregonians still support the plan, but no other state has seriously considered following Oregon's lead.

The use of cost-effectiveness analysis to ration access to costly high-tech services is common practice outside the United States, where government agencies such as England's National Institute for Clinical Excellence and Australia's Pharmacy Benefit Advisory Commission use clearly delineated cost-effectiveness criteria before approving access to drugs and other new technologies. Managed care organizations in the United States have also considered using cost-effectiveness criteria, whether as part of utilization review or when establishing drug formularies. Medicare is currently exploring whether to formalize the process.

Payers will have a massive body of cost-effectiveness research to draw on. Researchers have refined methods for comparing the cost-effectiveness of different interventions and have even developed scales with names like "Quality Adjusted Life Years" (QALYs) that permit the comparison of completely different treatments—hip replacement surgery versus corneal transplants, for example. This research is limited by some of the same data problems that plague quality measurement, especially the difficulty of creating a seamless electronic medical record. However, there is considerable merit to the idea of allocating health spending to the interventions with the highest benefit/cost ratios. As Oregon's Kitzhaber might have said, the question is not whether we should ration access to technology, it is how best to do it. Rationing based on cost-effectiveness criteria offers the potential to give us the most bang for our healthcare bucks.

The plans in place in Oregon, Hawaii, Maine, Massachusetts, and elsewhere may prove to be harbingers of change, where the states successfully expand coverage after generations of failure by the federal government. But many challenges remain if we are to expand access while simultaneously assuring efficiency and quality. In the last chapter, I offer a few ideas—some old and some new—for reviving the American healthcare system.

Reviving the American Healthcare System

Our physical and mental health is perhaps the nation's greatest asset. It behooves each community, therefore, to consider what plan will most effectively promote the health of its citizens.

—RAY WILBER, chairman of the Committee on the Costs of Medicare Care, 1932[1]

AMERICANS SPEND FAR MORE on healthcare than anyone else in the world. Yet there is unacceptable variation in the quality of care and millions of Americans face financial catastrophe should illness strike. If the healthcare system were a patient, we might say it was in critical condition.

This is not for want of remedies. Ever since the report of the Committee on the Cost of Medical Care, ideas for improving access while lowering cost and raising quality have emanated from the private and public sectors. Every candidate in the ongoing presidential campaign has offered their prescription. We do not need any more proposals for healing our healthcare system. There are more than enough to go around. What we need are ways to assure that the proposals already on the table have a better chance of succeeding.

Looking back at a century of health reform, it is easy to identify some common barriers to success:

- *Inadequate information.*
- *Inappropriate incentives.*
- *Too many opportunities to prosper by playing games instead of creating value.*
- *Unrealistic expectations about the cost of care.*

In this chapter, I offer some ideas about how to lower these barriers.

Laying the Foundation for Reform through Electronic Medical Records

We are a half-century into the computer age, though you might never know it if you were to look at the state of health information technology. Many providers still rely on paper records. Those who have computerized often have separate systems for clinical and billing data. There is no technology standard so providers cannot easily share clinical data. The result is that too many people make too many important medical decisions in an information vacuum. It is a sorry state of affairs that has exacted a heavy toll.

How heavy? Consider some of the most significant market-based initiatives of the past two decades, such as capitation, utilization review, integrated delivery systems, and physician-hospital organizations. None of these initiatives lived up to its promise. All faced the same common obstacle—the necessary information systems were lacking. Ongoing initiatives, including consumer-directed health plans, report cards, pay-for-performance, and cost effectiveness evaluation will also fall short of their potential if we do not improve our data systems. Better data will also go a long way toward curing what ails insurance markets. We may finally see the kind of risk adjustment of insurance premiums that Enthoven envisioned for his Consumer Choice Health Plan, and insurers would be more likely to participate in risk pools and brokerage arrangements such as the Massachusetts Connector.[2] If we want to make any significant progress in reforming the health economy, we must standardize and broadly implement integrated electronic medical records (EMRs). It is the foundation upon which all else will be built.

Obstacles to EMRs

Fewer than half of all hospitals and 20 percent of physicians have adopted an EMR system. Nursing homes, home care agencies, dentists, and other providers are even further behind. There are many vendors hawking their EMR systems, and each one has different data fields and variable names. Even if a doctor and a hospital both have an EMR, the chances are that they cannot exchange electronic information.

These problems stem from simple economics. Most providers have refused to adopt EMRs because vendors have failed to make a compelling business case for it. For a typical physician, adoption costs can exceed $40,000, with annual maintenance costs of $8,000.[3] Proponents claim that doctors can recover this investment through improvements in billing (i.e., increasing coding levels to maximize reimbursements) and better management of accounts receivable. Their claim must not be very convincing or doctors would be adopting EMRs at a much higher rate.

EMR proponents also point to tremendous potential cost savings; one study suggests that the savings from reducing unnecessary lab tests alone would exceed $30 billion annually.[4] Health IT expert J. D. Kleinke suggests that such savings represent a *losing* proposition for many providers.[5] He observes that any cost savings to society represents lost revenues to providers and wonders why providers would purchase a system that would drive down their revenues. Kleinke is probably correct in the short run. But if providers do adopt standardized EMRs, it will be easier for payers to implement payment systems that reward efficiency. When this happens, provider and consumer interests in reducing healthcare spending will be aligned and the overall benefits of EMR will more than offset the cost. But this is a chicken-or-egg problem—we will not see these long-run benefits of EMRs if providers have no short-run incentives to adopt them.

Even if vendors could make a business case for EMRs, providers may remain on the fence because of concerns about system compatibility. A few heavy hitting technology companies, including GE and Oracle, are beta-testing interoperability software that will enable partial integration of previously incompatible systems. This may coax some providers off the fence, but many others will undoubtedly wait for a unified standard.

I am not quick to recommend massive government intervention in the healthcare system, but chicken-or-egg problems and an absence of standards are two clues that the market, left to its own devices, may never give us EMRs. A closer look at the economics of standards suggests that a little push from the government may be all it takes to resolve this problem.

The Economics of Standards

Standards can emerge organically, such as when the VHS videocassette recorder gradually overwhelmed Betamax or when Microsoft's MS-DOS format beat Apple for supremacy among personal computer users. Both home video and personal computing were naturals for standardization because they display "network externalities." This means that the benefits to any one user of a given format depend on how many others use that format. Once a particular format reaches a "tipping point" in terms of market share, the entire market moves in that direction and the format becomes the industry standard. Much time and money can be wasted waiting for the tipping point, however, and some technologies display such weak network effects that standardization may never happen. This seems to be the case for EMR. Patients may gain a lot from standardization, but providers get very little. Thus there is little meaningful network externality effect and the market has no momentum to standardize.

To avoid inefficient and time consuming standards battles, industries often create standard-setting consortia that agree to a common format. The DVD consortium did this in the mid-1990s and the result was the fastest growing consumer electronics innovation in history. Standardization sometimes requires a push from the government. This is what happened with the creation of the high definition television standard. Fortunately the federal government is now pushing for standardizing EMR.

There is bipartisan agreement in Congress for the need to standardize EMR and President Bush has made this a national goal to achieve by 2014. Tremendous progress is already underway. The Healthcare Information Technology Standards Panel (HITSP), a consortium of over two hundred IT vendors, healthcare providers and payers, and public sector agencies, was formed in late 2005 under the auspices of the American National Standards Institute and chaired by Dr. John Halamka, the chief information officer of the Harvard Medical School. HITSP is developing a set of standards to "enable and support widespread interoperability among healthcare software applications."[6] In January 2007, the U.S. Department of Health and Human Services secretary, Michael Leavitt, accepted thirty consensus standards proposed by the HITSP. These standards will ensure compatibility across providers' office systems, and among providers' systems, laboratory systems and patient-centered systems such as those fostered by CDHPs. According to Halamka, the standards will "empower consumers to be stewards of their own health information."[7]

By January 2008, all new and upgraded federal health information systems will have to comply with these standards. The federal government should go further and require providers to adopt EMRs that use the same standard; a threat to withhold Medicare payments would be sufficient to make this a reality. I expect that the private sector would soon follow suit, as private payers often take their cue from Medicare.[8] Most hospitals already have or are considering adopting EMR and will only weakly oppose such a requirement. Physicians may require a bit of convincing.

It will cost a solo practitioner somewhere around $12,000 to $15,000 annually (including amortized upfront costs) to move to EMR. This is a big expense, even for a physician. If we are to get physicians on board with EMR, then the path of least resistance would be to subsidize adoption, perhaps by adding an EMR "factor" to the RBRVS. That is to say, all physician fees would increase by some nominal amount (likely less than 1 percent) to cover the cost.

This approach would meet with some opposition, however, because the EMR factor that is profit neutral for the average physician would not be sufficient to cover the costs for solo practitioners and small groups. Even so, I see no economic justification for giving solo practitioners a bigger subsidy. Solo practice is noneconomical; EMR is just one more diseconomy of scale. If patients want the personal touch and doctors want the luxury of solo practice, then they should bear the cost. Given the importance of gaining speedy acceptance of EMR, it still might be necessary to grease the skids. An extra $10 to $20 billion spread out over two to three years should be enough to pay for half the cost of putting EMR in every doctor's office, no matter what the size of the practice. This would represent less than 0.5 percent of total healthcare spending. The payback for society, in terms of the ability to implement meaningful healthcare reform, would be vastly higher.

Improving Data Collection

A big problem with administrative claims data is that it does not include sufficient risk adjusters or outcomes. This will be remedied once we have integrated EMRs. In the meantime, we can use the present claims system to gather additional clinical data. New York State requires hospitals to report a small number of risk adjusters for heart patients, in addition to traditional claims information. The result is the best report card in the nation. Medicare should do the same, requesting diagnosis-specific risk adjusters for every inpatient and outpatient. Medicare should also request more detailed outcomes data, such as the social and functioning status data that I describe below.

Confidentiality

Electronic health data systems contain confidential patient diagnostic information. Computer hackers could access this information with dire results. Individuals with chronic conditions might find it difficult to obtain insurance or employment. Many people could be subject to embarrassment, derision, or worse. Opponents of implementing standardized EMRs conjure up scenarios like these. But this describes the *current* state of affairs. Medicare administrative claims data is stored electronically and contains enough diagnostic information to allow anyone to wreak havoc with the lives of beneficiaries. The same is true for private insurance administrative claims. Fortunately the guardians of this data have been on their toes and there appear to have been no widespread instances of abuse. EMR will not make things worse. Centralized safeguards, including coding to mask individual identities, could make this information even more difficult to steal.

Unfortunately regulators have erected a host of barriers to information to data integration, all in the name of protecting privacy of medical information. Recent research shows that new privacy protection laws have significantly reduced the rate at which providers adopt EMR.[9] Concerns about confidentiality are valid, but have always been present. EMR does not raise the threat level, and regulations that limit the adoption of EMR will have disastrous consequences for the entire health system. When it comes to privacy protection, the cat is already out of the bag. Let's get the best cat we can.

Recapitulation

It is little exaggeration to say that every other major ongoing healthcare initiative depends on the success of EMR. EMRs must be our top priority. But there is a lot more we can do to revive our healthcare system.

Make CDHPs Work

There are only a handful of ways to counter the excesses of Marcus Welby era incentives. The government can put a lid on prices and limit access to technology. Done halfheartedly, as has been the case with rate setting and CON, this has little impact. Done all out, as is the case in Canada and elsewhere, costs can be kept under control, though queuing for care is an inevitable byproduct. In any event, a full-blown government takeover of the U.S. healthcare system seems no more likely to win congressional approval today than any time in our past, potential claims of "this time is different" notwithstanding. Private insurers have their own options for cutting costs. They can salary or capitate providers, "reversing" the economics as Kaiser once put it. But this solution has succumbed to the HMO backlash.

If we shift the focus of cost containment away from payers and providers, then we must put the onus on patients. This is what CDHP is supposed to be about. Amidst all the hoopla, the economic reality is that the financial incentives in today's CDHP plans are inadequate. CDHP deductibles are too low and 100 percent last-dollar coverage kicks in too soon. As a result, CDHPs will have little impact on any patient who is hospitalized or anyone with a chronic illness.

The solution is simple: Change the financial incentives. Instead of a 100 percent deductible of $5,000, try a 25 percent copayment up to a ceiling of $20,000.[10] Patients would face the same maximum expenditure of $5,000, thereby securing the same degree of financial security. But with this redesigned CDHP, almost all enrollees, even those with chronic illnesses or requiring hospitalization, will have an incentive to shop around for providers offering the best value. Shopping around is what makes markets work, because it forces providers to become more efficient.[11] Even patients who do not shop around will get the benefits from efficient providers.

A bit of experimentation could further strengthen CDHPs. If possible, copayments should be calibrated to make patients sensitive to the marginal expense of additional healthcare. For example, a diabetic who is sure to spend at least $20,000 annually should get the first $20,000 free and then face cost-sharing provisions up to $40,000. The current rules enabling tax deductibility of HSAs limit the ability of plans to experiment with copayments. Let's relax the rules.

Simplify the Financial Instruments

One goal of CDHPs is to make it easier for patients to be good healthcare consumers. But HSAs add a new layer of complexity to healthcare financing. Some enrollees are having difficulty getting payments from their HSAs to providers who are unaccustomed to this new financial instrument. I suspect that this problem will quickly sort itself out. But there is a second problem that may only get worse over time as HSAs grow into valuable retirement investment vehicles. Banks and brokerage houses are eager to get into the business of managing HSAs. As the business of managing HSAs grows alongside the business of managing individual retirement accounts, so, too, will the requisite administrative burdens and account management fees.

There is a simple solution. Congress should do away with HSAs and instead change the rules regarding IRAs. Employers should be permitted to contribute up to an extra $5,000 annually into their employee's tax deferred retirement accounts. Individuals may use their retirement accounts for uncovered medical expenses without penalty, up to an annual limit of $5,000. CDHPs can keep the same copayments and ceilings or experiment as I described above. This approach keeps all of the financial features of CDHPs and HSAs without creating yet another retirement account. The only caveat is that, like with CHDPs, wealthier taxpayers would be the biggest winners because they have the highest tax rates. If possible, we should couple this proposal with another change that will balance out the tax impact.

Level the Insurance Market Playing Field

HSAs are a "if you can't beat them, join them" approach to leveling the tax playing field. There are three problems with this approach. First, it does nothing to level the playing field for HMOs, for which big deductibles make little sense. Second, it continues to make health insurance artificially less expensive than all other goods and services, distorting purchases toward healthcare and away from everything else. Third, it has the largest distortionary effect for the wealthiest taxpayers who face the highest marginal income tax rates.

There is a "beat 'em" solution: eliminate tax deductibility for all health insurance. This would level the playing field while eliminating one of the most regressive elements of the tax code. Of course, eliminating a $200 billion tax break for the middle class and wealthy is a political nonstarter. In addition, research on insurance take up suggests that if we take away the tax benefits, more workers may choose to go without insurance.

Thirty years ago, Alain Enthoven proposed capping the deduction at the premium charged by the typical HMO. This would keep most of the tax subsidy intact and, at the same time, the tax code would no longer subsidize the purchase of excessively generous health insurance. Various versions of this idea have floated around ever since, most capping deductibility at or around the cost of the "median" plan in the market. If implemented today, this would give HMOs a fairer chance against more costly plans. It would also eliminate the unnecessary intermingling of health insurance with retirement investing that characterizes CDHP.

Although this proposal forces enrollees to bear the full incremental cost of expensive plans, it still gives a tax break to "median" plans relative to "cheap" ones. This is easily remedied by setting a lower cap on deductibility. But even this cannot disguise the regressivity of proposals that rely on tax deductions. We ought to move to a neutral or even a progressive tax system. Many economists believe that the best way to do this is to move from tax deductions to tax credits. I will discuss this a bit further when I explore options for covering more of the uninsured. First, I will offer other suggestions for improving efficiency and quality.

Sensible Pricing

It is staggering to think that the average American spends over $7,000 annually on medical care but has little idea of what anything costs. I am not sure if there is a simple solution to this problem—the unpredictability and complexity of the medical care process make it all but impossible for any individual patient to do a sensible job of comparison shopping. Even so, we should not cut too much slack for an industry whose pricing system seems deliberately designed to confuse patients. We could make great strides in improving efficiency if we paid more attention to pricing, not so much to give more information to consumers, but more to give the right incentives to providers.

In a textbook competitive market, prices are supposed signal to consumers the amount that goods and services cost to produce, so that no one purchases something that costs more than it is worth. Prices are also supposed to signal to producers the amount that goods and services are worth to consumers, so that producers do not produce things that have little value. This is how markets reach efficient outcomes. This is not how healthcare markets work and the resulting inefficiencies are massive. CDHPs address moral hazard distortions on the demand side. There are less well-known and equally pernicious distortions on the supply side.

Consider "per diem" payments in which hospitals receive a fixed price for each day a patient is in the hospital. Once a patient is medically ready for discharge, the price of extending the hospital stay vastly exceeds the value and the cost. Hospitals see this distorted pricing and try to keep their per diem patients longer than necessary. In contrast, the prospective payment system pays hospitals nothing for each extra day. A price of zero is obviously well below both value and cost, so hospitals try to discharge prospective payment patients too early. The pricing of heart surgery (and other specialty services) offers another example of distorted prices. It is often more valuable to treat the most severely ill cardiac patients, in the sense that they have the most to gain from a successful operation. Unfortunately these patients are also the most costly to treat. In practice, the price that hospitals receive for heart surgery often does not vary with severity. The result is that price does not provide the proper signal of value, giving hospitals a financial incentive to treat the least severely ill. This seems to be a big motivation behind the establishment of specialty heart hospitals, whose detractors accuse of cherry picking the healthiest (re: most profitable) patients.

Payers know about these distortions and are taking a few steps in the right direction. A few private payers set lower per diems for the last few days of an inpatient stay. Medicare is refining DRG adjustments to assure that specialty hospitals cannot easily prosper by cherry picking. These are small but important steps toward eliminating the tactics that providers and payers currently use to arbitrage the system. But many distortions remain, none better exemplified than in the so-called overuse of the emergency room.

The ER Myth

Nowhere is the gap between price and cost bigger than for routine care delivered in the emergency room. Patients who go to the ER for routine care must wait for a lull in the action, when the medical staff is not attending to more urgent cases. When that lull arrives, patients are treated by doctors and nurses who would otherwise be waiting for the next emergency. The incremental cost of their time is next to nothing. But the hospital's price is astronomical. This is why insurers try to prevent their enrollees from visiting ERs even though the cost to the healthcare system is negligible. Hospitals could fix this problem by billing routine care at marginal cost and billing true emergencies to cover the cost of the standby capacity that has been waiting to handle them. The same story is true, more or less, for hospital-based outpatient care. Prices bear no relation to cost and the result is that outpatients are driven away from hospitals.

Ironically, in our zeal to push everything away from the hospital, we have failed to reduce the costs of hospital infrastructure while adding billions of dollars for outpatient infrastructure. There is nothing wrong with community-based clinics or with patients who value convenience. But the system should not provide financial incentives to deliver care in inefficient ways. It is no wonder that healthcare costs have continued to skyrocket even as we push more and more care to outpatient settings.

Other Pricing Remedies

There are many other examples of pricing distortions with pernicious effects. Prospective payment punishes hospitals that treat patients with above average medical needs. Economists who have studied inpatient pricing unanimously agree that payers should move to a two-part payment system that includes (1) a fixed fee per admission (adjusted for the DRG) that is less than the current fee, and (2) some percentage of the total cost of treatment. This would simultaneously reduce gaming and increase the quality of care given to the sickest patients.

In the same vein, the DRG classification system needs refining. There are currently 590 DRGs, with considerable variation in medical needs within each one. This means that within any diagnosis, some patients are more profitable than others resulting in cherry picking and other unwanted behaviors. Payers are not too concerned about this because they feel that with fixed payments, their overall costs will be unaffected. This is short-sighted. These games drive up total system costs and often place patients in hospitals that do not ideally meet their needs. Health services researchers have field-tested a variety of methods for refining risk adjusters. Payers should embrace them.

Finally the practice of setting different prices for each element of the medical care process can lead to numerous inefficiencies, because providers try to maximize their own reimbursements, rather than reduce total costs. This (and most other pricing problems) can be fixed by moving to a single episode of illness payment.

Episode of Illness Payments

There has been considerable effort over at least two decades to design "episode of illness" payments that assign a lump sum payment to a provider organization for each episode of illness treated. For example, a provider organization might receive $40,000 for a hip replacement, which would cover the cost of diagnosis, surgery, and rehabilitation. This would give the organization responsibility for finding the lowest-cost way to delivery the full gamut of services. The physician-hospital organizations of the 1980s and 1990s were developed along these lines, but payments were calibrated only for age and sex and PHOs had inadequate internal monitoring and compensation systems. As a result, it was difficult for the PHO to hold each member physician accountable for cost containment. I think that EMRs will greatly improve the ability of organizations to implement episode-of-illness payment systems. Episode-of-illness payments may yet be resurrected.[12]

Keep Pushing on Quality

As we continue to pay more attention to healthcare costs, we had better not neglect quality. The good news is that payers and employers are not just talking about quality; they are taking bold steps to measure and reward the best providers. The bad news is that they have a long way to go in terms of measurement and compensation systems. The worse news is that they need patients to help, but most patients seem blissfully unaware of the quality movement.

Toward Better Report Cards

All too often, we measure what we can, not what we should. Perhaps the best known example of this is the push to measure school performance on the basis of test scores. The result is predictable—teaching to the test with little apparent improvement in anything that is not captured by standardized testing. The healthcare report card movement often succumbs to the same trap. Everyone understands that the ideal report card should measure the outcomes that matter most (e.g., mortality, quality of life) and use comprehensive risk adjusters (i.e., those available on medical records). But most report cards measure one or two secondary outcomes (i.e., postsurgical complications) and use minimal risk adjusters (i.e., those available in administrative claims.) We might be better off if we measured nothing at all!

New York State's surgery mortality report cards are better than most because the state obtains crucial risk adjustment data from the hospital medical records. Other states should follow suit. This may invite upcoding, but the virtues of rich risk adjustment should outweigh such criticism. The proof is in the pudding. There may be some gaming going on in New York, but hospitals there are less likely to invoke the "holy writ" that their patients are sicker and instead have engaged in the difficult task of actually improving quality.

New York can do even better, and the rest of the nation can follow their lead.[13] New York should use all statistically valid risk adjusters, including race and prior health spending, not just those that have a direct medical link to outcomes. This will have the twin virtues of increasing the precision of the rankings and eliminating some of the gaming. States should also explore constructing report cards based on diagnosis (e.g., heart failure), not the chosen procedure (e.g., heart surgery). This will further limit gamesmanship. Perhaps the most important step is to measure a broader set of outcomes. Mortality is important. For many conditions, other outcomes matter even more. Can an asthma patient return to work? Can a hip replacement patient climb stairs? Is the cancer patient in pain? Once we get the answers to these questions, we can produce meaningful outcome report cards for wide range of procedures and conditions, not just high risk surgery.

Once again, health services researchers have field-tested the necessary metrics. John Ware and Cathy Sherbourne have pioneered and validated a comprehensive outcomes measurement tool, the SF-36 patient questionnaire. The thirty-six questions generate eight different outcomes scores, including physical functioning (such as ability to climb stairs), social functioning (such as ability to work), mental health, and bodily pain.[14] Researchers have also developed disease specific surveys, such as the asthma impact survey. Unfortunately providers rarely administer the SF-36 (or the two-minute SF-12 or the new, even shorter, SF-8) to their patients. Let's find a way to collect this information every year.

Harvard's David Cutler has even loftier ambitions. He proposes creating National Health Accounts (NHAs). Similar to the gross domestic product, which measures the sum total of our economic output, NHAs would measure the sum total of our nation's health, relying on metrics such as Quality Adjusted Life Years (QALYs) and the closely related Healthy Years Equivalents (HYEs). Cutler's plan to track the QALY score of the nation is ambitious and audacious. But think of the benefits. By tracking each individual's health status, as measured by their QALY scores, we can assess the overall quality of care that patients are receiving and say goodbye to today's narrowly focused report cards that miss the forest for the trees. By tracking the entire population's QALY scores we can determine how well the overall health system is functioning. These are worthy goals.

Go Slow with P4P

Americans enthusiastically embraced the efforts of their physicians to assure quality. Payers are now assuming responsibility for quality assurance through their P4P programs. I am not sure if this is what patients want.

Patients already have their own P4P mechanism—it is called repeat purchase. If we do not like our doctors, we look for new ones. If we want our doctors to provide smoking cessation advice or book an appointment within twenty-four hours—two popular P4P metrics—we can take our business elsewhere when they do not. We do not need our payers intervening in such decisions.

Some P4P metrics are more sophisticated and it might be asking too much for patients to pay attention to things like CPOE adoption. But I am leery of P4P micromanagement. As we learned from the failures of utilization review, it is a big step from informing providers about what works to paying them to do what works. I believe that providers want to do the right thing. If they choose not to abide by the latest P4P metrics, then more often than not it is because they are putting their money and time where they think it will do more good.

Theory and emerging evidence also suggest that payers should take multitasking seriously. I pose the following challenge to any payer who is currently engaged in P4P. Find two measurable tasks, call them A and B, that compete for a provider's time or money. Implement a P4P scheme that rewards A and measure whether providers cut back on B. If so, then there is a problem. The solution is not to reward B. There is always a task C and D and E and so forth. And if payers reward the entire alphabet, why give doctors any discretion? This is the wrong way to go.

It is far more prudent to reward outcomes. Do not worry that the link between provider actions and patient outcomes is sometimes indirect. Weak outcomes-based incentives can have powerful effects. Providers will still gain by improving quality. Besides, outcomes-based rewards promote overall improvements in quality, because they differentiate among providers who are superior in intangible ways, such as diagnostic skill. Task-based P4P will never do this.

We could do without P4P altogether if patients would respond more strongly to report cards. Despite some encouraging evidence from New York State, it seems that most report cards go unheeded. It is hard to blame patients who still rely on their doctors to guide them through the healthcare system. It is our doctors who must do a better job of reacting to report cards. If Dr. Welby ever found out that Lang Memorial Hospital had unacceptably high surgical mortality rates, I am sure that he would have told his patients and complained bitterly to the surgical staff. It is the doctors more than the patients who need to leave Lake Woebegone. They could start by spending a few minutes a day examining report cards. Even better, medical schools could provide more training in the statistics of report cards, so that doctors can do a better job of evaluating them. If doctors are to be our agents in this information age, they need more than just medical training.

Keep Some Regulations Jettison the Rest

The list of healthcare regulations is longer than the list of healthcare acronyms in the appendix. I will examine a few that are salient to the success of our overall system.

What Works

Like it or not, the U.S. approach to healthcare depends on competition and there can be no competition without competitors. The antitrust laws are therefore essential to the system's success. If anything, the courts have been too eager to accept discredited ideas that competition in healthcare "doesn't work." Fortunately the U.S. Department of Justice and the Federal Trade Commission have been diligent in assembling the evidence demonstrating the benefits of provider competition and seem poised to convince skeptical judges and juries. The antitrust agencies should be just as diligent in assuring that payers remain competitive.

Insurance markets require additional oversight lest they fall victim to cream skimming and adverse selection. Employer-sponsored coverage still works for most Americans and COBRA and HIPAA guaranteed renewability and other rules sustain risk pools and increase portability. Until we find a more comprehensive approach (which may retain an important role for employers), this hodgepodge of regulations is far better than nothing.

Medicare funding continues to be based on an intergenerational social contract that will soon confront unpleasant demographic realities, with not enough workers supporting too many beneficiaries. Congress already knows about both the problems and the limited set of viable solutions for Medicare's looming budget crisis. There is no time to act like the present, but I am scarcely the first to offer such advice and, like those before me, I expect my words will go unheeded.

As long as traditional Medicare endures, the Center for Medicare and Medicaid Services will necessarily have its hands in the marketplace. Just as private insurers must set rules governing payments to providers and access to services, so, too, must Medicare. The list of innovative rules originating with Medicare is impressive, and the willingness of the private sector to mirror Medicare's practices is telling. Medicare introduced the DRG system for paying hospitals and the RBRVS system for doctors. Most MCOs followed suit. Medicare created the Professional Review Organizations that spun off private utilization review agencies. Medicare is pushing for information technology standards and exploring how to incorporate cost-effectiveness analysis into drug pricing. Perhaps I am hopelessly biased, but I think that one reason for Medicare's successful track record as a regulator is that the program has a long history of relying on the best and brightest minds from academia to advise, develop, and implement program changes without getting too heavy handed.[15] This approach to regulation seems to have worked.

What Doesn't Work

Even as the FTC and DOJ try to maintain competition, many states have tried to undermine it. Starting in the 1990s, some states have required MCOs to contract with "any willing provider," effectively eviscerating selective contracting. In most states, the rules apply only to retail pharmacy, but in a few states they also apply to hospitals and doctors. The broadening of networks in response to the managed care backlash took the pressure off of other states to enact similar rules, but provider lobbying groups are resurrecting the idea. Legislators should ignore them. A few states have considered doing away with competition altogether by giving doctors permission to openly collude. Fortunately these proposals have generally not gone far and even if they are enacted, they may not preempt federal antitrust laws.

Certificate of Need laws are the most egregious anticompetitive regulations, artifacts of bygone days when most patients had indemnity insurance and most hospitals received cost-based reimbursement. CON now serves as a wasteful barrier to much needed competition. Hospitals that obtained precious bed licenses decades ago are protected from competition for the indefinite future, regardless of how well they meet the needs of their communities. Many states have dropped their CON laws. The rest of the nation should follow suit.

I have recently heard two new justifications for CON from legislators in states that do not adequately fund Medicaid or cover the uninsured. One argument is that CON protects safety net hospitals from competition. With CON, legislators can sustain the hidden cross-subsidies of the preselective contracting era, rather than raise the taxes necessary to properly fund Medicaid and cover the uninsured. This is political subterfuge. The irony is that legislators will have to raise taxes anyway, because Medicaid and Medicare HMOs have to raise their premiums to pay the rates commanded by monopoly hospitals.

Legislators would also like to prevent entry by specialty hospitals that might cherry pick the most profitable patients, leaving community hospitals with the burden of caring for Medicaid patients and the uninsured. There is some merit to this.[16] But once again, CON is being used to overcome other shortcomings in the system and we all pay higher prices as a result. Our legislators should stop applying Band-Aids on top of Band-Aids.

States have also been eager to regulate insurance markets. Insurance benefits mandates drive up premiums for exactly those buyers who can least afford it—small businesses and individuals who do not enjoy ERISA exemptions. About ten states allow small firms to purchase "Mandate-lite" plans. Forty others need to join them. At the same time, the federal government should exempt Association Health Plans from state mandates (much as ERISA exempts self-insured firms.) This would do far more to help small firms buy low-cost health insurance than all the purchasing pools put together.

In the tradition of all "two handed economists," I do have a few misgivings about eliminating all mandates. Insurers who offer stripped down policies stand to enjoy favorable risk selection. I would require a minimum set of coverage requirements, such as those included in Medicare Parts B and D (i.e., including prescription drugs). This would exclude a myriad of politically motivated mandates that plague state coverage rules.

If we mandate nothing else, it should be a broad set of preventive healthcare services. It is a dirty little secret of the industry that employers and insurers lack adequate incentives to cover prevention. The logic is air tight: why should employers and insurers pay for services today that will prevent spending by some other employer or insurer years from now? The problem is even worse for children's preventive services; the odds of the insurer enjoying the payoff from encouraging healthy childhood behaviors are nil. This is a classic problem in economics and has a classic solution. If individually selfish behavior leaves everyone worse off, then we should promote "selflessness." This is how we limit pollution, keep the highways safe, and raise money for the public defense. We ought to mandate that all insurers cover preventive measures. We should go one further, overwriting ERISA to force self-insured plans to do the same. An expert panel could routinely review the evidence to determine which preventive measures merit coverage; not every preventive service is cost-effective.

Covering the Uninsured

At some point in the late 1960s, health policy makers must have thought that they had solved the access problem. The vast majority of Americans had coverage through their employers. Medicare and Medicaid covered the elderly, the disabled, and many of the indigent. Nonprofit hospitals, community health centers, and government providers of last resort provided a safety net for the millions who remained uninsured. To a large extent, this uniquely American approach to healthcare reflected America's values, accepting modest inequities in access in exchange for a largely free market system. Only it turns out that the inequities in access were not modest. We did not have a safety net so much as a torn and tattered patchwork quilt. In the remainder of this book, I will describe how we can cover the uninsured while still maintaining competition.

From Tax Deductions to Tax Credits

When the federal government made health insurance tax deductible after World War II, it catalyzed an already growing private health insurance market. But it also distorted the economics of the insurance market, placing lower-cost insurance plans at a competitive disadvantage. With HIPAA of 1997, Congress restored some balance in the tax treatment of insurance by allowing individuals to create taxexempt HSAs for their CDHPs. This does nothing to restore competitive balance for other low-cost plans, however. President Bush's has proposed a uniform tax deduction for any health insurance policy. This would level the playing field but maintains regressivity and will do little to expand coverage to the uninsured. Many low-income individuals decline to take up insurance even if their employers are paying 75 percent or more of the premium. A tax deduction that amounts to no more than 25 percent of the premium for most wage earners is not going to improve take up. This will require a different approach.

Leading economists including Mark Pauly and Jonathan Gruber favor moving away from tax deductions and toward tax credits. With tax credits, individuals who purchase insurance would be eligible for a federal income tax refund based on the price of the insurance and their income. Tax credits have many advantages over other options. Tax credits sever the link between employment and the funding of coverage, thereby limiting labor market spillovers. The parameters of the credit can be chosen to assure a level playing field and balance the desires for a neutral or progressive tax structure, higher take up, and limited budget impact. In fact, economists estimate that tax credits are far more cost effective than tax deductions.

Although tax credits are the best way to encourage take-up, there is no way to assure 100 percent take-up short of having the government pay 100 percent of the premium. Consider that in some states, insurance for a family of four can cost $12,000 or more. If the tax credit was set at $9,000 per household, then families would still need to come up with $3,000 to pay for coverage. Some families would choose not to do so.

It will be prohibitively costly to rely solely on the carrot of the tax credit to assure universal coverage. We need some sticks. The biggest stick is purchase mandates. All individuals earning at least twice the poverty level should contribute toward a relatively low-cost health insurance plan. If they refuse to purchase insurance, they should pay a penalty enforced through the tax code. The amount of the mandate should vary by income, of course. There is no other way to prevent those with means from free riding on a market-based system. Anyone without health insurance is a freeloader in the making.

Pay or Play

I still expect most Americans will turn to their employers to purchase health insurance for them. But many employers may balk, preferring to free ride on the system. Just as purchase mandates will prevent free riding by individuals, a "pay-or-play" rule would prevent free riding by employers. Employers either provide group insurance or pay a tax. Tax credits would be granted only to individuals whose employers elect not to play. Massachusetts is trying this combination and California's Governor Schwarzenegger has proposed a similar approach. No one yet knows whether a tax credit sufficient to assure individual take-up will also cause a wholesale withdrawal of employer sponsored coverage. Massachusetts will provide us with a natural experiment.

I like the pay-or-play approach for several reasons. First, it maintains the group market that works reasonably well for most working Americans. Second, it can be calibrated to be roughly revenue neutral for most firms. Third, it keeps employers (and through them, their employees) actively interested in the health economy. I would rather decentralize insurance purchasing among employers, each of whom is competing for employees, than vest it with local governments.

The Fork in the Road

If we sweep aside the details, there are essentially two divergent paths that we can take to cover the uninsured. We can expand coverage in the private sector, through an Enthoven-style voucher scheme, or a combination of an employer mandate, individual mandate, and tax credits. The alternative it to adopt a publicly financed single-payer system. Congress has wrestled with these two choices for decades with only one breakthrough, the creation of Medicare and Medicaid. The real action in healthcare reform today is taking place in the states, where the prospects are encouraging. No one can predict the fate of the ongoing experiments in Maine and Massachusetts. But at least we will have experiments to study and learn from.

This is just the beginning. Half of the states are considering health reform initiatives. If anything is standing in the way, it is the justifiable fear among state lawmakers that the new taxes required to fund expansion of coverage will drive businesses to neighboring states. There is a simple way to prevent this. Congress should mandate that all states reach targets for the number of uninsured, say, below 5 percent within 5 years. Congress could tie compliance to a set of financial carrots and sticks, as it does with Medicaid. To prevent a race to the bottom, Congress should also specify a minimum benefit package. It would then be up to each state to devise the most effective way of meeting these coverage goals.

Experimentation—allowing states to respond flexibly to critical policy problems—is the essence of American federalism.[17] Some states will follow Massachusetts's lead and adopt a market-based system. Others may opt for government control. President Bush endorses this federalist approach and is even open to the possibility that government-controlled systems outperform market-based systems.[18] So am I.

Unless we institute a hard spending cap, no expansion in coverage will come for free. Congress will have to grease the skids to get states to go along. Congress should therefore cap the tax deductibility of health insurance, or move from tax deductibility to tax credits. By reducing the tax subsidy there should be enough money to go around, and I expect that most states will be eager to run with it.

Democrats are likely to oppose this approach for two reasons. First, it will not guarantee universal coverage. The fact is that anything short of a single-payer system will fall short of universal coverage. Some businesses will fail to either pay or play, and some individuals will refuse to purchase anything less than fully subsidized insurance. Second, most states are likely to try market-based reforms, as these have the smallest tax burden. Perhaps a compromise is possible. Some Democrats have proposed raising the SCHIP income threshold to 400 percent of the federal poverty level. Republicans object that under this proposal, 70 percent of America's children would have government coverage. Even so, the actual cost of expanding SCHIP coverage would be relatively small; with the exception of neonates (most of whom are already covered under Medicaid or SCHIP), medical costs for children tend to be modest. SCHIP expansion thus might prove to be a relatively low-cost yet critical piece of a more comprehensive plan to cover the uninsured, one that might allow all of the stakeholders in the longstanding debate about healthcare reform to finally find common ground.

With government insuring the young and the old, we would rely on states to find ways to assure that all adults under age sixty-five have coverage, with partial funding coming from Congress. A similar compromise was struck when Congress created the federal Medicare program but gave control of Medicaid to the states. After forty years of gridlock, it could not hurt to try the same approach.

If I Had to Choose

In the last week of my health economics class, my students discuss healthcare reform. After assessing the pros and cons of various options, my students invariably ask whether I prefer a government or market-based solution. The federalist approach gets me off the hook.

As a researcher, I can wait a few years and see which solution is most effective. But if federalism is not possible, I know what choice I would make.

As much as I believe in the power of markets as a force for quality improvement and efficiency, the performance of healthcare markets remains mixed. At the same time, there is much to be said for a single-payer system. It is our best chance to get close to 100 percent coverage. It will be equitable. We may be able to cut 10 percent or more out of the overall healthcare budget simply by limiting administrative costs. And legislators can place a hard cap on healthcare spending, limiting future growth.

Many will criticize such a government takeover of the financing of the system, and not without cause. Good things rarely happen when U.S. politicians meddle excessively in any sector of the economy and the specter of socialized medicine would loom large. But this criticism must be weighed against the success of Medicare. Moreover, this proposal falls far short of socializing medicine, because providers will remain in the private sector. If we set the initial budget at the current level of health spending, we can even avoid Canadian-style rationing (at least for now).

If we instead expand the private sector, there is no guarantee that we can cover all the uninsured. Nor could we guarantee cost containment. If anything, expanding insurance through the private sector is likely to drive up total spending, as millions of currently uninsured Americans gain full access to the system. Without the hard spending cap of a single-payer system, healthcare costs could continue to climb.

The arguments in favor a single-payer system are very seductive. I sometimes feel the tug, until I consider the nuances. For one thing, there is nothing inherently wrong with spending more money on healthcare, provided that we spend our money wisely. Competition, when it works, is the best way to allocate our healthcare dollars. In addition, a single-payer system must be financed through taxes that will inevitably place a drag on the economy. These are reasonably compelling arguments for redoubling our efforts to support competitive healthcare markets. But it is when I look at the evolution of our healthcare system over the past century that I fully appreciate the dangers of a single-payer system and I am finally able to resist its temptation.

Technological Change

My colleague Burton Weisbrod argues that the most important long-run engine of our healthcare system is technological change.[19] It is hard to look at the history of the healthcare system and disagree. The X-rays and antiseptics introduced at the end of the nineteenth century made it possible for surgeons to ply their trade, but also drove up costs and led the Committee on the Costs of Medical Care to recognize the need for health insurance. The remarkable list of innovations from the mid-twentieth century until today have saved countless lives and added immensely to the quality of life, but once again these have come at a considerable financial cost. The next generation of medical innovation may produce even greater health benefits, even as we worry about having the wherewithal to afford them. No debate about national health reform is complete without considering the consequences for innovation.

A good starting point is to ask whether new medical technology has been worth the cost. I recall a fascinating discussion of this question at a conference hosted by Northwestern University about a decade ago. One of the featured speakers was Jim Mortimer, the president of the Midwest Business Group on Health. An audience member asked if society was better off with 1990s technology at 1990s costs, or 1980s technology at 1980s costs. Without hesitation, Mortimer said that he would rather have 1980s technology at 1980s costs. I suspect he would give the same answer if the comparison were brought up to date.

Mortimer must have done some kind of cost-benefit analysis in his head and concluded that the benefits of a decade's worth of new technology, in terms of longevity and quality of life, were not worth the extra cost. We do not have to rely on Mortimer's snap judgment. It is possible to quantify the benefits of new technology, in dollars, and directly perform the required cost-benefit analysis.

David Cutler and several of his colleagues have performed exactly this calculation.[20] They have estimated the benefits, both in terms of life-years saved and QALYs, from technological improvements in the treatment of a wide range of diseases, including heart disease and cancer. They have drawn on survey research and economic studies to put a dollar value on the health improvements.[21] Finally they have compared the dollar value of benefits against the increase in medical costs.

Cutler et al. confirm that new technologies are very costly, but the benefits outweigh the costs by as much as five to one. That is a remarkable return on investment and it is hard to find another sector of the economy that offers anything close to it. There is no doubt that much of what we spend on technology is wasted in unnecessary tests and procedures. Even accounting for this waste, the benefits are huge. We should all want today's technology at today's costs. It is worth every penny.

We are on the cusp of yet another wave of medical innovation. Advances in biotechnology and pharmacogenomics will revolutionize the diagnosis and treatment of disease by allowing doctors to decode the genetic causes of illness and customize treatments to increase drug efficacy and minimize adverse drug reactions. Nanomedicine will enable doctors to use microrobots to monitor and repair organ systems at the molecular level. Device manufacturers are miniaturizing pacemakers, defibrillators, and brain stimulators to permit noninvasive procedures for a broader population. The FDA recently approved the first temporary implantable artificial heart for patients awaiting heart transplants. It will not be long before patients receive permanent implantable artificial hearts. And thanks to the lessons learned in the development of artificial skin for burn patients, it is only a matter of time before it is possible to grow entire organs. We do not yet know which of these breakthroughs will prove to have widespread practical value, but it is certain that the practice of medicine in the not too distant future will look a lot different than it does today. This is unless the Luddites have their way and halt technological change in its tracks.

Much of the impetus for ongoing innovation comes from basic research funded by the National Institutes of Health and other public sector agencies. NIH funding is declining for the first time in recent memory. This is a terrible mistake that Congress must quickly rectify. The far more costly and time consuming process of developing innovations and bringing them to market will remain in the private sector.

Needless to say, private sector companies will not invest in innovation unless they can expect a reasonable profit, and here is where our choices for covering the uninsured become critical.[22]

For better or for worse, when medical R&D companies look to see where the opportunities for profits lie, they look to the United States. Although market forces here offer some restraints on the prices and availability of medical technology, the regulatory controls of other nations are far stricter. As a result, companies rely on U.S. profits to recover their R&D costs. Any major reforms of the U.S. healthcare system would therefore have a massively disproportionate effect on the pace of technological change worldwide.[23]

Expansion of coverage through the private sector is likely to have minimal impact on incentives for R&D or the pipeline of innovations. There is no guarantee that the benefits of new technologies will continue to outweigh the costs, of course, though a century of experience suggests they will. But if we nationalize the financing of healthcare, then sooner or later (probably sooner), legislators will face an imperative to hold the line on spending growth. We can expect them to follow the lead of other nations and set strict limits on spending for medical technology. This will cause technology firms to cut back R&D spending. No one can be sure how this will affect the pipeline of innovation, but it cannot be good.[24]

I suspect that legislators who want to nationalize healthcare financing will simply ignore the impact of today's regulations on tomorrow innovations, adopting a "what we don't know won't hurt us" approach to healthcare reform. It might even turn out that the most important innovations will still reach the market, even with tight-fisted federal budget controls. But no one can be certain of this, and no federalist experiment can provide the answer.

Coda

There are times when I think about the creeping incrementalism that has characterized our efforts to fill in the healthcare safety net and despair of ever making a serious dent in the problem. At these moments, I understand that a private health insurance system will never achieve

100 percent coverage and I feel ready to endorse a single-payer system. But then I think about my children (and their children yet unborn) and I ask whether I want to deny them medical technologies as yet undreamed of.

I am not ready to give up on market-based healthcare. We must do a much better job of covering the uninsured but we can do that without ripping everything up. Let us not be so single-minded in the pursuit of access today that we ignore how our choices will affect the entirety of the health system in the future. There is too much at stake.

An Alphabet Soup of Healthcare Acronyms

AMA: American Medical Association. Industry trade group that long opposed national health reform and managed care. It has softened its stand on health reform.

CCHP: Consumer Choice Health Plan. A proposal for national health insurance based on market principles. Developed by Alain Enthoven.

CCMC: Committee on the Costs of Medical Care. Published in 1932 a series of prescient reports on U.S. healthcare system.

CDHP: Consumer Directed Health Plan. An insurance plan that features a high deductible and a tax-advantaged Health Savings Account.

CHP: Comprehensive Health Planning Act of 1964. Encouraged states to engage in facilities planning.

CMS: Center for Medicare and Medicaid Services. Federal agency that administers Medicare and coordinates administration of Medicaid with the states.

COBRA: Comprehensive Omnibus Budget Reconciliation Act of 1983. Made it easier for workers to keep insurance after changing jobs.

CON: Certificate of Need. Requirement that hospitals obtain planning approval before expanding or building a new facility.

COSE: Council of Small Enterprises. Successful small business health insurance purchasing pool started in Cleveland in the 1970s.

CPOE: Computerized physician order entry. Computer system for tracking drug prescription and use in the hospital. Expensive but effective tool for reducing medication errors.

DRG: Diagnosis Related Group. Classification method introduced by HCFA in 1983 as part of the PPS. Used to set hospital reimbursements based on patient's condition and medical needs.

EMR: Electronic Medical Records. Long a dream of policy makers and may soon be a reality.

ERISA: Employee Retirement Income Security Act of 1974. Exempted self-funded employer-sponsored insurance plans from state insurance laws, including benefits mandates.

FMLA: Family and Medical Leave Act of 1993. Guarantees that workers can keep their health insurance coverage for up to twelve weeks if they leave work for illness, birth, or adoption of a child, or to care for a seriously ill family member.

FPL: Federal Poverty Level: Currently the FPL annual income is approximately $10,000 for an individual and $20,000 for a family of four.

GHC: Group Health Cooperative of Puget Sound. An early HMO.

HIP: Health Insurance Plan of New York. Another early HMO.

HCFA: Health Care Financing Organization. The old name for CMS.

HCTC: The Health Coverage Tax Credit program. Created in 2002, it provides tax credits worth up to 65 percent of the cost of insurance to workers who lose their jobs or take early retirement in industries deemed to have been displaced by foreign trade.

HIE: Health Insurance Experiment. The randomized study of how co-payments affect health spending and outcomes conducted by the RAND Corporation.

HIPAA: Health Insurance Portability and Accountability Act of 1996. Made it easier for displaced workers to continue insurance coverage.

HIPC: Health Insurance Plan of California. An unsuccessful small business health insurance purchasing pool. Started in California in 1992; shut down in 2006.

HMO: Health Maintenance Organization. A form of managed care that relies on reversing provider incentives to reduce unnecessary care. Critics claim that HMOs go too far and limit access to necessary care.

HSA (prior to 1990): Health Systems Agency. Local planning board responsible for administering CON laws.

HSA (after 2000): Health Savings Account. An account that an individual may draw from to pay for medical bills. Unused moneys roll over to the next year and, after age sixty-five, may be used for non-healthcare spending. Basically a rechristened MSA.

IDS: Integrated Delivery System. A system in which several hospitals own physician practices, other provider organizations, and offer their own capitated health plans.

IOM: Institutes of Medicine. Their two reports on healthcare quality spawned the current report card and pay for performance movements.

MSA: Medical Savings Account. An account that an individual may draw from to pay for medical bills. Unused moneys roll over to the next year and, after age sixty-five, may be used for nonhealthcare spending.

NHI: National Health Insurance. Still a pipedream.

OAA: Old Age Assistance program. Created in 1935, the earliest precursor to Medicare.

PCP: Primary care physician, i.e., Dr. Welby.

PHO: Physician Hospital Organization. A vertically integrated organization designed to accept capitated payments from insurers in exchange for comprehensive physician and hospital services.

PPO: Preferred Provider Organization. A form of managed care that relies on selective contracting to contain spending.

PPS: Prospective Payment System. Introduced by Medicare in 1983. Pays hospitals a flat fee per admission with the fee adjusted according to the patient's DRG.

PRO: Peer Review Organizations. Established to monitor compliance with the rules of the Medicare PPS.

PSRO: Professional Standards Review Organization. Part of the 1970s planning process. Precursors to PROs and utilization reviews.

QALY: Quality Adjusted Life Year. Scale used to measure overall health of an individual or entire population.

QOF: Quality and Outcomes Framework. Pay for performance program in the United Kingdom.

SCHIP: State Children's Health Insurance Program. A federally mandated/state-administered program to expand health insurance to low-income children.

TANF: Temporary Assistance for Needy Families. Created as part of the Welfare Reform Law of 1996. TANF assured Medicaid eligibility for pregnant women and their children while developing a plan for self-sufficiency.

UR: Utilization review. Third-party oversight of medical decision making, including preadmission screening and second surgical opinion programs.

✚ NOTES ✚

Introduction

1. Source: Third Bush-Kerry debate, in Tempe, AZ, October 13, 2004.
2. Clinton 2004.
3. Ginzberg 1977.
4. Stevens and Stevens 1974.

Chapter One
An Accidental Healthcare System

1. Source: Woolley and Peters 2007.
2. Temin 1988.
3. Stevens and Stevens 1974.
4. Starr 1982.
5. Burrow 1977.
6. Ibid., 151 and 152.
7. Committee on the Costs of Medical Care 1972, 19. (Hereafter referred to as CCMC 1972.)
8. Temin 1988.
9. The average $239 cost in 1928 would amount to about $2,700 today. Per capita income has increased six-fold during this time. Hence the $239 bill would represent the same percentage of income in 1928 as would a $16,200 medical bill today.
10. CCMC 1972, 21.
11. We do not always avoid risk, of course, but taking risks by playing poker or buying a lottery ticket involves an element of fun and fantasy that does not apply to medical spending.
12. CCMC 1972, 24.
13. Ibid., 109.
14. http://www.ssa.gov/history/ces.html.

15. Social Security Administration, "Report of the Committee on Economic Security." Issued January 1935 and obtained from the Social Security Administration Web site: http://www.ssa.gov/history/reports/ces.html.

16. Friedberg 1998.

17. Myers 1970.

18. Stevens and Stevens 1972.

19. Some economists argue that nonprofits may provide higher levels of "hard to measure" attributes such as training of personnel. The evidence on whether nonprofits really behave this way is mixed, with some studies suggesting that many nonprofits behave like "for profits in disguise."

20. Stevens and Stevens report that in 1960, the average elderly New Yorker receiving old-age income assistance had an annual medical bill of $700.

21. Health Insurance Association of America 1962.

22. Beito 1994.

23. Temin 1988.

24. Falk, Rorem, and Ring 1933.

25. Anderson 1975, 36.

26. Ibid.

27. Aetna actually offered its first health insurance product in 1899. It was offered only to individuals who already had life or accident coverage and was intended mainly as a marketing tool. Source: Aetna's corporate Web page: http://www.aetna.com/about/aetna/aag/history.html.

28. Source: Health Insurance Association of America 1959.

29. For more discussion, especially of the legal barriers to the creation of the Blues, see Cunningham and Cunningham 1997.

30. Pauly 1997.

31. The health benefits offered by many employers did not take the form of insurance as defined by the IRS, which complicated the IRS effort to rule on tax treatment (Thomasson 2003, 1374–75). See also, Comment 1954, 222–47.

32. Selden and Gray 2006, 1568–79.

33. Blendon and Benson 2001, 33–46.

Chapter Two
Paging Doctor Welby

1. Enthoven 1978, 650–58.

2. According to one survey, 70 percent of Americans had a "great deal" of confidence in those running the healthcare system. By the 1990s, that figure hovered near 30 percent (Blendon and Benson 2001, 33–46).

3. Fuchs 1974.

4. Roemer 1961, 36–42.

5. This is a variant of an economic concept known as Say's Law, namely that supply creates its own demand. Roemer actually found that hospitals only filled about half the new beds, so the law should be "A bed built is a bed half filled."

6. Arrow 1963, 941–73.

7. Ideally free markets promote efficient production and competitive pricing. Goods are produced at the lowest possible cost and sold to consumers at marginal costs. In turn, consumers purchase only those goods that are valued at more than their cost. This assures that an economy gets the most out of its available resources.

8. Though one could give up happiness to insure against health, for example by cutting back on dessert.

9. Arrow also noted the crucial role of nonprofit hospitals, stating "The very word profit is a signal that denies the trust relations." (1963, 208).

10. Evans 1974, 162–73.

11. Though not very relevant when Evans did his research, it is also true that physicians paid a fixed salary have an incentive to under prescribe.

12. Satterthwaite 1982.

13. It is also possible that patients in shortage areas were undertreated, though inducement theorists do not push this interpretation. Inducement could also be considered a response to malpractice, but the theory and much of the evidence predates such concerns.

14. Several papers give this line of argument. For example: Pauly and Satterthwaite 1981, 488–506 and Dranove and Wehner 1994, 61–73. One study that seems to confirm the inducement hypothesis is by Gruber and Owings, who show that the rate of caesarian sections increases with the supply of obstetricians. The magnitude of this effect is very small, however (Gruber and Owings 1996, 99–123).

15. For example, see, Barro and Beaulieu 2003 and Gaynor et al. 2004, 915–31.

16. Examples of such studies include Office of Inspector General, 1989 and Hillman et al. 1990.

17. Hemenway et al. 1990, 1059–63.

18. For a review of the older literature on hospital economies of scale, see Long 1985, 25–44.

19. For a summary, see Luft et al. 1990.

20. Pauly 1968, 531–37.

21. For example roughly two-thirds of physicians surveyed in 1955 acknowledged that health insurance increased the willingness of their patients to be hospitalized and undergo surgery. See Freidson and Feldman 1958.

22. As Nixon's plan became more expansive, responsibility for the research was transferred to the Department of Health, Education and Welfare (now the Department of Health and Human Services).

23. A partial list of RAND HIE participants (with subsequent academic positions) includes Robert Brook (UCLA), Emmett Keeler (UCLA), Arlene Leibowitz (UCLA), Willard Manning (University of Chicago), and Charles Phelps (University of Rochester). Newhouse is a professor at Harvard University and has also advised numerous federal healthcare agencies.

24. The enrollees lived in one of six locales including big cities, suburbs, and small cities.

25. Some participants in Seattle were enrolled in the Group Health Cooperative of Puget Sound, a large Health Maintenance Organization.

26. A thorough review can be found in Newhouse et al. 1993.

27. The picky reader will point out that one can never "get to" infinity through finite price increases. The less picky reader will understand the point my colleague was making.

28. By this time, the lines between Blue Cross and Blue Shield had blurred, as many Blue Cross plans sold medical coverage and many Blue Shield plans sold hospital coverage.

29. Robinson and Luft 1985, 333–56.

30. Weisbrod 1991, 523–52.

31. Mullan 2004.

32. Ibid.

33. Rothschild and Stiglitz 1976, 629–50. Both Rothschild and Stiglitz have had illustrious careers in academia. Rothschild is a chaired professor at Princeton and a fellow of the American Academy of Arts and Sciences (AAAS). Stiglitz is a chaired professor at Columbia University, a fellow of the AAAS, and served as the chairman of the Council of Economic Advisors under President Clinton.

34. These numbers are drawn from two large federally sponsored surveys, the Survey of Income and Program Participation (SIPP) and Medical Expenditure Panel Survey (MEPS). The latest figures may be slightly higher than what is reported here.

35. Source for Medicare and Medicaid enrollments: Health Insurance Association of America 1989.

36. Medicaid also provides aid to the indigent blind.

37. Source: Kaiser Family Foundation and Health Research and Education Trust 2005.

38. Medical underwriting involves predicting the medical expenditures for an individual or group and setting premiums accordingly.

39. Bundorf and Pauly 2006, 650–73.

40. Although it has proven difficult to produce a reliable estimate of the effect of insurance on bankruptcy rates, there is little doubt that the former is a major predictor of the latter.

41. Institutes of Medicine of the National Academies 2003.

42. This provision was a response to employer mandates that had been enacted by Hawaii. The law granted an exemption for Hawaii, which proved essential to Hawaii's subsequent enactment of an employer pay-or-play requirement.

43. For example, the conservative National Center for Policy Analysis cites a Milliman and Robertson analysis of just twelve mandates and concludes that they could increase insurance costs by 15 to 30 percent. The NCPA does not say that this would occur only if the benefits would not otherwise be offered. See NCPA 1997.

44. Jensen and Morrisey 1999.

45. Public finance economists Jonathan Gruber and Brigitte Madrian provide an excellent overview of this literature, from which I draw the results cited herein. See Gruber and Madrian 2002.

Chapter Three
Therapy for an Ailing Health Economy

1. Tunney 1971, 3.

2. Most insurers will not reimburse hospitals unless they are accredited by the nongovernmental Joint Commission on Accreditation of Healthcare Organizations.

3. "An Interview with Paul Ellwood" 1997.

4. Williams 1991.

5. Crowley 1996, 139.

6. HMOs have no greater incentive to keep their patients healthy than do standard indemnity plans. Both prosper when medical costs are low.

7. Crowley 1996.

8. Cutting 1971, 20.

9. Williams 1971, 17.

10. Williams 1971.

11. Economist Katherine Ho offers data suggesting that negative perceptions of quality remain an important obstacle to entry by Kaiser and the GHC outside of their traditional West Coast bases. See Ho 2006.

12. Coggeshall 1965, 26.

13. Somers and Somers 1977, 251.

14. The most widely cited study is Salkever and Bice 1976, 185–214.

15. Morrisey 1999.

16. Conover and Sloan 1998.

17. This example appears in Demlo 1983.

18. The program also covered patients in a separate Maternal and Child Health program.

19. Reischaver 1979.

20. Dranove and Cone 1985.

21. Assaf et al. 1993.

22. Golden and Kurkjian 1994; Thomas 1994.

23. Lipman 1995.

24. Morrisey, Sloan, and Valvona 1988.

25. See Staiger and Gaumer 1992, Cutler 1995, and Shen 2003a.

26. Sussman and Langa 1993.

27. For example, see Angelleli, Grabowski, and Gruber 2006 for evidence that quality in nursing homes is a public good.

28. Dranove and White 1998.

29. Schwartz, Colby, and Reisinger 1991.

30. Source: State Health Access Data Assistance Center 2006.

31. Estimates of crowd out range as high as 60 percent. The seminal paper on crowd out is Cutler and Gruber 1996. For more recent evidence see Lo Sasso and Buchmueller 2004 and Gruber and Simon 2007.

32. This result is cited in Madrian 1998.

33. Gruber and Madrian 1996.

34. Gruber and Madrian 1997.

35. Gruber and Madrian 2002.

36. Kaiser Family Foundation and Health Research and Education Trust 2007.

37. For a review of this literature, see Chollet 2004.

Chapter Four
The Managed Care Prescription

1. Both quotes from Hall and Findlay 1997.

2. Berg 1983; Barron 1984.

3. Quoted in Rosenbaum 1984.

4. Newhouse et al. 1993.

5. Newhouse 2006.

6. To my knowledge, there is no systematic evidence on the impact of these cost-sharing provisions on total medical spending. The impact could not have been profound; spending continued to increase.

7. Source: U.S. Department of Health and Human Services 2003 and author's own calculations.

8. Luft 1978.

9. Ibid.

10. Ginsburg 2000.

11. See Chassin 1996 for further discussion of physician skepticism about quality improvement.

12. Miller and Luft 1994.

13. See, for example, Cutler and Sheiner 1997.

14. Dranove and White 1998.

15. Barro and Beaulieu 2003.

16. Gaynor, Rebitzer, and Taylor 2001.

17. Wickizer, Wheeler, and Feldstein 1989.

18. Cutler, McClellan, and Newhouse 2000. This is a high-powered research team. Cutler was an advisor to the Clinton healthcare task force and is currently dean of the Harvard University College of Arts and Sciences; McClellan is a Stanford professor who took time out to run the FDA and CMS under President George W. Bush; Newhouse, a Harvard professor considered by many to be the "dean" of health economists, led the RAND study and has headed the panel that advises Medicare.

19. See Flood et al. 1998.

20. I was Enthoven's doctoral student between 1979 and 1983. Most of this discussion is based on personal communications with Enthoven.

21. Unlike the Rothschild-Stiglitz model, enrollees would still pay the same amount regardless of their own health needs.

22. Source of quote: Personal communication with Alain Enthoven.

23. Source: At this conference on health reform that I attended, Enthoven debated Clinton advisor Paul Starr. Enthoven was clearly disappointed at the ways in which his ideas had morphed into such a highly regulated scheme.

24. The first article in a major newspaper commenting about a backlash to HMOs or managed care appears to have appeared in the February 12 edition of the *St. Petersburg Times*. On May 19, the *New York Times* ran a front page article by noted healthcare writer Milt Freudenheim entitled "HMOs Cope with a Backlash on Cost Cutting."

25. Ad hoc Committee to Defend Health Care 1997.

26. Pham 1997.

27. Source: Harris Polls, cited in Blendon and Benson 2001.

28. Source: Ibid. This survey question had been asked since 1978.

29. Gawande et al. 1998.

30. Hellinger 1996.

31. Miller and Luft 1997.

32. Miller and Luft 2002.

33. Reschevsky, Hargraves, and Smith 2002.

34. Chernew, Scanlon, and Hayward 1998; O'Neill 2002.

35. Dranove and Satterthwaite 1992.

36. Long after Patient Bill of Rights legislation died, Americans continued to support government standards to "protect the rights of patients in HMOs." See Pew Research Center 2001.

37. "Aetna" 2001.

38. In 2002 Rowe replaced Donaldson as CEO.

39. Hawkins 2000.

40. Ho 2005.

41. Source: Current Population Survey, various years.

42. For a summary of this research, see Town and Vogt 2006.

43. American Medical Association 2006.

44. This also assumes that the insurance industry would have survived intact at the near zero profit levels it was achieving back in 2000.

45. Source: U.S. Department of Health and Human Services. The increase for nurses between 2000 and 2004 was 23.5 percent, with the trend forecast to hold through 2005.

46. Claxton et al. 2005.

47. Gruber and Washington 2003.

48. Gruber 2007.

49. Institutes of Medicine 1999; Institutes of Medicine 2000.

Chapter Five
Self-Help

1. Goodman 2004.

2. The term "Health Savings Account" was coined by Edward Shapiro in 1980. For a fuller account of the history of HSAs, see Bowen 2005.

3. Worthington 1978.

4. Hixson 1980.

5. Goodman and Musgrave 1992. The book was reissued in 1994 with a different subtitle: *Patient Power: The Free-enterprise Alternative to Clinton's Health Plan.*

6. Christmas Clubs used to be a major savings vehicle. Individuals would deposit a little bit of money into their Christmas Club account every month and then withdraw the accumulated total in December to purchase presents.

7. Nowadays that individual would be guaranteed by law the right to continued coverage. I will have more to say about this in chapter 7.

8. These are due for an increase in 2007.

9. For a description of the frustrations many enrollees are experiencing, see Fuhrmans 2007.

10. For a summary of this literature, see Buntin et al. 2006.

11. Hall and Havighurst 2005.

12. Sullivan and Sharon 2006.

13. AHIP Center for Policy and Research 2006.

14. Fronstin and Collins 2006.

15. A well-known problem with surveys of this kind is that individuals often do not know what kind of plan they are enrolled in (for years this has plagued efforts to measure enrollments in HMOs versus PPOs.) For example, my employer Northwestern University began offering a new "Value Plan" this year, complete with high deductibles and an MSA. While Northwestern has held countless educational sessions about the new offering, some of my colleagues who have signed up for the Value Plan did not realize that it is a CDHP or even that it has an HSA. And these are business economists!

16. Kaiser Family Foundation and Health Research and Education Trust 2007.

17. U.S. Government Accountability Office 2006.

18. Sullivan and Sharon 2006.

19. Buntin et al. 2006.

20. United Health Group Press Release, July 12, 2006.

21. Buntin et al. 2006, w523.

22. While these studies control for characteristics of enrollees that are observable to the researcher (e.g., age), they do not control for unobservable enrollee characteristics that might affect both the decision to enroll in a CDHP and costs. (For example, the enrollee would know about a recent change in health status but the researcher would not have this information.) This implies that the results of these studies may suffer from "selection bias" and are therefore unreliable.

23. Berenson 2005.

24. I will ignore the very real possibility that individuals equate higher prices with higher quality, which would mitigate any incentive to shop for the lowest price provider.

25. There are few if any hamburger "outliers"; customers who use fifty packets of ketchup or find some other way to dramatically drive up the cost of the hamburger.

26. Shleifer 1985.

Chapter Six
The Quality Revolution

1. Brook 1998.

2. The field of quality evaluation is evolving rapidly. Rather than try to provide a comprehensive, up to the minute review of all the latest research, this chapter introduces the essential theoretical concepts and highlight some of the key research findings. I hope that the framework I present in this chapter will allow the reader to synthesize new research as it emerges.

3. Brook et al. 1983.

4. Source: IOM Press release, http://www.iom.edu/CMS/28312/5010/30506.aspx. Searched 6/14/2007.

5. Brook 1998.

6. Institutes of Medicine 1999.

7. Institutes of Medicine 2000.

8. Source: http://www.healthgrades.com/AboutUs/. Searched 2/22/2007.

9. The Web sites are www.hospitalcompare.hhs.gov and http://www.medicare.gov/NHCompare/Home.asp.

10. Shearer and Cronin 2005.

11. Weiler et al. 1993.

12. Donabedian 1980.

13. The seminal paper is Luft, Bunker, and Enthoven 1979. A follow-up study partially resolves some issues of causality. See Luft, Hunt, and Maerki 1987.

14. More recent studies suggest that there is substantial learning for heart surgery; it remains to be seen whether learning is equally important for other procedures. See Huckman and Pisano 2006 and Ramanarayanan 2007.

15. Schneider and Epstein 1996.

16. Quoted in Burton 1999.

17. Dranove and Satterthwaite 1992.

18. For example, "Cardiac Surgery Outcomes Improve in New York Hospitals," Press Release from Healthcare Association of New York, October 31, 2005.

19. Dranove, Kessler, McClellan, and Satterthwaite 2003.

20. Werner 2005. A version of this paper appears as Werner, Asch, and Polsky 2005.

21. Both race and prior hospitalization are indirect indicators of medical need; the New York statisticians restrict their risk adjusters to direct indicators such as blood pressure that are drawn from medical records.

22. Brennan et al. 1991.

23. Geraci et al. 1999.

24. Werner and Bradlow 2006.

25. Accessed 7/16/2007.

26. Mennemeyer, Morrisey, and Howard 1997.

27. Mukamel et al. 2004–5; Dranove and Sfekas 2007. There is also recent evidence that enrollees respond to managed care report cards. For example, see Scanlon et al. 2002.

28. This view is explicitly incorporated into the 1970 legislation creating the French health insurance system, the "Carte Sanitaire."

29. Merritt 2006.

30. I am indebted to Professor Joel Shalowitz, who teaches Kellogg's course on international health systems, for this example.

31. An oft-cited article on multitasking published in a management journal casts the problem in a very similar way. The title of the article: "On the Folly of Rewarding A, while Hoping for B" (Kerr 1995).

32. Holmstrom's first paper on agency is mandatory reading for every economics Ph.D. student and he has written many influential papers on agency since then. See Holmstrom 1979. Milgrom's book on the economics of organizations, coauthored by my former advisor John Roberts (another Nobel candidate) inspired the academic field of the economics of strategy. See Milgrom and Roberts 1992. Milgrom is also known for his research on auctions and on game theory.

33. Holmstrom and Milgrom 1991.

34. Poon et al. 2004.

35. Klasco 2003.

36. Needleman et al. 2002. Twenty-five nurses working eight-hour weekday shifts would add approximately two hundred nursing hours per day. A typical hospital has about 150 inpatients on a given weekday; thus, the added staffing represents an additional 1.33 hours per patient, enough to make a measurable impact on quality according to Needleman's findings.

37. For evidence of the kind of gaming that occurs, and a broader review of this literature, see Figlio and Getzler 2002 and Cullen and Reback 2006.

38. Petersen et al. 2006.

39. Shen 2003b.

40. Hagland 2006.

41. Lindenauer 2007.

42. For a detailed discussion of this program and its results, see Galvin 2006.

43. Mullen, Frank, and Rosenthal 2006.

44. Lu 2007.

Chapter Seven
Mending the Safety Net

1. "Statement from Risa Lavizzo-Mourey, M.D., MBA, RWJF President and CEO, Regarding Release of Federal Estimates of Number of Uninsured Americans," News release from Robert Wood Johnson Foundation, Princeton, NJ, 8/29/2006.

2. The vast majority of seniors have enrolled and most reported the process to be easy or fairly easy. See Weir 2007.

3. For a nice discussion of AHP features, see Kofman et al. 2006.

4. Source: Kaiser Family Foundation and Health Research and Educational Trust 2006.

5. Gruber and Lettau 2004.

6. Simple comparisons of premiums paid by small and large employers often show no difference, but these comparisons do not adjust for benefits or differences in risk.

7. There were fifty-one licensed small group carriers in Illinois in 2004. Not all of these do business in the Chicago area and many will not offer a PPO product analogous to that obtained by Northwestern University. Even so, the market has many competitors and market forces are at play. Source: Letter from the U.S. Government Accountability Office to Senator Olympia Snowe, subject "Private Health Insurance: Number and Market Share of Carriers in the Small Group Health Insurance Market in 2004." Letter dated 10/13/2005. The letter reports that there are over two dozen small group carriers in the median state.

8. Jack Meyer and Lise Rybowski provide an in-depth look at these purchaser cooperatives (Meyer and Rybowski 2001).

9. Yegian et al. 2000.

10. For an example of the death spiral in the private sector, see Cutler and Zeckhauser 1997.

11. Source: Personal conversation between Steve Millard and my research assistant, Christa Van der Eb.

12. National Economic Council 2006.

13. Source: Web site www.statehealthfacts.org, sponsored by the Henry J. Kaiser Family Foundation.

14. Minnesota would still have the smallest percentage of uninsured even without the risk pool.

15. Infectious diseases are an obvious exception but account for small percentage of total health spending.

16. Source: www.statehealtfacts.org.

17. Pauly has written extensively on the topic. For example, see Patel and Pauly 2002.

18. Herring and Pauly 2006.

19. For an excellent discussion of the politics of state health reform, see Brown and Sparer 2001.

20. Kaye 2005.

21. Source: United States Small Business Administration, 2006, *Small Business Profiles for the States and Territories*.

22. ERISA permits Hawaii to regulate self-insured firms. It is the only state that has this exemption. In fact, the Hawaii employer mandate prompted the ERISA legislation.

23. Ostram 1994.

24. Dirigo is Latin for "I direct."

25. "Health Care For All? Not Quite" 2007.

26. Cited in Bragdon 2006.

27. There have been occasional complaints that Anthem Blue Cross, the state's Dirigo carrier, is either actively or passively discouraging enrollments. For example, see Langley 2006.

28. Anyone who claims that premiums have nothing to do with costs or competition would have to explain why insurers do not charge twice their current rates or even higher. Even monopolists pass along portions of cost increases and decreases to their customers.

29. Quoted in Belluck 2006.

30. Moffit and Owcharenko 2006.

31. Woolhandler and Himmelstein 2006.

32. The Robert Wood Johnson Foundation keeps an up-to-date compilation of state coverage initiatives. See http://www.statecoverage.net.

33. Source: Speech given by Secretary of Health and Human Services Michael Leavitt at American Enterprise Institute, Washington, DC, 4/24/2007.

34. Hill and Wolfe 1998.

35. Abramowitz 1992.

Chapter Eight
Reviving the American Healthcare System

1. Committee on the Costs of Medical Care 1972, x.

2. See Pope et al. 2004 and Ash, Ellis, and Kramer 2001 for examples of ongoing research and applications of risk adjustment.

3. There is a range of estimates of the cost of EMR. These figures are drawn from Miller et al. 2005.

4. Walker et al. 2005.

5. Kleinke 2005.

6. Source: ANSI Web site searched 1/31/2007: http://www.ansi.org/standards_activities/standards_boards_panels/hisb/hitsp.aspx?menuid=3 #News.

7. Quoted in "Standards Panel Delivers Interoperability Specifications to Support Nationwide Health Information Network," PR Newswire, November 1, 2006.

8. Most private insurers use some variant of Medicare's billing system. Both DRGs and the Resource-based Relative Value Scale started with Medicare before moving to the private sector. Utilization review service agencies got their start as Medicare Professional Review Organizations.

9. Miller and Tucker 2007.

10. I am not wedded to these exact figures and I am confident that plans will experiment to find the range that works best.

11. The RAND study was never designed to capture this effect, but it is likely to be huge.

12. Renowned policy expert Jeff Goldsmith offers similar hope and concern about episode-of-illness payments, but does not acknowledge the role of information technology (Goldsmith 2007).

13. The state also needs to do a better job of generating statistics showing how it is doing. Their current methods suffer from inherent statistical biases due to the failure to account for potential gaming. The state has been hostile to such criticism, bordering on defensiveness. The state should not confuse a discussion about valid statistical measures with a rejection of their program.

14. Ware and Sherbourne 1992.

15. The list of CMS/HCFA administrators reads like a Who's Who in health services research, including Carolyn Davis, Gail Wilensky, Bruce Vladeck, and Mark McClellan. The list of advisors is equally impressive.

16. U.S. Government Accountability Office 2003.

17. Nivola 2005.

18. Speech given by Secretary of Health and Human Services Michael Leavitt at American Enterprise Institute, Washington, DC, 4/24/2007 and personal communication with Secretary Leavitt.

19. Weisbrod 1991.

20. Cutler 2005.

21. This is not out of line with valuations used in Canada, Australia, and England when health agencies consider whether to pay for new technology.

22. There is considerable research to back this up. For example, see Finkelstein 2004 and Acemoglu and Linn 2004. Unfortunately the research is not refined enough to tell us the kinds of research projects that would be most affected by a cutback in industry profits.

23. Other nations "free ride" on technology developed for the potential profits of the U.S. market. The same might occur under the federalist approach, where a state with tight budget controls gains access to drugs developed for the potential profits in other states.

24. Industry critics such as Marcia Angell, former editor-in-chief of the *New England Journal of Medicine*, correctly point out that drug companies earn rates of return well above the norms for other industries and spend as much money marketing their innovations as they spend on R&D (Angell 2004). Moreover a lot of R&D leads to "me-too" drugs that only marginally expand treatment opportunities. But it is difficult to envision a way to restrain industry profits without restraining incentives to innovate. Other nations have rules that pay companies higher prices for truly innovative products (as judged by the regulators). Even so, these innovative products command lower prices elsewhere than they do in the United States.

Abramowitz, M. 1992. "Oregon Plan Would Ration Health Care, Cover Every Resident." *Washington Post*, June 14, B4.

Acemoglu, D., and J. Linn. 2004. "Market Size in Innovation: Theory and Evidence from the Pharmaceutical Industry." *Quarterly Journal of Economics*, 119:1049–90.

Ad hoc Committee to Defend Health Care. 1997. "For Our Patients, Not for Profits: A Call to Action." *Journal of the American Medical Association* 278, 21:1733–38.

"Aetna: A leader makes up for lost time." 2001. *Modern Physician* (January):19.

AHIP Center for Policy and Research. 2006. "January 2006 Census Shows 3.2 Million People Covered by HSA Plans." Washington: America's Health Insurance Plans.

American Medical Association. 2006. *Competition in Health Insurance: A Comprehensive Study of U.S Markets: 2005 Update. Chicago: American Medical Association.*

"An Interview with Paul Ellwood." 1997. *Managed Care* (November).

Angell, M. 2004. "Excess in the Pharmaceutical Industry." *Canadian Medical Association Journal* 171, 12.

Angelleli, J., D. Grabowski, and J. Gruber. 2006. "Nursing Home Quality as a Public Good." NBER working paper no. 12361.

Anderson. 1975. *Blue Cross Since 1929: Accountability and the Public Trust.* Cambridge, MA: Ballinger Publishing, 36.

Arrow, K. 1963. "Agency and the Welfare Economics of Medical Care." *American Economic Review* 53, 5:941–73.

Ash, A., R. Ellis, and M. Kramer. 2001. "Finding Future High-cost Cases: Comparing Prior Cost Versus Diagnosis-based Methods." *Health Services Research* 36, 6:194–206.

Assaf et al. 1993. "Possible Influence of the Prospective Payment System on the Assignment of Discharge Diagnoses for Coronary Heart Disease." *New England Journal of Medicine* 329, 13:931–35.

Bragdon, T. 2006. "Maine's State-Run Health Plan Faltering." *Health Care News* (January).

Barro, J., and N. Beaulieu. 2003. "Selection and Improvement: Physician Responses to Financial Incentives." NBER working paper no.10017.

Barron, J. 1984. "General Motors Proposes Changes in its Employee Health Program." *New York Times*, A18.

Beito, D. 1994. "Lodge Doctors and the Poor." *The Freeman* 44, 5.

Belluck, P. 2006. "Massachusetts Sets Health Plan for Nearly All." *New York Times*, April 4.

Berenson, R. 2005. "Which Way for Competition: None of the Above." *Health Affairs* 24, 6:1536–42.

Berg, E. 1983. "Major Corporations Ask Workers to Pay More of Health Costs." *New York Times*, September 12, A1.

Blendon, R., and J. Benson. 2001. "Americans' Views on Health Policy: A Fifty-year Historical Perspective." *Health Affairs* 20, 3:33–46.

Bowen, W. 2005. *Policy Innovation and Health Insurance Reform in the American States: An Event History Analysis of State Medical Savings Account Adoptions (1993–96)*. Ph.D. Dissertation, Florida State University.

Brennan, T. et al. 1991. "Incidence of Adverse Events and Negligence in Hospitalized Patients: Results of the Harvard Medical Practice Study." *New England Journal of Medicine*, 324–70.

Brook, R. 1998. "Managed Care is Not the Problem, Quality Is." *Journal of the American Medical Association* 278, 19:1612–14.

Brook, R. et al. 1983. "Does Free Care Improve Adults Health? Results from a Randomized Controlled Trial." *New England Journal of Medicine* 309:1426–34.

Brown, L., and M. Sparer. 2001."Window Shopping: State Health Reform Politics in the 1990s." *Health Affairs* 20, 1:50–67.

Bundorf, M. K., and M. Pauly. 2006. "Is Health Insurance Affordable for the Uninsured?" *Journal of Health Economics* 25, 4:650–73.

Buntin, M. et al. 2006. "Consumer-Directed Health Care: Early Evidence about Effects on Cost and Quality." *Health Affairs*, 25:w516–30.

Burrow, J. 1977. *Organized Medicine in the Progressive Era*. Baltimore: Johns Hopkins University Press.

Burton, T. 1999. "Heart-Care Assessment Finds Reputation and Reality Don't Necessarily Match." *Wall Street Journal Interactive Edition*, April 22.

"Cardiac Surgery Outcomes Improve in New York Hospitals." 2005. Press Release from Healthcare Association of New York, October 31.

Catlin, A. et al. 2007. "National Health Spending in 2005: The Slowdown Continues." *Health Affairs* 26, 1:142–53.

Chassin, M. 1996. "Improving the Quality of Care." *New England Journal of Medicine* 335, 14:1060–63.

Chernew, M., D. Scanlon, and R. Hayward. 1998. "Insurance Type and Choice of Hospital for Coronary Artery Bypass Graft Surgery." *Health Services Research* 33, 3:447–66.

Clinton, H. 2004. "Now Can We Talk About Health Care?" *New York Times*, April 18. Available at: http://query.nytimes.com/gst/fullpage.html?sec= health&res=9A00E7DE1E38F93BA25757C0A9629C8B63 (Accessed March 12, 2007).

Chollet, D. 2004. *The Role of Reinsurance in State Efforts to Expand Coverage.* Academy Health Issue Brief 5, 4.

Claxton, G. et al. 2005. *Employer Health Benefits.* Menlo Park, CA: Kaiser Family Foundation and Health Research and Education Trust.

Coggeshall, L. 1965. *Planning for Medical Progress through Education.* Washington, DC: Association of American Medical Colleges, 26.

Comment: "Taxation of Employee Accident and Health Plans Before and Under the 1954 Code." 1954. *Yale Law Journal* 64, 2 (December):222–47.

Committee on the Costs of Medical Care. 1972(reprint of 1932 report). *Medical Care for the American People.* New York: Arno Press.

Conover, C., and F. Sloan. 1998. "Does Removing Certificate-of-Need Regulations Lead to a Surge in Health Care Spending?" *Journal of Health Politics, Policy, and Law* 23, 3:455–81.

Crowley, W. 1996. *To Serve the Greatest Number.* Seattle: University of Washington Press, 139.

Cullen, J., and R. Reback. 2006. "Tinkering towards Accolades: School Gaming under a Performance Accountability System." In *Improving School Accountability: Check-ups or Choice*, edited by T. Gronberg and D. Jansen. Advances in Applied Microeconomics, 14. Amsterdam: Elsevier Science.

Cunningham, R., and R. Cunningham. 1997. *The Blues: A History of the Blue Cross and Blue Shield System.* Dekalb, IL: Northern Illinois University Press.

Cutler, D. 1995. "The Incidence of Adverse Medical Outcomes under Prospective Payment." *Econometrica*, 63:29–50.

———. 2005. *Your Money or Your Life: Strong Medicine for America's Health Care System.* New York: Oxford University Press.

Cutler, D., and J. Gruber. 1996. "Does Public Insurance Crowd Out Private Insurance?" *Quarterly Journal of Economics* 111, 2:391–430.

Cutler, D., and L. Sheiner. 1997. "Managed Care and the Growth of Medical Expenditures." Harvard University, working paper.

Cutler, D., M. McClellan, and J. Newhouse. 2000. "How Does Managed Care Do It?" *Rand Journal of Economics* 31, 3:526–48.

Cutler, D., and R. Zeckhauser. 1997. "Adverse Selection in Health Insurance." NBER working paper W6107.

Cutting, C. 1971. "Historical Development and Operating Concepts." In *The Kaiser-Permanente Medical Program*, edited by A. Somers. New York: Commonwealth Fund, 20.

Demlo, L. 1983. "Assuring Quality in Health Care." *Evaluation and the Health Professions* 6, 2:161–96.

Donabedian, A. 1980. *Exploration in Quality Assessment and Monitoring*, Vol. 1: *The Definition of Quality and Approaches to Its Assessment*. Ann Arbor, MI: Health Administration Press.

Dranove, D., and A. Sfekas. 2007. "Do Report Cards Move Market Share? Yes and No." Northwestern University, unpublished working paper.

Dranove, D., and K. Cone. 1985. "Do State Rate Setting Programs Really Lower Hospital Expenses?" *Journal of Health Economics* 4:159–65.

Dranove, D., and M. Satterthwaite. 1992. "Monopolistic Competition when Price and Quality are Imperfectly Observable." *RAND Journal of Economics* 23, 4:518–34

Dranove, D., and P. Wehner. 1994. "Physician-induced Demand for Childbirth." *Journal of Health Economics*, 13:61–73.

Dranove, D., and W. White. 1998. "Medicaid Dependent Hospitals and Their Patients: How Have They Fared?" *Health Services Research* 33, 2:163–85.

Dranove, D., D. Kessler, M. McClellan, and M. Satterthwaite. 2003. "Is More Information Better? The Effects of Report Cards on Cardiovascular Providers and Consumers." *Journal of Political Economy* 111, 3:555–88.

Enthoven, A. 1978. "Consumer-choice Health Plan." *New England Journal of Medicine*, 298:650–58.

Evans, R. 1974. "Supplier-induced Demand: Some Empirical Evidence and Implications." In *The Economics of Health and Medical Care*, edited by Mark Perlman. London: MacMillan, 162–73.

Falk, I., C. R. Rorem, and M. Ring. 1933. *The Costs of Medical Care*. Chicago: University of Chicago Press.

Figlio, D., and L. Getzler. 2002. "Accountability and Disability: Gaming the System." NBER working paper no. 9307.

Finkelstein, A. 2004. "Static and Dynamic Effects of Health Policy: Evidence from the Vaccine Industry." *Quarterly Journal of Economics* 119, 2:527–64.

Flood, A. et al. 1998. "How Do HMOs Achieve Savings?" *Health Services Research* 33, 1:79–100.

Freidson, E., and F. Feldman. 1958. *Public Attitudes toward Health Insurance*. Health Information Foundation Research Series, 5.

Friedberg, Leora. 1998. "The Effect of Old Age Assistance on Retirement." NBER working paper no. 6548.

Fronstin, P., and S. Collins. 2006. "The 2nd Annual EBRI/Commonwealth Fund Consumerism in Health Care Survey." The Commonwealth Fund, December.

Fuchs, V. 1974. *Who Shall Live?* New York: Basic Books.

Fuhrmans, V. 2007. "Health Savings Plans Start to Falter." *Wall Street Journal*, June 12, D1.

Galvin, R. 2006. "Pay-for-Performance: Too Much of a Good Thing? A Conversation with Martin Roland." *Health Affairs Web Exclusive*, September 6, w412–19.

Gawande et al. 1998. "Does Dissatisfaction with Health Plans Stem from Having No Choices?" *Health Affairs* (September–October):184–94.

Gaynor, M. et al. 2004. "Physician Incentives in Health Maintenance Organizations." *Journal of Political Economy* 112, 4:915–31.

Gaynor, M., J. Rebitzer, and L. Taylor. 2001. "Incentives in HMOs." NBER working paper no.8522.

Geraci, J. et al. 1999. "The Association of Quality of Care and Occurrence of In-Hospital, Treatment-Related Complications." *Medical Care* 37, 2:140–48.

Ginsburg, M. 2000. "A Survey of Physician Attitudes and Practices Concerning Cost-effectiveness in Patient Care." *Western Journal of Medicine* 173: 390–94.

Ginzberg, E. 1977. *The Limits of Health Reform*. New York: Basic Books.

Golden, D., and S. Kurkjian. 1994. "The Fraud Factor: Hidden Costs of Health Care." *Boston Globe*, July 31, 1.

Goldsmith, J. 2007. "Physicians and Hospitals: Can They Cooperate to Control Costs?" *Health Affairs Blog*, January 19.

Goodman, J. 2004. "Health Savings Accounts Will Revolutionize American Health Care." National Center for Policy Analysis Brief Analysis no. 464.

——. 2007. "Physicians and Hospitals: Can They Cooperate to Control Costs?" *Health Affairs Blog*, January 19.

Goodman, J., and G. Musgrave. 1992. *Patient Power: Solving America's Healthcare Crisis*. Washington, DC: Cato Institute.

Gruber, J. 2007. "Universal Coverage Rx: Tax-Code Changes, Money, Insurance Pools and a Mandate." *On My Mind: Conversations with Economists*. University of Michigan, interview with Jonathan Gruber.

Gruber, J., and B. Madrian. 1996. "Health Insurance and Early Retirement." In *Advances in the Economics of Aging*, edited by D. Wise. Chicago: University of Chicago Press.

—— 1997. "Employment Separation and Health Insurance Coverage." *Journal of Public Economics* 66, 3:349–82.

Gruber, J., and B. Madrian. 2002. "Health Insurance, Labor Supply, and Job Mobility: A Critical Review of the Literature." NBER working paper no. 8817.

Gruber, J., and E. Washington. 2003. "Subsidies to Employee Health Insurance Premiums and the Health Insurance Market." NBER working paper no. W9567.

Gruber, J., and K. Simon. 2007. "Crowd-out Ten Years Later: Have Recent Public Insurance Expansions Crowded Out Private Health Insurance?" NBER working paper no. 12858.

Gruber, J., and M. Lettau. 2004. "How Elastic is the Firm's Demand for Health Insurance?" *Journal of Public Economics* 88, 7:1273–94.

Gruber, J., and M. Owings. 1996. "Physician Financial Incentives and the Diffusion of Cesarian Section Delivery." *RAND Journal of Economics* 27, 1:99–123.

Hagland, M. 2006. "Pay-for-performance Programs Show Results, Spur Development." *Health Care Strategic Management* 24, 2:1–3.

Hall, M., and C. Havighurst. 2005. "Reviving Managed Care with Health Savings Accounts." *Health Affairs* 24, 6:1490–500.

Hall, M., and S. Findlay. 1997. "Clinton Panel To Write Patients' Bill of Rights." *USA Today*, March 27, 1A.

Hawkins, J. 2000. "HMO Moves to Mend Fences with Doctors." *Physician Executive* 26, 1:7.

Health Insurance Association of America. *Sourcebook of Health Insurance Data*, various years.

"Health Care for All? Not Quite." 2007. *Business Week Online*, April 16.

Hellinger, F. 1996. "The Impact of Managed Care on Market Performance: A Review of New Evidence." Agency for Health Care Policy and Research, mimeo.

Hemenway, D., et al. 1990. "Physician Response to Financial Incentives: Evidence from a For-Profit Ambulatory Care Center." *New England Journal of Medicine* 322:1059–63.

Herring, B., and M. Pauly. 2006. "The Effect of State Community Rating Regulations on Premiums and Coverage in the Individual Health Insurance Market." NBER working paper no. 12504.

Hill, S., and B. Wolfe. 1998. "Testing the HMO Competitive Strategy." *Journal of Health Economics* 16:261–86.

Hillman, B. et al. 1990. "Frequency and Cost of Diagnostic Imaging in Office Practices: A Comparison of Self-referring and Radiology-referring Physicians." *New England Journal of Medicine* 323:1604–5.

Hixson, J., ed. 1980. *The Target Income Hypothesis and Related Issues in Health Manpower Supply*. Bethesda, MD: U.S. Department of Health, Education and Welfare, Health Resources Administration.

Ho, Katherine. 2005. "The Welfare Effects of Restricted Hospital Choice in the U.S. Medicare Care Market."

——. 2006. "Barriers to Entry of a Vertically Integrated Health Insurer: An Analysis of Welfare and Entry Costs." Unpublished manuscript.

Holmstrom, B. 1979. "Moral Hazard and Observability." *Bell Journal of Economics* 10, 1:74–91.

Holmstrom, B., and P. Milgrom. 1991. "Multitask Principal-Agent Analyses: Incentive Contracts, Asset Ownership, and Job Design." *Journal of Law and Economic Organization* 7(Spring):24–52.

Huckman, R., and G. Pisano. 2006. "The Firm-specificity of Individual Performance: Evidence from Cardiac Surgery." *Management Science* 52, 4:473–88.

Institutes of Medicine. 1999. *To Err Is Human: Building a Safer Health System.* Washington, DC: National Academy of Sciences.

——. 2000. *Crossing the Quality Chasm: A New Health System for the 21st Century.* Washington, DC: National Academy of Sciences.

Institutes of Medicine of the National Academies. 2003. *Hidden Costs, Value Lost: Uninsurance in America.*

Jensen, G., and M. Morrisey. 1999. "Mandated Benefit Laws and Employer-Sponsored Health Insurance." Health Insurance Association of America.

Kaiser Family Foundation and Health Research and Education Trust. Various years. "Employer Health Benefits: Annual Survey." Menlo Park: Henry J. Kaiser Family Foundation.

Kaplan, R. 1995. "Utility Assessment for Estimating Quality-Adjusted Life Years." In *Valuing Health Care: Costs, Benefits, and Effectiveness of Pharmaceuticals, and Other Medical Technologies,* edited by F. Sloan. Cambridge: Cambridge University Press, chap. 3, 31–60.

Kaye, N. 2005. *Medicaid Managed Care: Looking Forward, Looking Back.* National Academy for State Health Policy (June).

Kerr, S. 1995. "On the Folly of Rewarding A, while Hoping for B." *Academy of Management Executive* 9, 1:7–14.

Klasco, R. 2003 "CPOE: Why Don't We Get It?" *Health Management Technology* (August).

Kleinke, J. D. 2005. "Dot-Gov: Market Failure and the Creation of a National Health Information Technology System." *Health Affairs* 24, 5:1246–62.

Kofman, M., et al. 2006. "Association Health Plans: What's All the Fuss About?" *Health Affairs* 25, 6:1591–602.

Langley, R. 2006. "Exposing the Myth." *Bangor Daily News,* December 25, A8.

Lindenauer, P. et al. 2007. "Public Reporting and Pay for Performance in Hospital Quality Improvement." *New England Journal of Medicine* 356, 5:486–96.

Lipman, L. 1995. "FBI Chief: Health-care Fraud Endemic." *Denver Post*, March 22, A13.

Long, M. 1985. "A Reconsideration of Economies of Scale in the Health Care Field." *Health Policy* 5:25–44.

Lo Sasso, A., and T. Buchmueller. 2004. "The Effect of the State Children's Health Insurance Program on Health Insurance Coverage." *Journal of Health Economics* 23, 5:1059–82.

Lu, Feng Susan. 2007. "Does Information Disclosure Improve Quality? Evidence from a Nursing Home Quality Initiative." Northwestern University, unpublished manuscript.

Luft, H. 1978. "How do Health Maintenance Organizations Achieve Their 'Savings?' " *New England Journal of Medicine* 298, 24:1336–43.

Luft, H. et al. 1990. *Hospital Volume, Physician Volume, and Patient Outcomes: Assessing the Evidence*. Health Administration Press Perspectives. Ann Arbor, MI: Health Administration Press.

Luft, H., J. Bunker, and A. Enthoven. 1979. "Should Operations Be Regionalized? The Empirical Relation between Surgical Volume and Mortality." *New England Journal of Medicine* 301, 2:1364–69.

Luft, H., S. Hunt, and S. Maerki. 1987. "The Volume-Outcome Relationship: Practice-Makes-Perfect or Selective Referral Patterns." *Health Services Research* 22, 2:157–82.

Madrian, B. 1998. "Health Insurance Portability: The Consequences of COBRA." *Regulation* 21, 1:27–33.

Mennemeyer, S., M. Morrisey, and L. Howard. 1997. "Death and Reputation: How Consumers Acted upon HCFA Mortality Information." *Inquiry* 34 (Summer):117–28.

Merritt, R. 2006. "Despite Health Insurance, People often Forgo Using Lifesavings Beta Blockers." *Medical News Today*, September 17.

Meyer, J., and L. Rybowski. 2001. "Business Initiatives to Expand Health Coverage for Workers in Small Firms." Commonwealth Fund Publication 475.

Milgrom, P., and J. Roberts. 1992. *Economics, Organization, and Management*. New York: Wiley Press.

Miller, A., and C. Tucker. 2007. "Privacy Protection and Technology Diffusion: The Case of Electronic Medical Records." Available at SSRN: http://ssrn.com/abstract=960233.

Miller, R. et al. 2005. "The Value of Electronic Health Records in Solo or Small Group Practices." *Health Affairs* 24, 5:1127–37.

Miller, R., and H. Luft. 1994. "Managed Care Plan Performance Since 1980: A Literature Analysis." *JAMA* 271 19:1512–17.

———. 1997. "Managed Care Performance: Is Quality of Care Better or Worse?" *Health Affairs* 16, 5:7–25.

Miller, R., and H. Luft. 2002. "HMO Plan Performance Update: An Analysis of the Literature, 1997–2001." *Health Affairs* 21, 4:63–86.

Morrisey, M. 1999. "State Health Care Reform: Protecting the Provider." In *American Health Care: Government, Market Processes, and the Public Interest*. Oakland, CA: The Independent Institute.

Morrisey, M., F. Sloan, and J. Valvona. 1988. "Medicare Prospective Payment and Post-Hospital Transfers to Subacute Care." *Medical Care* 26, 9:837–53.

Moffit, R., and N. Owcharenko. 2006. "Understanding Key Parts of the Massachusetts Health Plan." Web memo no. 1045.

Mukamel, D. B., D. L. Weimer, J. Zwanziger, S. F. Gorthy, and A. I. Mushlin. 2004–5. "Quality Report Cards, Selection of Cardiac Surgeons, and Racial Disparities: A Study of the Publication of the New York State Cardiac Surgery Reports." *Inquiry* 41:435–46.

Mullan, F. 2004. "Wrestling with Variation: An Interview with Jack Wennberg." *Health Affairs Web Exclusive*, October 7.

Mullen, K., R. Frank, and M. Rosenthal. 2006. "Can You Get What You Pay For? Pay-for-Performance and the Quality of Healthcare Providers." Unpublished manuscript.

Myers, R. 1970. *Medicare*. Bryn Mawr: McCahan Foundation.

National Economic Council. 2006. *Reforming Health Care for the 21st Century*. Report prepared for President George W. Bush, February 15.

NCPA. 1997. "The Cost of Health Insurance Mandates." Brief Analysis 237.

Newhouse, J. et al. 1993. *Free for All? Lessons from the RAND National Health Insurance Experiment*. Cambridge, MA: Harvard University Press.

Needleman, J. et al. 2002. "Nurse-staffing Levels and the Quality of Care in Hospitals." *New England Journal of Medicine* 346, 22:1715–22.

Newhouse. 2006. "Reconsidering the Moral Hazard-Risk Avoidance Tradeoff." *Journal of Health Economics* 25, 5:1005–14.

Nivola, P. 2005. "Why Federalism Matters." Brookings Institution Policy Brief no. 146.

Office of Inspector General. 1989. *Financial Arrangements Between Physicians and Health Care Businesses*. Washington, DC: Department of Health and Human Services.

O'Neill, L. 2002. "How Far Do Medicare HMO Patients Travel? 2002, Implications for Access and Quality." *Abstract Academy for Health Services Research Policy Meeting* 19:9.

Ostram, C. 1994. "Facts in Hand, Mrs. Clinton Sees No Reason to Alter State's Plan." *Seattle Post-Intelligencer*, July 24, A10.

Patel, V., and M. Pauly. 2002. "Guaranteed Renewability and the Problem of Risk Variation in Individual Insurance Markets." *Health Affairs Web Exclusive*, August 28.

Pauly, M. 1968. "The Economics of Moral Hazard: Comment." *American Economic Review* 58, 3:531–37.

———. 1997. *Health Benefits at Work*. Ann Arbor: University of Michigan Press.

Pauly, M., and M. Satterthwaite. 1981. "The Pricing of Primary Care Physicians' Services: A Test of Consumer Information." *Bell Journal of Economics* 12, 2:488–506.

Petersen, L. et al. 2006. "Does Pay for Performance Improve the Quality of Health Care?" *Annals of Internal Medicine* 145, 4:265–72.

Pew Research Center. *News Interest Index Poll*, conducted June 2001.

Pham, A. 1997. "HMOs seek cure to image malady." *Boston Globe*, June 12, C1.

Poon, E. et al. 2004. "Overcoming Barriers to Adopting and Implementing Computerized Physician Order Entry Systems in U.S. Hospitals." *Health Affairs* 23, 4:184–90.

Pope, G. et al. 2004. "Risk Adjustment of Medicare Capitation Payments Using the CMS-HCC Model." *Health Care Financing Review* 25, 4:119–41.

Porter, M. 1980. *Competitive Strategy*. New York: Free Press.

Ramanarayanan, S. 2007. "Does Practice Make Perfect: An Empirical Analysis of Learning-by-Doing in Cardiac Surgery." Northwestern University, unpublished manuscript.

Reischauer, R. 1979. Testimony before the Subcommittee on Oversight, U.S. House of Representatives, June 27.

Reschevsky, J., J. Hargraves, and A. Smith. 2002. "Consumer Beliefs and Health Plan Performance: It's Not Whether You Are in an HMO but Whether You Think You Are." *Journal of Health Politics, Policy, and Law* 27, 3:353–77.

Robinson, J., and H. Luft. 1985. "The Impact of Hospital Market Structure and Patient Volume on Average Length of Stay and the Cost of Care." *Journal of Health Economics*, 4: 333–56.

Roemer, M. I. 1961. "Bed supply and hospital utilization: a natural experiment." *Hospitals* 35(November):36–42.

Rosenbaum, D. 1984. "Chrysler, Hit Hard by Costs, Studies Health Care System." *New York Times*, March 5, A1.

Rothschild, M., and J. Stiglitz. 1976. "Equilibrium in Competitive Insurance Markets: An Essay of Imperfect Information." *Quarterly Journal of Economics*, 80:629–50.

Salkever, D., and T. Bice. 1976. "The Impact of Certificate of Need Controls on Hospital Investment." *Milbank Quarterly* 54, 2:185–214.

Satterthwaite, M. 1982. "Competition and Equilibrium as a Driving Force in the Health Services Sector." Paper prepared for the ARA/Wharton Conference on the Future of the Service Economy, November 19.

Scanlon, D. et al. 2002. "The Impact of Health Plan Report Cards on Managed Care Enrollment." *Journal of Health Economics*, 21:19–41.

Schneider, E., and A. Epstein. 1996. "Influence of Cardiac-surgery Performance Reports on Referral Practices and Access to Care. A Survey of Cardiovascular Specialists." *New England Journal of Medicine* 335, 4:251–56.

Schwartz, A., D. Colby, and A. Reisinger. 1991. "Variation in Medicaid Physician Fees." *Health Affairs* 10(Spring):131–39.

Selden, T., and B. Gray. 2006. "Tax Subsidies for Employment-related health Insurance: Estimates for 2006." *Health Affairs* 25, 6:1568–79.

Shearer, A., and C. Cronin. 2005. "The State of the Art of Online Hospital Public Reporting." Report Prepared for the CMS Hospital Three State Pilot Project, 2nd Edition, July.

Shen, Y. 2003a. "The Effect of Financial Pressure on the Quality of Care in Hospitals." *Journal of Health Economics*, 22:243–69.

———. 2003b. "Selection Incentives in a Performance-based Contracting System." *Health Services Research* 38, 2:535–52.

Shleifer, A. 1985. "A Theory of Yardstick Competition." *RAND Journal of Economics* 16, 3:319–27.

Social Security Administration. "Report of the Committee on Economic Security." Issued January 1935 and obtained from the Social Security Administration Web site: http://www.ssa.gov/history/reports/ces.html.

Somers, A., and H. Somers, eds. 1977. "The Philadelphia Medical Commons: The choices ahead." In *Health and Health Care*. Germantown, MD: Aspen Systems Corporation, 251.

Staiger, D., and G. Gaumer. 1992. "Quality of Care in Hospitals: Post-admission Mortality under Medicare's Prospective Payment System." Unpublished manuscript.

Starr, P. 1982. *The Social Transformation of American Medicine*. New York: Basic Books, 126.

State Health Access Data Assistance Center. 2006. "The State of Kids Coverage." Prepared for the Robert Wood Johnson Foundation.

Stevens, R., and R. Stevens. 1974. *Welfare Medicine in America*. New York: Free Press.

Sullivan, P., and C. W. Sharon. 2006. "Consumer-Driven Health Plans Gaining Stronger Presence." Aon Consulting/ISCEBS Survey, June.

Sussman, E., and K. Langa. 1993. "The Effect of Cost-containment Policies on Rates of Coronary Revascularization in California." *New England Journal of Medicine* 329, 24:1784–89.

Temin, P. 1988. "An Economic History of American Hospitals." In *Health Care in America*, edited by T. Frech. The Pacific Research Institute.

Thomas, J. 1994. "Senator: Health Care Fraud Costs Staggering." *St. Petersberg Times*, July 9, 6a.

Thomasson, Melissa A. 2003. "The Importance of Group Coverage: How Tax Policy Shaped U.S. Health Insurance." *American Economic Review* 93, 4: 1374–75.

Town, R., and W. Vogt. 2006. "How Has Hospital Consolidation Affected the Price and Quality of Hospital Care?" Robert Wood Johnson Foundation Polity Brief.

Tunney, J. 1971. U.S. Congress, Senate, Committee on Labor and Public Welfare, Subcommittee on Health, *Health Care Crisis in America, Hearings* before the Subcommittee on Health of the Committee on Labor and Public Welfare, 92nd Congress, first session, 3. Cited in Stevens, R., and R. Stevens, 1974, *Welfare Medicine in America*. New York: Free Press.

U.S. Department of Health and Human Services. 2003. *Health, United States.*

U.S. Government Accountability Office. 2006. "Consumer-Directed Health Plans: Small but Growing Enrollment Fueled by Rising Cost of Health Care Coverage." GAO-06–514, April 28.

United Health Group Press Release, July 12, 2006.

Walker, J. et al. 2005. "The Value of Health Care Information Exchange and Interoperability." *Health Affairs Web Exclusive* (January):W5–10.

Ware, J., and C. Sherbourne. 1992. "The MOS 36-Item Short-Form Health Survey (SF-36): I. Conceptual Framework and Item Selection." *Medical Care* 30, 6:473–83.

Weiler, P. et al. 1993. *A Measure of Malpractice*. Cambridge, MA: Harvard University Press.

Weir, D. 2007. "Most Seniors Now Have Drug Coverage." University of Michigan, unpublished report.

Weisbrod, B. 1991. "The Health Care Quadrilemma: An Essay on Technological Change, Insurance, Quality of Care, and Cost Containment." *Journal of Economic Literature* 29, 2:523–52.

Werner, R. 2005. "The Impact of Quality Report Cards on Racial Disparities and Health Outcomes." University of Maryland, unpublished manuscript.

Werner, R., D. Asch, and D. Polsky. 2005. "Racial Profiling: The Unintended Consequences of Coronary Artery Bypass Graft Report Cards." *Circulation* 111:1257–63.

Werner, R., and E. Bradlow. 2006. "Relationship between Medicare's Hospital Compare Performance Measures and Mortality Rates." *JAMA*, 296:2694–702.

Wickizer, T., J. Wheeler, and P. Feldstein. 1989. "Does Utilization Review Reduce Unnecessary Hospital Care and Contain Costs?" *Medical Care* 27, 6:632–47.

Williams, G. 1991. *Kaiser-Permanente Health Plan: Why it Works.* Oakland, CA: Kaiser Foundation.

Woolhandler, S., and D. Himmelstein. 2006. "Massachusetts' Mistake." Available at: http://www.tompaine.com/articles/2006/04/07/massachusetts_mistake .php (Accessed April 7, 2006).

Woolley, J., and G. Peters. 2007. *The American Presidency Online.* Santa Barbara, CA: University of California (hosted), http://www.presidency.ucsb .edu/ws/?pid=12892

Worthington, P. 1978. "Alternatives to Prepayment Finance for Hospital Services." *Inquiry* 15(September):246–54.

Yegian, J. et al. 2000. "The Health Insurance Plan of California: The First Five Years." *Health Affairs* 19, 5:158–65.